MW01234794

Locating
the
Proper
Authorities

Locating the Proper Authorities

The Interaction of Domestic and International Institutions

Daniel W. Drezner, Editor

THE UNIVERSITY OF MICHIGAN PRESS

Ann Arbor

Copyright © by the University of Michigan 2003
All rights reserved
Published in the United States of America by
The University of Michigan Press
Manufactured in the United States of America
⊗ Printed on acid-free paper

2006   2005   2004   2003   4   3   2   1

A CIP catalog record for this book is available from the British Library.

Library of Congress Cataloging-in-Publication Data

Locating the proper authorities : the interaction of domestic and
   international institutions / Daniel W. Drezner, editor.
        p.   cm.
     Includes bibliographical references and index.
     ISBN 0-472-11289-9 (cloth : alk. paper)
      1. International relations—Congresses.   2. Comparative government—
   Congresses.   3. International relations—Public opinion—Congresses.
   I. Drezner, Daniel W.

   JZ43 .L63   2002
   327.1—dc21   2002032034

Contents

Part 3. Persuasion

Acknowledgments

The idea for this book started with the observation that Robert Putnam's pathbreaking work on two-level games has led to an unbalanced development in research about the interaction between domestic and international institutions. A great deal of work has built on Putnam to show how domestic politics can constrain the ability of states to cooperate internationally. However, there has been much less work on the flip side of Putnam's argument—that foreign policy leaders can use international institutions as a means of circumventing or co-opting domestic opposition.

From this idea came a three-day conference in Boulder, Colorado, in June 1999 entitled "The Interaction of Domestic and International Institutions," where eight papers were presented and the larger points debated. Six of these papers, thoroughly revised, along with Duncan Snidal and Alexander Thompson's concluding chapter, make up the present volume.

From the origins of the idea for the book to its publication, the contributors and I have accumulated several debts. Steve Chan was instrumental in turning my idea into a tangible conference proposal. Funding for the 1999 conference was provided by grants from the University of Colorado at Boulder's Council on Research and Creative Work and its Institute for International Relations. Jana Murphy and Nicole Wittenstein made sure that the trains ran on time at the conference, which allowed the contributors to focus on the larger themes. The contributors were fortunate to have an able corps of discussants—Steve Chan, Kathryn Hochstetler, Helen Milner, and Dimitris Stevis. Their advice proved indispensable in our later revisions. Two other participants presented papers but later withdrew from the project because of other obligations. We are grateful to Delia Boylan and Stephen D. Krasner, whose papers and critiques were both constructive and stimulating.

In the process of turning the conference papers into this edited volume, the contributors are grateful to Jeremy Shine, political science editor at the University of Michigan Press. Jeremy's tenacity and patience proved most valuable during the review process. The two anonymous reviewers for the Press provided excellent suggestions for revisions. Kevin Rennells was instrumental in converting this book from bytes to pages. I am also grateful to Bonnie Weir for her vital contributions at the final stages of publication.

Everyone mentioned here is absolved from any errors contained in this book. This includes the two computers that I used to compose and compile this work: the Compaq Deskpro, serial number 6731BPM5Q888, and the Dell Inspiron 3500, serial number 24969312A. These machines were kind enough not to crash.

From this project's inception, I received a steady drumbeat of advice from my colleagues and peers on the mechanics of this project. The content of this advice was remarkably uniform: edited volumes serve little purpose but to act as a constant drain on the editor's time and resources. In response, I took on a much more ambitious project. The first day of the conference was also my first day as a dog parent. For not chewing up anything related to this project, this book is dedicated to Chester Drezner, a very sweet three-year-old beagle.

Introduction: The Interaction of International and Domestic Institutions

Daniel W. Drezner

Following the third wave of democratization, several prominent international relations scholars predicted a growing sensitivity to the preference of domestic actors in world politics (Simmons 1995; Moravcsik 1997). With a larger role for public opinion and interest groups to play in the crafting of foreign policies, fewer states would be prepared to incur significant domestic costs for the sake of international cooperation (Milner 1997). Robert Putnam's (1988) two-level games approach stressed that domestic institutions could block agreements that diverged too much from their preferences. In short, the primacy of domestic politics would lead to a fraying of multilateral collaboration.

The events of the past decade suggest that life has not been this simple. Across the globe, there are examples of recalcitrant domestic groups acquiescing to costly international obligations. President Clinton dispatched ground troops to Haiti, Bosnia, and Kosovo to enforce UN Security Council resolutions, despite significant congressional resistance and tepid public support (see Schultz, this volume). European Union (EU) governments, in order to meet the Maastricht Treaty's criteria for the European Monetary Union, pursued painful contractionary fiscal and monetary policies in the face of double-digit unemployment (Rotte 1998). In the Pacific Rim, several countries reformed their financial sectors and curtailed cheap loans to corrupt elites to comply with International Monetary Fund (IMF) conditionality requirements (Haggard 2000). Despite significant domestic political costs, most of these states have adhered to most of the IMF policies. When a moderately popular coup d'etat occurred in Paraguay, the relevant officers backed down when threatened with exclusion from the regional free-trade association, MERCOSUR (see Pevehouse, this volume).

What accounts for the trumping of domestic interests by international institutions? The question is not a trivial one; the growth of complex interdependence (Keohane and Nye 1978) and the continued globalization of heretofore domestic issues (Goodman and Pauly 1993; Vogel 1995; Cerny 1995; Rodrik 1997; Slaughter 1997; Braithwaite and Drahos 2000) imply more conflicts between international and domestic institutions in the near future. In the last decade, the growth in the literature on the interaction between domestic and international politics has been impressive (Rogowski 1989; Snyder 1991; Cowhey 1993; Evans, Jacobson, and Putnam 1993; Keohane and Milner 1996; Pahre and Papayoanau 1997; Milner 1997; Moravcsik 1998). Beginning with Putnam (1988), both comparative politics and international relations scholars have investigated how the global system empowers and constrains domestic interest groups, how domestic interests affect a state's international bargaining position, and how Janus-faced decision makers mediate between the second and third images of politics (Waltz 1959).

Despite all this attention to domestic-global interactions, significant gaps remain in our knowledge. While international organizations (IOs) have acted as effective crowbars to override the preferences of domestic institutions, these institutions' responses to multilateral pressure have varied from acquiescing to standing firm. What explains this variation? How are international institutions used to influence domestic politics?[1] Which domestic actors use IOs in this capacity? Under what conditions will such attempts at influence be initiated? Under what conditions will they be successful? What are the long-run implications for the distribution of authority between domestic and international institutions?

The goal of this book is to address these questions and to suggest some answers. It does so by parsing the interaction of domestic and international institutions along two dimensions. The first dimension is the way in which international institutions are used to influence domestic politics. The chapters here explore three possible avenues of influence: contracting, coercion, and persuasion. The second dimension defines the actors who use the international institution to advance their ends. External actors will often use IOs as a means of influencing the domestic politics of another country. Just as often, however, domestic agents within the nation-state will use the international institution as a way of circumventing domestic opposition.

The potential value that this volume adds to the existing body of knowledge is considerable.[2] It offers a clear typology of transnational institutional interactions and provides a useful analytic lens on the subject. It fleshes out the variety of functions that international institutions have in domestic-international bargaining. It provides a fuller description of how domestic institutions are responding to globalizing pressures. It adds a number of (non-European) cases to the body of evidence on the interaction between the second and third images of politics. Finally, it puts forward a set of testable hypotheses distinct from the extant literature.

This introduction will set the theoretical table. For all of the research on political institutions, there has been surprisingly little work on how institutions from different levels of analysis bargain with each other, what resources they bring to the negotiating table, and what determines the outcome of these bargains. A look at the different causal mechanisms through which international organizations influence domestic institutions, as well as the motivations behind the actors using these IOs, will help to frame the rest of the chapters in this volume.

The introduction is divided into five sections. The first section surveys the existing literature on the subject and points out gaps that need to be addressed, while the second section lays out the common assumptions of the chapters in this volume. The third section describes the typology of interactions between democratic and international institutions. The fourth section posits some initial hypotheses on the relationship between international and domestic institutions. The final section previews the rest of the chapters in this volume.

The Literature

The relationship between domestic and international institutions has not gone unexplored in political science. The two-level games approach has made great strides in the study of domestic-international interactions, helping to bridge the intellectual gap between the studies of international relations and comparative politics (Milner 1998). The neoliberal institutionalist approach emphasizes the role of international institutions and their ability to foster international cooperation in the face of domestic impediments (Moravcsik 1991). The constructivist paradigm demonstrates how international regimes can construct norms that permeate domestic structures (Klotz 1995; Finnemore 1996b). Each of these efforts has its drawbacks, however. Puzzles and paradoxes remain.

Robert Putnam's (1988) original article on the two-level games approach has provided a plethora of useful hypotheses. However, his primary focus is on how domestic political opposition affects the ability of leaders to bargain at the international level. Putnam says remarkably little about the reverse effect: how policy initiators can use international bargaining to affect domestic politics. He does provide two ways in which international negotiations can affect the domestic political environment—synergistic linkage across issue areas and the reverberation of international norms into the domestic stage—but these remain underspecified (446–47, 454–56). How exactly can international actors use persuasion to change domestic constituencies' minds? When is issue linkage possible, and when is it not? Follow-up work has fleshed out the two-level games approach (Evans, Jacobson, and Putnam 1993) but as Moravcsik (1993, 5–9) acknowledges, this effort has not really focused on how international institutions can affect the domestic political terrain.[3]

The two-level games approach suffers from three additional flaws. First, the scholarship on domestic-international linkages generates a curious picture of the relevant actors in world politics. The work on two-level games presumes that nation-states are the primary actors in international bargaining, albeit occasionally constrained by domestic politics. The case studies in Evans, Jacobson, and Putnam (1993) primarily describe states making bargains with each other in the face of domestic constraints.[4] No doubt, much of international politics consists of interstate bargains, but much of it consists of bargaining with international organizations. Negotiations with IOs are qualitatively distinct from negotiations with other nation-states. The distinction arises from negotiating over the distribution of power versus the distribution of authority (Claude 1966; Milner 1991; Hurd 1999). Interstate bargains are frequently discrete, one-shot affairs. Their impact may be lasting, but unless new regimes are created through these bargains, it is rare for these negotiations to strip domestic institutions of their authority or legitimacy. Bargains with international organizations, however, permit a greater intrusion into the domestic affairs of nation-states. Historically, states have ceded sovereign powers to international regimes, including the monitoring of human rights conventions, exclusive economic zones, and conditionality requirements on loans made by international financial institutions (Krasner 1995a, 1999).

International organizations derive, from their very existence, some form of collective legitimacy. Public opinion polls in the United States have shown that, ceteris paribus, there is greater support for foreign military action when the action is taken under the auspices of an international organization (Kull 1996; Sobel 1996). Even Hans Morgenthau (1985, 34) has acknowledged the legitimacy of IOs as well as its effects:

> legitimate power has a better chance to influence the will of its objects than equivalent illegitimate power. Power exercised . . . in the name of the United Nations has a better chance to succeed than equivalent power exercised by an "aggressor" nation or in violation of international law.

Beyond the United Nations (UN), other international organizations gain legitimacy through a reputation for expertise (such as the IMF) or through recognition of its ability to set global standards (such as the Basle Committee on Banking Supervision). It is conceivable that in granting IOs concessions domestic institutions also relinquish authority. Bargaining with international organizations is intrinsically distinct from bargaining with other nation-states because it involves the legitimacy of different authorities.

International organizations are distinct from nation-states in another way. The constructivist (Checkel 1997; Klotz 1995) and sociological (DiMaggio and Powell 1983; Ikenberry and Kupchan 1990) paradigms endow IOs with the added power of altering the identities of constituent actors. Repeated interaction between IOs and domestic institutions can lead to new forms of intersubjective understanding. Andrew Cortell and James Davis Jr. (1996) observe that domestic actors will appeal to international norms as a way of pushing their domestic agenda. Mower (1964) has shown that IOs will actively attempt to inculcate norms into the domestic politics of member states; in this volume, Jon C. Pevehouse and Alastair Iain Johnston demonstrate that IOs can transmit or reinforce norms to domestic actors.

A second flaw in the two-level games approach is that there is a lack of imagination about the role that international actors can play in domestic bargaining. Issue linkage and moral suasion are important roles for international actors. But there are a plethora of possible roles. International organizations can provide a way for states to display credible commitments because they wish to avoid the costs in reputation of reneging from a multilateral commitment. In a world of uncertainty, international actors provide a means of signaling preferences and/or outcomes. Through the promotion of epistemic communities, international actors can provide expertise and knowledge to uninformed domestic actors. International institutions affect multilateral bargaining through the threat of coercion or the proffering of targeted bribes. IOs can also provide domestic actors with a source of legitimacy and/or a source of socialization that leads to greater intersubjective understandings. This variety of roles for international actors extends well beyond Putnam's typology or that of neoliberal institutionalists (Keohane 1984).

Finally, another flaw in the two-level games approach is its emphasis on the ratification of major agreements and not on the more routine forms of interaction between international and domestic institutions. Theoretically, there would appear to be no need to distinguish between the two. Empirically, however, there is a significant difference. For most regimes where domestic politics are relevant, the calculus of compliance changes drastically after the ratification of an agreement. As Peter Cowhey (1993, 302) observes, "Divided powers make it harder to initiate commitments and also harder to reverse them."[5] The threat of exit from an international regime after its creation is often a hollow one. Domestic institutions or interests might voice their discontent at adhering to a regime norm, but this rarely translates into action. For example, multilateral economic sanctions lacking the support of an international regime easily fall apart if domestic political forces prefer to trade with the targeted country. Sanctions supported by an international regime experience few defections because these domestic groups are deterred by the authoritative presence of an international organization (Drezner 2000). EU governments have been able to invoke the Maastricht Treaty's goal of European monetary integration to impose harsh macroeconomic policies with reduced domestic political costs (Rotte 1998). Attempts by U.S. trade bureaucracies to circumvent the U.S.-Canada Free Trade Agreement were thwarted (Goldstein 1996). Recalcitrant domestic groups can still subvert policies pushed by IOs, but their ability to do so must be placed in the context of an iterated series of bargains with the international organization that are not disrupted by the threat of exit. Examining how domestic institutions interact after treaties have been signed is just as important as studying their preratification role (Underdal 1998).

Domestic institutions will be concerned about ceding power to international sources of authority. Congress has long been wary about presidents' using North Atlantic Treaty Organization (NATO) or UN authorization to bypass congressional approval of the use of force. Judith Goldstein (1996) has shown the resistance of U.S. trade courts and bureaucracies in response to the U.S.-Canada Free Trade Agreement. David Vogel (1995) has documented the resistance of regulatory agencies in EU countries to cede their authority to the supranational European Commission. Nonexecutive political institutions within developing countries are finding their powers greatly constrained by the stringency of IMF structural adjustment loans. As other issues such as environment protection, intellectual property rights, tax evasion, money laundering, and labor standards require international negotiation and cooperation, domestic agents will have their own reasons to care about the relationship between international and domestic institutions. Kal Raustiala (1997a) notes that the structure of these domestic institutions determines the extent to which a country complies with international regulatory regimes. More research is needed on how domestic institutions react to international pressures.

The two-level games approach does a fair job of characterizing the power and preferences of domestic actors but leaves the international dimension underspecified. The neoliberal institutionalist and constructivist approaches have focused more on the role of international organizations in world politics, but their weakness is the absence of domestic politics from their stories. Both approaches offer explanations for the purpose and power of international institutions. For liberals, international regimes reduce transaction costs and can act to monitor and enforce agreements (Axelrod and Keohane 1985). However, the neoliberal approach presumes either that the nation-state is a unitary actor (Keohane 1984) or that domestic actors can only fashion national preferences in a once-off maneuver (Moravcsik 1997). How different domestic institutions respond to international regimes remains an unanswered question.

The constructivist approach has done a better job of relating how international institutions can disseminate norms that permeate domestic institutions (Finnemore 1996b; Cortell and Davis 1996; Klotz 1995). However, there are three drawbacks to the constructivist approach. First, this paradigm has a great deal of difficulty describing why (or when) certain norms are successfully transplanted across nations while others are unsuccessful. For example, why has the chemical weapons taboo spread but the prohibition of napalm has not? Second, there is a disturbing lack of agency in the constructivist literature. In part this is because this approach relies more upon structural forces than agency to explain change. However, a central tenet of this approach is the mutual interactions of structures and agents (Wendt 1987; Checkel 1997). There is little in the constructivist paradigm about why domestic actors might embrace certain norms but reject others. Finally, the causal mechanisms for the spread of norms are too passive. Finnemore (1996b, 1996c), for example, assumes that domestic institutions mimic accepted global practices without understanding the logic of those practices. The act of persuasion, so important to the prevalence of certain norms, is more complex than this (see Johnston, this volume).

International relations scholars do appreciate the importance of both domestic and international institutions, but their studies of them have bifurcated. The two-level games approach does an able job of describing the effect of domestic institutions on international bargaining but leaves the international dimension underspecified and has a limited explanatory domain. Neoliberal and constructivist approaches do a better job of describing the role of international institutions but fail to examine how these institutions handle their domestic counterparts.

These flaws in the literature have not gone unnoticed. As Lisa Martin and Beth Simmons (1998, 747–49) observe, "in privileging the state as an actor, we have neglected the ways in which other actors in international politics might use institutions . . . and the ways in which the nature or interests of the state itself are potentially changed by the actions of institutions. . . . Overall, as we work towards a more sophisticated specification of the causal mechanisms through which institutions can influence behavior, we will have to pay much more attention to domestic politics than studies of international institutions have thus far." The goal of this volume is to take that challenge seriously.

The Common Assumptions

Clearly, more work is needed on the interactions between international and domestic institutions. There are several ways to tackle this problem. The contributors to this volume will address this issue from a set of common assumptions. This does not mean, however, that the authors have a common set of views with regard to the issue. Rather, the authors take as given the following set of simple propositions to narrow the areas of debate to a manageable range.

The first and driving assumption behind this project is that the growth of global interactions has created a situation of complex interdependence (Keohane and Nye 1978), outstripping the capacity of most nation-states to unilaterally regulate their own affairs. In economic affairs, technological innovations as well as political steps toward economic liberalization have led to an explosion of cross-border transactions, a ten thousandfold increase since 1980. This increase in international interactions has generated a concomitant rise in global externalities. These externalities range from the standardization of product labeling to the enforcement of copyright and patent law to environmental pollution. Most states are unable to manage these externalities without multilateral coordination, resulting in an increased demand for global policy coordination (Braithwaite and Drahos 2000; Keohane 1983). This increased demand for regimes has not been confined to economic matters. The proliferation of weapons of mass destruction, and the improvement in delivery mechanisms for those weapons, has increased the demand for security regimes as well. Globalization does not mean the demise of the nation-state, but it may imply that nation-states are more constrained in their ability to pursue autonomous policies.[6]

The second assumption is that actors can be divided into policy initiators and policy ratifiers. Policy initiators have significant agenda-setting powers. These actors are endowed with the first-mover advantage of proposing a change in the status quo on some policy dimension. Policy ratifiers do not have first-mover advantages, but they do have the ability to veto proposals made by policy initiators. Therefore, initiators must take into account the preferences and powers of ratifiers when they propose policy changes.[7]

This typology of initiators and ratifiers is similar but not identical to the two-level games literature typology of center of governments and policy constituencies (Evans, Jacobson, and Putnam 1993). The two-level games approach presumes that the center of government is a policy initiator. This is frequently true, but there are policy dimensions where the center of government acts like a ratifier. Subnational units might be the policy initiator, needing the approval of executives to have access to international resources (see Blanchard, this volume). Bureaucracies within the executive branch can act as both initiators and ratifiers. Also, there may be states where the initiator and ratifier have such similar preferences that the distinction is uninteresting. Some parliamentary democracies and totalitarian states would fall under this category. However, such unified nation-states are increasingly rare, so the distinction remains a useful one.

The third assumption is that international institutions do not have to be policy initiators to matter in their interactions with domestic institutions. There are clear examples, particularly in the epistemic community literature (Haas 1992a, 1992b), where an international organization acts as the policy initiator. Nevertheless, even authors who emphasize the importance of nonstate actors generally acknowledge that the policies of international organizations are determined by member states and not through some decision-making process separate from those states (Strange 1996; Moravcsik 1999).

That international institutions do not have to be policy initiators does not render them unimportant. They possess attributes that policy initiators lack on their own. These attributes can include expertise, prestige, legitimacy, material resources, credibility, effective signaling capacities, and enforcement powers. The chapters in this volume will reveal a number of different functions for these organizations. IOs also matter because, even if they are policy implementers rather than policy initiators, they will act in different ways than a great power acting without IO auspices. Neorealists explicitly assume that state leaders can force international institutions into line by fiat (Mearsheimer 1994–95); a constitutional approach assumes command by law. The principal-agent theory (Grossman and Hart 1983; Pratt and Zeckhauser 1985; Tirole 1986) as well as the new economics of organization (Moe 1984, 1991; McCubbins, Noll, and Weingast 1987; Banks 1989) suggest it is not that simple. International institutions promulgate rules that create expectations of compliance by all actors. Even great powers incur costs by violating those rules (Milgrom, North, and Weingast 1991; Ikenberry 2000).[8] At the very least, international institutions have some degree of insulation from power politics. Indeed, this is often the source of their legitimacy.[9] With this insulation, IOs alter the range of available bargaining strategies, changing the nature of the interaction. International institutions are thus an important intervening variable, even if not an independent one (Krasner 1983).

These assumptions are plausible enough to be noncontroversial. They are simple enough to generate interesting descriptions of institutional interactions without getting bogged down in needless arcana. With these assumptions in mind, the next section sets up a typology of institutional interactions.

A Typology of Institutional Interactions

There are two variables that help to categorize the range of interactions between domestic and international institutions. The first variable is the identity of the policy initiator. The second variable is the influence mechanism through which the international organization interacts with domestic institutions.

The first relevant variable is whether the policy initiator is a domestic or external actor. External initiators are distinct from domestic initiators because they exist outside the rules, norms, or procedures that govern a given territory and therefore lack the legal or moral standing to employ those mechanisms of governance. A domestic policy initiator will use international institutions as a way of increasing its leverage over the domestic ratifying institution. One reason for this tactic is for states to acquire IO expertise; another might be to acquire its legitimacy (Claude 1996). However, it is possible for the policy initiator to be an actor external to the nation-state in question. The United States' use of NATO to intervene in Bosnia and Kosovo would fall under this category, as would Russia's use of the Commonwealth of Independent States to intervene in the former Soviet republics. Other nation-states, nongovernmental organizations (NGOs), or multinational corporations might use international institutions as a mechanism to influence the target state. External policy initiators choose international organizations because they are denied access through domestic political channels. Acting through an international organization becomes their best option.

Internal and external policy initiators will use international organizations as a means for achieving policy outcomes that would otherwise be unfeasible. There is, however, a distinction between external and internal initiators in the matter of information. Domestic initiators are assumed to have more information about the policy environment of the target country. External initiators often lack the tacit knowledge that only comes through experiencing the political processes of the target country firsthand.

The second relevant variable is the influence mechanism through which international institutions will be used to influence domestic institutions. There are three types of influence that will be explored in this volume: contracting, coercion, and persuasion. These three influence mechanisms have been selected because each presumes some form of strategic interaction.[10]

The distinctions between contracting, coercion, and persuasion have been discussed elsewhere (Krasner 1999; Hurd 1999). Nevertheless, it is worth defining these types of interactions.[11] Contracting is an interaction in which all of the negotiating parties can be made better off relative to the status quo, with no actor being made worse off. Each possible outcome is Pareto improving. Contracting is therefore analogous to most market transactions, in which either all parties benefit from the transaction or there is no transaction, leaving no one worse off than before. Actors make their choices based purely on their own calculations of self-interest and do not need to worry about other actors punishing them should they choose not to cooperate. In this type of interaction, actors influence each other through the proffering of incentives, but not through the threat of sanctions.[12]

Contracting is the common mode through which international political economy scholars characterize interactions with international organizations. International institutions enhance their power, prestige, and reputation through the acceptance of their advice by nation-states and the successful creation of common norms. An analysis of the regime governing stratospheric ozone shows that the United Nations Environmental Program (UNEP) enhanced its influence through the acceptance by member states of its scientific conclusions (Haas 1992b). The Montreal Protocol widened the power and influence of the epistemic community that the UNEP helped create. Cooperation also generates a virtuous cycle. As more states cooperate with the relevant IO, chain-ganging behavior increases the incentive of other states to follow suit (Martin 1992; Drezner 2000).

Similarly, nation-states benefit from the reduced uncertainty of cooperation with an IO. One fear of globalization is that states will be forced to engage in race-to-the-bottom tactics to attract investment (Wallach and Sforza 1999; Tonelson 2000). Capital will flow to the areas where it can receive the greatest return on its investment. To some, this means the relaxation of labor, environmental, taxation, and human rights standards. Cooperation at the multilateral level, facilitated by international regimes, can help to prevent this phenomenon (Vogel 1995). Domestic institutions can use international organizations to retain some policy-making autonomy, leading to a win-win scenario for both sets of institutions. States can further benefit in the form of increased multilateral assistance from IOs to ensure cooperation.

Like contracting, coercion is choice theoretic; it presumes actors have clear definitions of their self-interest and will pursue their ends accordingly. The difference, as Hurd (1999, 386) notes, is the ability of other actors to influence decision making: "self-interest [contracting] involves *self-restraint* on the part of an actor . . . whereas coercion operates by *external* restraint." Coercive exchanges allow for the possibility outcomes that leave at least one actor worse off than the status quo. This does not imply that all coercive transactions end with Pareto-worsening outcomes. Rather, it is the prospect of such an outcome occurring that endows some actors with coercive power (Gruber 2000).

International organizations can use coercive practices to enforce multilateral agreements or to authorize member states to engage in coordinated coercion. The World Trade Organization (WTO) authorizes the use of trade sanctions to combat illegal trading practices. The Montreal Protocol permits member states to sanction countries that violate controls on chlorofluorocarbon (CFC) production. The UN Security Council has authorized both economic sanctions and the use of force to contain rogue states such as Iraq and Yugoslavia. Regional organizations such as the Organization of American States or the Economic Community of West African States have also applied coercive pressure in the interest of maintaining regional stability. Since the 1970s, many of these IOs have used coercive tactics to alter the target state's domestic institutions, through the enforcement of human rights treaties (Krasner 1995a).

Coercion is also a likely tactic when distributional conflicts arise. As Stephen D. Krasner (1991) points out, frequently the problem in international relations is not getting to the Pareto frontier but rather knowing where on the Pareto frontier to be. When states have already cooperated to the point where they are at the frontier, any attempt to increase one's utility comes at the expense of other actors. By definition, this kind of interaction has a coercive component. The question that both international and domestic institutions must ask is whether the joint gains of cooperation are worth the costs of acquiescing on an issue. For the IMF, is sustained cooperation with Russia worth the price to its reputation in the face of repeated Russian defections from agreements?[13] For the U.S. trade bureaucracy, are the benefits of free trade with Canada outweighed by the transfer of its authority to the binational panels set up to arbitrate trade disputes? At the Pareto frontier, international and domestic institutions face a zero-sum bargaining game where both sides are better off cooperating, but any improvement in their situation comes at the expense of the other.

It would be natural but erroneous to associate contracting tactics with the neoliberal paradigm and coercive tactics with the neorealist paradigm. As neoliberals describe cooperation, most agreements, once made, have a coercive element in order to enforce them. Similarly, realists permit purely contractual agreements between actors; two states agreeing to ally together to balance against a greater power, for example, are engaging in a contractual relationship that benefits both parties. It would be more appropriate to parse contracting and coercion in a temporal sense. Contracting occurs in situations when actors find themselves in an inefficient equilibrium and try to improve upon it. Coercion occurs postagreement, to ensure that all the actors adhere to the new equilibrium.[14]

Unlike contracting or coercing strategies, persuasion allows for the possibility that the internal preference ordering of actors can be changed through new modes of intersubjective understanding.[15] In the contracting or coercive approaches, actors ensure cooperation by manipulating the material external environment of incentives and disincentives. The persuasive approach reorders the internal values of the actor (Hurd 1999). The observed outcome of cooperation might be identical to the outcomes observed through contracting or coercion, but the causal mechanism is distinct.

There are several components to persuasion. For actors to be persuaded, they must be introduced to new concepts or analogies that alter their perceptions of the world. Like the man in Plato's cave, actors that lack information may develop a distorted set of perceptions.[16] If they receive new information, or new methods to process the information, their conceptual tool kit can be expanded, altering their preferences over issues in the process. For example, the initial Soviet resistance to the antiballistic missile (ABM) treaty in the early 1970s was predicated on the belief that defensive weapons were appropriate in an age of nuclear deterrence. Only after the United States altered its nuclear doctrine, and American negotiators persuaded the Soviets that an ABM defense would increase the temptation of launching an offensive strike, did the Soviets change their mind (Nye 1987).

Persuasion can also occur through the creation of social ties that generate nonmaterial incentives to go along with other transnational policy elites. There are multiple examples of persuasion mattering in international affairs. Through the auspices of an IO emanation, the United Nations Conference on Trade and Development's (UNCTAD) Intergovernmental Group of Experts on Restrictive Business Practices, most developing states have altered their preferences on global antitrust policy to fit better with developed world practices (Sell 1998). The UN's provision of new scientific and moral concepts helped to place environmental cooperation onto the global agenda (Haas 1992b). The Financial Stability Forum has promulgated a compendium of international financial standards that has strengthened the supervision and self-regulation of banking sectors across the globe. Persuasion has worked across a wide range of issue areas.

Persuasion, like coercion or contracting, is choice theoretic. Persuasion requires a greater degree of social interaction than does either contracting or coercion.[17] But persuasion also has important elements of strategic interaction. The persuading actor acts strategically in choosing the forum to engage in persuasion. As Alastair Iain Johnston's chapter notes, there may be a trade-off between forums that are well suited for persuasion and forums that are well suited for contracting or coercion. The actor targeted for persuasion needs to calculate whether there is a sufficient level of intersubjective understanding to warrant a change in the ordering of preferences over ends. If an actor is successfully persuaded, it then acts strategically in deciding whether to persuade other actors within the nation-state or to exploit principal-agent divisions as a way of altering the nation-state's foreign policy outputs. Persuasion requires a higher degree of social interaction, but there are still strategic components.

All international institutions use some mix of contracting, coercion, and persuasion in their interactions with nation-states. Parsing these mechanisms out is useful, however, if for no other reason than to observe the pattern of use and success of all of these mechanisms. The next section develops some preliminary hypotheses on this typology of institutional interactions.

Some Hypotheses about Institutional Interactions

With our typology of interactions, we can consider a more analytical set of questions to answer: Which IO mechanism will policy initiators use to interact with domestic institutions? Are internal or external initiators more likely to succeed in their influence attempts? What is the long-term cumulative effect of the use of international institutions? The full answers to these questions are left to the ensuing chapters. At this stage, however, it is possible to propose some tentative hypotheses that address these issues.

The first set of hypotheses deals with the relationship between state structure and the incentive for domestic policy–initiating institutions to use the contracting process. International relations theory has recognized the importance of state structure in the past but primarily through the variable of state strength. Strong states remain autonomous from societal pressures; weak policy-making states are more susceptible to societal pressures (Katzenstein 1978; Desch 1996). Just as important for our concerns, however, is the autonomy of state institutions *from each other* (Risse-Kappen 1995b; Drezner 2001). In parliamentary democracies, for example, the legislative and executive branches are closely linked; the policy-initiating and policy-ratifying institutions are essentially fused. In presidential systems, both branches of government must often approve a particular policy; they both have veto points. In federal nation-states, like Brazil, Germany, and the Russian Federation, central governments have much less freedom of movement in some issue areas as compared to unitary states like France, Japan, or Ukraine. Other domestic institutions that can increase the number of ratifying institutions include civil services within bureaucratic units and independent judiciaries.

We define states with multiple ratifying institutions as decentralized and those with relatively few veto points as centralized. In a fully centralized system there is only one veto point, and the initiator and ratifier are the same (for example, the dictator). Centralized states endow great power at the leadership level, but there are few independent sources of governing authority in these states. The simplest case of a decentralized system is with one ratifier and one (different) initiator. Highly decentralized systems have many ratifiers and may have multiple initiators. Decentralized states have multiple, interdependent centers of authority.

How does this state structure affect attitudes toward international institutions? In both types of states, policy-initiating institutions will use the contracting capabilities of IOs but for different reasons. Initiators from centralized states will use international institutions to establish credible commitments. Because centralized states can reverse policies at will, their credibility is limited (North and Weingast 1989). IOs can act as a surrogate ratifying institution when domestic ratifying institutions are weak or nonexistent. Jon C. Pevehouse shows in this volume how this helps democratizing states consolidate their political reforms.

Initiators from decentralized states need international institutions for a different reason. Decentralized states have a greater ability to credibly commit, but policy makers also face more roadblocks to policy implementation. International institutions can provide the necessary resources to implement a policy that would have been impossible in the domestic realm. If the international institution prefers policies that conflict with the ratifiers but not with initiator, the latter will prefer an internationalization strategy. Furthermore, by locking in a policy through an international institution, the initiator helps to increase the costs to a state's reputation of reversing course. With decentralized states, international institutions expand the ex ante choice set by reducing the number of ex post options.

Domestic state structure affects how policy initiators use international institutions, but so does the organizational structure of international institutions. International relations theory has tended to treat all international organizations in an undifferentiated manner, although this is slowly changing (Koremenos, Lipson, and Snidal 2001). International organizations differ according to whether the membership is open or restricted; whether decisions are made via unweighted voting, weighted voting, or consensus mechanisms; whether the organization has centralized or decentralized resources; and whether the IO is endowed with enforcement powers or not.

IOs vary according to structural dimensions, making them useful in different situations. The ideal IO structure for contracting may differ from the ideal structure for coercion, which may differ from an IO designed for persuasion. Institutionalists, for example, talk about the need for strong, centralized enforcement and monitoring capabilities to coerce wayward actors; as Alastair Iain Johnston notes in his chapter, these qualities may make persuasion much more difficult. Similarly, an IO will be more effective at coercion when the membership is large (Drezner 2000), but this also raises the transaction costs of contracting (Axelrod and Keohane 1985).

That said, there are certain traits common to the successful use of international organizations by policy initiators. For example, the more select the membership criteria, the more valuable the IO becomes. Selectivity can give an international organization enhanced stature to its members, making its actions more relevant. The importance of selectivity can be seen in Jon C. Pevehouse's emphasis on "democratic" IOs or in Alastair Iain Johnston's emphasis on the small size of the Association of Southeast Asian Nations (ASEAN) Regional Forum. Another useful trait for contracting, coercion, and persuasion is a well-respected secretariat. If an IO staff is held in high esteem, it will be easier to achieve consensus among the organization's members in dealing with the targeted state. This can be seen in Jean-Marc F. Blanchard's chapter in this volume on the role of the United Nations Development Programme (UNDP) in the formation of the Tumen River Area Development Programme (TRADP).

Another hypothesis concerns the relationship between the location of the policy initiator and the likelihood of a successful bargain. A relatively straightforward prediction would be that, ceteris paribus, external policy initiators will have less success in their interactions with domestic institutions than will domestic policy initiators. There are three reasons for this. First, a domestic policy initiator should possess more accurate information about the preferences of policy ratifiers, the relevant interest groups, and public opinion in general. It should therefore make fewer errors than an external policy initiator. Second, an external policy initiator must overcome the perception that it is intruding into another country's sovereignty; otherwise its pressure could be perceived as illegitimate. Such a scenario would incur rally-round-the-flag effects in the targeted state. This issue is one reason why external policy initiators will work through international institutions to manipulate another state's domestic institutions. Even with this shielding, however, external initiators will usually lack the legitimacy that domestic policy initiators have.[18] Third, an external policy initiator has no guarantee that any domestic interest groups or institutions will share their preferences. When a domestic policy initiator internationalizes its approach, this implies that a segment of the targeted state supports a change in policy. The same cannot be presumed when the policy initiator is external to the state.

The final hypothesis deals with the long-term effects of the interaction between international and domestic institutions. Repeated interactions should inevitably enhance the power of policy initiators at the expense of ratifying institutions. Why? The transfer of authority from domestic to international institutions has an asymmetric effect on the domestic institutional balance. The governance structure of most international organizations apportions voting power to member states. Policy-initiating institutions within these states often control these votes. These institutions will also have enhanced influence and knowledge gained through their day-to-day interactions with the international organization. Thus, although the transfer of authority from domestic to international institutions weakens the power of all domestic institutions, policy initiators will retain more influence over the international organization through their voting power and routinized interactions. To be sure, ratifying institutions can influence the behavior of international organizations through the denial of funding or through restrictions on how country representatives should vote on particular issues.[19] However, this influence is indirect and constrained by principal-agent problems. Over the long term, there should be a burgeoning "democracy deficit" as more power shifts away from ratifying institutions.

This hypothesis, combined with the work done on bargaining and two-level games, highlights a central irony about the power of foreign policy leaders. Schelling (1960), Putnam (1988), and others have pointed out that foreign policy leaders can use the recalcitrance of domestic ratifying institutions as a way to extract more concessions from other negotiating partners. This volume suggests that leaders can also use the resources of international organizations to force acquiescence from domestic ratifiers. The irony is that, although numerous scholars have highlighted the increasing power of subnational actors and international organizations, foreign policy leaders can play these new actors off each other as a way of enhancing their own power.

The hypotheses in this section are tentative at best, but they provide a useful flashlight with which to illuminate the presentations in this volume.

The Rest of the Book

As noted previously, a great deal has been written on the interaction between domestic and international politics. However, this volume distinguishes itself from the previous literature in several ways. First, it pushes beyond the use of two-level game metaphors and generates more concrete theories on how the interaction between second-image and third-image institutions affects international relations. Second, it creates a useful typology of institutional interactions. Third, because the topic addresses issues that have been handled in a variety of methodological and theoretical ways, the contributors run the gamut in terms of their approaches. Fourth, the chapters run the empirical gamut, from the use of military force to regional economic development.

Finally, the cases discussed are non-European. While the EU is a phenomenon worthy of extensive study, there is an unfortunate tendency to generalize from a case with extreme values for some of the relevant variables. This type of approach can lead to flawed generalizations (Collier and Mahoney 1996). The cases under discussion in this volume include studies of North America, East Asia, and newly established democracies. These areas have been neglected in studies of institutional interaction.

The first two chapters look at the ability of policy initiators to exploit the contracting capabilities of international institutions. Jon C. Pevehouse examines how policy initiators within democratizing states use international organizations as a means of consolidating the reform process. Pevehouse observes that initiators will use international institutions as a means of locking in reforms and as a means of compensating elites that are out of power, reducing the temptation to seize power by extraconstitutional means. Not all international institutions can perform this function, but those with an essentially democratic character and membership are well suited to this task. Pevehouse argues that international institutions raise the costs of defections from democracy in the future and guarantee that all elites within a democratizing society benefit from the reform process.

Jean-Marc F. Blanchard looks at the transnational politics behind the TRADP, a regional organization in Northeast Asia bordering China, Russia, and North Korea. China has been eager to develop the borderland, and the project has received assistance from the United Nations Development Programme. However, Russia has proven to be a stumbling block to development. Blanchard shows that this is not due to resistance from Moscow but rather to resistance from the Primorski Kray region of Russia that is directly affected by TRADP. The governor of the region, as the ratifier, has vetoed further development because of the threat to his own power base and the region's mistrust of China's motives. In this case, the external policy initiator cannot overcome the resistance of the domestic ratifier, despite the Pareto-improving outcome.

The next two chapters develop game-theoretic models to demonstrate how the contracting and coercion techniques can be used. Eric Reinhardt looks at how domestic policy initiators can use their knowledge of General Agreement on Tariffs and Trade (GATT)/WTO procedures as a way of getting protectionist ratifiers to liberalize trade rules. Reinhardt uses a game-theoretic model to show that initiators are capable of using an international institution's implicit threat of coercion by its members to extract concessions from an otherwise recalcitrant legislature. However, this comes at a price; initiators will also be forced at times to acquiesce to ratifying institutions because it does not want to incur the transaction costs of the WTO's adjudication process. Contrary to the claim of neoliberal institutionalists, in some cases high transaction costs in international organizations help to strengthen cooperation. Reinhardt backs up these hypotheses with compelling statistical evidence.

Kenneth A. Schultz looks at how the Clinton administration was able to use international organizations to blunt congressional opposition to participation in armed humanitarian interventions. He argues that the resort to IOs helps to commit the president to military action by bolstering popular support for an operation and by increasing the costs of backing down. This commitment device magnifies the president's power by forcing congressional opponents to choose between stopping an ongoing operation—thereby risking blame if things go badly—or taking only symbolic steps. Thus, international institutions can help the policy initiator expand its policy menu in the face of opposition from the ratifier.

The next chapter explores the persuasion mechanism more fully. Alastair Iain Johnston examines how China's membership in the ASEAN Regional Forum and the UN have altered Chinese foreign ministry's perceptions of security issues. Johnston first explores the microprocesses of how persuasion works. He then shows that China has acquired a new understanding of important Western security concepts through the ASEAN Regional Forum and demonstrates how foreign ministry bureaucrats have adopted these concepts in the crafting of foreign policy. China's participation in UN negotiations of a Comprehensive Test Ban Treaty has socialized Chinese diplomats to the point where China has been willing to cooperate with other states in the region on nuclear testing to a surprising extent.

The concluding chapter by Duncan Snidal and Alexander Thompson reviews the lessons learned from the models and cases presented in the volume. It evaluates the contributions made by this volume to our understanding of transnational institutional interactions. The hypotheses posed in these chapters are evaluated in light of the empirical support, and avenues for further research are mapped out.

Notes

1. In the interest of style, I will use the terms "international organization," "international regime," and "international institution" interchangeably. This comes at some cost to analytical precision, but the distinctions between these terms have been previously discussed in the literature. On the distinction between international regimes and international organizations, see Young 1980, Krasner 1983, and Keohane 1989. As used here, the term "international institution" encompasses both regimes and organizations, which is why it will be the dominant term in this text.

2. The concluding chapter by Duncan Snidal and Alexander Thompson addresses the extent to which this potential is fulfilled.

3. Schoppa (1997) is an exception, but he confines his bargaining analysis to the U.S.-Japan relationship, restricting the generalizability of his approach.

4. Kahler 1993 is a notable exception.

5. See also Drezner 1998 and Underdal 1998, 18–19.

6. It should be pointed out that the effect of globalization is unequal across nation-states. States with sufficiently large internal markets and security forces are less vulnerable to the dictates of global markets. Less developed

countries, on the other hand, have fewer independent resources to cope with globalization and are thus more likely to seek out the support of international organizations.

7. There are other roles that actors can play in the policy process, including facilitation and implementation. These roles are discussed but not stressed in this volume.

8. For example, despite the United States' preeminent role in NATO, the United States felt compelled to play by NATO's rules during the Cuban Missile Crisis (Risse-Kappen 1995a) as well as in the decision to intervene in Bosnia (Holbrooke 1998).

9. This suggests an intriguing paradox. For great powers, the more autonomous the IO, the more useful its legitimacy. The more autonomous the international institution, however, the less influence the great power has over its policy.

10. This is not an exhaustive typology; Finnemore (1995), for example, discusses mimicking, a different causal mechanism from those listed here.

11. It should be stressed that particular influence attempts combine elements of each of these ideal types.

12. Note that this criterion does not exclude the possibility of one actor offering additional incentives to ensure cooperation. A Pareto-improving agreement implies that winners receive sufficiently large benefits such that they can compensate any other agent's losses and still increase their own utility.

13. See Stone 1997 on this very conundrum.

14. Fearon (1998) uses a similar typology.

15. As used in this introduction, the term "persuasion" encompasses both the persuasion and the social influence mechanism discussed in Johnston's chapter.

16. This does not imply that actors with complete information cannot develop different perceptions. However, persuasion is of little use in this scenario.

17. Coercion and contracting have elements of social interaction (Wendt 1999). Coercion and contracting strategies require some degree of intersubjective understanding, such as the mutual recognition of interdependence and common knowledge of the game structure.

18. For an exception, see Schoppa 1997.

19. Examples of this include U.S. legislation in the 1970s authorizing U.S. representatives in multilateral development banks to vote against aid to countries that violated certain human rights practices.

Part 1. Contracting

Democratization, Credible Commitments, and Joining International Organizations

Jon C. Pevehouse

International institutions and organizations have become the center-piece of the heated debate between realists and neoliberals over the past two decades. Realists and their neorealist counterparts contend that institutions have little influence on state behavior and are simply epiphenomenal to outcomes in world politics (Mearshimer 1994–95; Grieco 1988). Neoliberals argue that institutions provide essential functions to facilitate cooperation that would not otherwise occur between rational, egoistic actors (Keohane 1984; Keohane and Martin 1995). Although there are no easy answers in this debate, part of the question of whether institutions matter for international cooperation turns on why sovereign states join these organizations in the first place. The neoliberals argue that, if international institutions and organizations are indeed epiphenomenal, why do so many states continue to join and form these structures? As the neoliberals readily admit, however, no one has a clear answer to this question (Keohane and Martin 1995).

The purpose of this chapter is to provide one part of the answer to the question of why states join IOs.[1] I will argue that membership in certain types of international organizations are coveted by certain states in the international system for reasons that have little to do with traditional concerns of international cooperation. Specifically, newly democratized states desire membership in "democratic" international organizations—that is, IOs where the vast majority of members are recognized as democracies. Moreover, they join and attempt to join these organizations not for reasons typically outlined by neoliberals (decreased transaction costs, creation of forums and sidepayment opportunities for international bargains, and so forth) but for domestic political reasons. In a nutshell, leaders in nascent democracies need to make credible commitments to democratic reform, including liberal economic reform. Membership in an international institution allows

25

them greater credibility and policy leverage vis-à-vis potential opponents in the new democratic system. Thus, they join institutions in an attempt to secure democracy.

To test this theory, I conduct a large-N statistical investigation of the determinants of joining "democratic" international organizations (defined subsequently). I find that democratization, ceteris paribus, is a significant predictor of accession to these organizations. The chapter will proceed as follows. First, I briefly review what the existing neoliberal and international organizations literature has to say concerning why states join IOs; second, I outline the issue of why leaders in new democracies have a difficult time achieving credible commitments to reform; third, I review why certain types of IOs can provide that credibility to nascent democracies; and finally, I conduct an empirical test of this hypothesis, evaluating the influences on joining "democratic" IOs from 1950 to 1992.

Why Join International Organizations?

International organizations are ubiquitous in modern international politics. Although few would disagree that these organizations are increasing in number, opinions would differ on their potential to influence in international politics. Before delving into a discussion of international organizations, however, we must define what we mean by an IO. I adopt the definition of Shanks, Jacobson, and Kaplan (1996, 593), who view IOs as "associations established by governments or their representatives that are sufficiently institutionalized to require regular meetings, rules governing decision-making, a permanent staff, and a headquarters." This definition places IOs as a subset within the concept of international institutions. Thus, debates about the effectiveness of international institutions include, but are not limited to, international organizations.

My concern in this work is less with the theoretical debate between those who do and those who do not believe in the efficacy of institutions in engendering cooperation among states. Rather, I address the puzzle previously outlined; why would a state choose to join an international organization? Such decisions can be costly politically and especially economically.[2] Yet, why do states seem anxious to join such institutions, given that they (a) are costly and (b) may or may not be important in facilitating interstate cooperation?

For most work on international organizations, the prevailing assumption is that states join IOs to help solve coordination problems, persuade other states to change their preferences, or help enforce bargains (see Martin 1992). Much of this work has evolved in the fields of international political economy and security studies. Traditional work in the field of international organization still describes the role of IOs as pursuing "common or converging national interests of the member states" (Feld and Jordan 1994, 10). IOs, for the vast majority of this literature, reflect concerns with international politics that cannot otherwise be dealt with domestically (Archer 1992, 48).

My contention is that the push for accession to an IO can come from the domestic political arena, especially in states that have recently undergone a transition to democracy. This is not to say that the international forum is unimportant. Certainly the impetus behind the formation of many international and regional organizations is conditions that states feel they can cope with only as a group. I would argue, however, that many IOs are formed with one eye on the domestic political process. If for no other reason, leaders must watch for a domestic backlash against membership itself.[3] More important, much of the "action" in an international organization consists of nonmember states attempting to join the organization. IOs can serve a variety of purposes, but seldom do states apply for membership to an existing organization simply to solve a coordination or collaboration problem with another state (which is already a member). To explain such decisions, one must turn to domestic politics.

There is surprisingly little work on the domestic determinants of IO membership. The scholarship that does exist concentrates mostly on the political economy of regionalism. Specifically, work by Milner (1988) and Busch and Milner (1994) argues that domestic firms have demanded regional trade organizations due to factors such as the export dependence of firms, firm multinationality, and the structure of intraindustry trade (Busch and Milner 1994, 268–70). Thus, the confluence of international or regional economic conditions and the preferences of firms within a state give rise to international organizations that may impact international cooperation but find their impetus domestically.

A similar argument is made by Etel Solingen (1994) with regard to the security arena. Her work argues that whether or not a state joins regional security arrangements (specifically, nonproliferation agreements) is a function of the nature of domestic political coalitions within a state. Thus, "internationalist" coalitions of favoring domestic economic liberalization will join institutions to maximize the benefits received from institutions. International institutions can "bank-roll" domestic coalitions (Solingen 1994, 168). Joining regional security frameworks, therefore, is driven by the domestic political concerns of the liberalizing coalitions. These works serve as an excellent starting point to make the broader economic and political argument I put forth.[4] Namely, joining and creating international organizations have as much to do with domestic political imperatives (including the demands of firms) as they do with solving international coordination problems.

Finally, there is a body of literature that discusses how IOs can be used strategically by actors in their domestic political battles. Although this work does not usually seek to explain the formation of or accession to an IO, the general theories are similar. Much of these hypotheses grow out of the two-level games literature in discussing the political dynamics between the international bargaining and the domestic ratification games (Putnam 1988; Evans, Jacobson, and Putnam 1993). Judith Goldstein (1996), for example, has argued that mechanisms instituted by the North American Free Trade Agreement (NAFTA) have been utilized by the president to achieve a policy outcome that would have otherwise been opposed by Congress. Xinyuan Dai (1999) has argued that domestic environmental groups use international organizations as a source for assistance during policy battles with governments that would not otherwise support environmental protection. For these authors, IOs serve an instrumental purpose for domestic political actors or coalitions—to help them achieve a certain goal in domestic politics rather than a goal of international cooperation.

Although this literature provides an excellent starting point for this chapter, there is little scholarship on the relationship between democracy and IO involvement.[5] There has been speculation and many brief references to the relationship between IOs and democracy, but no systematic empirical study of this association exists. In their work discussing IOs, interdependence, and militarized disputes, Bruce Russett, John Oneal, and David R. Davis (1998) find, in their dyadic data set, that the higher the democracy score of the least democratic state in the dyad, the more likely these states are to be involved in an IO. They do not discuss this finding, and the variable itself is only a control for their test of the effect of military conflict on IO involvement (that is, their endogeneity tests).

Shanks, Jacobson, and Kaplan (1996) find that states that have become more democratic (over an eleven-year period) tend to belong to *fewer* international organizations, although, as they point out, they do not control for the type of organization. They speculate that their finding grows out of the collapsed Eastern bloc IOs that ended shortly after the breakup of the Soviet Union (Shanks, Jacobson, and Kaplan 1996, 609–10). Moreover, they only speculate as to why many democratizing states outside the Eastern bloc actually increased their IO portfolio over the same time period. This chapter attempts to provide the answer to this question. The next section discusses the problems confronted by democratizing states and why internal measures to deal with these issues are not always credible or successful.

Democratization and Credible Commitments

New democracies face a variety of political and economic challenges throughout their existence (Linz and Stepan 1996). Their early years, however, bring the most severe obstacles (Power and Gasiorowski 1997). These challenges tend to arise from two groups that emerge in the aftermath of the initial transitions: distributional winners and losers. Institutions have distributional consequences for many actors (Knight 1992), and it is not surprising that when institutions change so do the identity of the winners and losers. These winners and losers may consist of groups, political parties, even individuals. Winners can attempt to turn their (often newfound) power into a permanent political advantage. As Lane (1979) and Przeworski (1991) point out, political power gives rise to increasing returns to scale: political power begets more political (and economic) power. This "temptation of power" can result in biased institutions, the exclusion of certain groups from the democratic process, a freezing of the pace of reform, and even a reversal of earlier liberalization (Hellman 1998). Why would winners bias emerging democratic institutions, especially if they are winning in the short term? In many cases these new democrats feel their ability to advance reform slipping, and they usurp power to further the cause of reform. Stephan Haggard and Robert Kaufman (1995, 8) allude to this dynamic when they argue that "the fact that so many leaders in new democracies have acted autocratically in crisis situations implies that such behavior cannot be explained simply in terms of personal ambition or lack of concern for democratic institutions." Often, the explanation lies in the inability of leaders to make credible commitments to liberal reform.[6]

The form of this "autocratic" action in a crisis varies: taking control of the state by canceling elections, suspending reform, or even cracking down on potential antiregime forces can occur in these situations. The lack of the ability to make a credible commitment to democratic reforms on the part of regime leaders can undermine democratic consolidation. How can a commitment problem hinder the consolidation process? There are multiple answers to this question, but first I will discuss why such a commitment problem is especially acute in transitional states.

There are three main sources of credibility problems for new democratic states.[7] These credibility issues arise with regard to both economic and political liberalization but are particularly acute in states undergoing a dual transition. The first problem is time-inconsistent preferences. A regime's optimal policy ex ante may differ from its evaluations of proper policy ex post (Rodrik 1989b). The regime is reform oriented, but because of exogenous conditions or as a result of reform itself the government contemplates or undertakes a reversal of previous reform. This type of reversal is most common in the economic realm, where governments often rescind reforms in response to internal opposition (Krueger 1978). Although this is not a problem faced only by new democracies, the high turnover rate of leadership in major groups and/or parties within new democracies exacerbates the probability of ex post policy reversals (Calvo and Frankel 1991).[8] It is important to note that simply the perceived threat of reversal is what is important to regime opponents and economic interests (both international and domestic). That is, opponents and investors will make decisions based on their ex ante calculations of the likelihood of reversal at the time of policy implementation, regardless of the eventual outcome.

The second source of a lack of credibility is information related. Regimes can and do begin reform that they have no intention of completing (that is, those who freeze reform or bias institutions for their own power).[9] There are certain benefits that accrue to those who make certain economic reforms (e.g., loans, increased investment) that can give governments an incentive to appear as reformist (Frye 1997). Given that the regime is relatively new, external and internal actors have even less information about the true type of government in power. This uncertainty over the type of government (sincere versus dissembling) can limit the benefits of reform for those who are sincere. Thus, earnest reformers would benefit from sending a credible signal to distinguish themselves from fraudulent reformers.

Last and most important, new regimes lack a reputation for having self-restraint and honoring commitments (Diermeier et al. 1998;

Linz 1978). Established governments have built a reputation for honoring commitments to reform, protecting property rights, and so forth. New regimes have no track record and thus foster few expectations that commitments will be credible. Compounding this problem is that during many transitions existing institutions are cast aside by the winners, which can create a slippery slope to less credibility for these actors.[10] Thus, any reputation that may exist for those in power will be negative: "After any transition from authoritarian rule, the emergent democracy will be a regime in which not all significant political actors will have impeccable democratic credentials" (Whitehead 1989, 78). Since the winner's past behavior consisted of gutting or severely altering domestic institutions, its ability to signal credible commitments in the posttransition period will be limited.

Democratization and its attendant credibility problems create immense difficulties in both the political and economic realms. In the political realm, elites often have a deep mutual distrust for one another in the transitional period (Burton, Gunther, and Higley 1992). This absence of trust flows directly from the lack of reputation for keeping agreements and is compounded by the uncertainty of the transitional environment. It can have disastrous consequences for democracy. If regime opponents do not believe that political reform or economic liberalization efforts are sincere, they are unlikely to lend support to the new regime. They may become active against the regime, even turning to violent measures (Crescenzi 1999) or allying with other disaffected groups in society.[11] Regardless of the option the opposition chooses, they force the regime into a response.

It is this forced reaction on the part of the regime that can further undermine democracy and escalate the distrust between winners and losers. A cycle of distrust can develop, weakening the already fragile democracy: "[I]f each political sector concludes that the democratic commitment of the other is lukewarm, this will reduce the motivation of all, and so perpetuate the condition of fragility" (Whitehead 1989, 94). Winners feel they are losing control of the state. They feel that a segment of the population has turned against them and cannot be trusted. Opposition groups refuse to be placated since they no longer trust any promises of future reform. As Gunther, Diamandouros, and Puhle (1995, 9) note, this lack of respect for the governing elite's authority "could be compatible with an abridgment of democracy that might ultimately culminate in its transformation into a limited democracy or authoritarian regime." Thus, the bias in institutions does not result from the preferences or the greed of actors in the new regime per se but is a consequence of the lack of trust and a credible commitment to democracy.

One example of this dynamic is the suspension of democracy by Peruvian president Alberto Fujimori in 1992. Faced with an armed opposition group as well as a judicial and legislative branch he could not trust, Fujimori suspended the legislature and installed his own government. He justified the coup on the grounds that he needed more power to fight "legislative and judicial corruption" (Galvin 1992). A major reason the legislature had become so opposed to Fujimori was their worry over his potentially dictatorial style: dubbed the "Little Emperor" by many Peruvian observers, he often accused "special interests" of making too many demands on the state (Hayes 1992). The distrust among Peruvian elites was a major reason behind Fujimori's action (Gunther, Diamandouros, and Puhle 1995, 9).

Another scenario for the weakening of reform flowing from the lack of a credible commitment to reform arises in the economic realm. Two groups of economic actors can react negatively to a lack of credibility in economic reform. First, international investors and corporations are hesitant to invest if they feel reform may be short lived (Frye 1997). This reluctance has economic implications for young governments, which are often in dire need of capital. At best, such a credibility gap slows the process of investment. At worst, a lack of capital inflow can lead to balance of payments problems, especially if domestic actors perceive the same credibility gap.

Second, domestic economic agents will alter their behavior if they sense the same credibility problem. Many economists argue that when domestic business and consumers are confronted with market (especially trade) liberalization that is not credible, they will overbuy in the short term, assuming that reform is ephemeral (Calvo 1986; Rodrik 1989a). This phenomenon can lead to current account deficits, which in combination with the lack of capital flow from outside the state can create pressures to reverse liberalization. Rodrik (1989a, 756) goes further, contending that the resulting distortion of domestic prices can lead to losses in overall welfare. This overbuying domestically, along with a decline in capital inflow, can create a difficult balance of payment situation for these young democratic governments.

Now the regime is in a potential catch-22. It can stick with reform that can continue to impose economic hardships on the fledgling regime, prompting declines in economic performance. These declines can then spawn increased opposition from economic elites, prompting an economic crisis or worse (for example, seeking to supplant the current regime). Conversely, it can limit or reverse economic reform, damaging its (already shaky) reputation with internal and external business interests. This can, in turn, limit investment flow to the state, further eroding economic performance.[12] The regime thus faces a choice between further undermining its reputation with investors or sticking with reform that is eroding its economic performance.

Faced with such dismal choices in either the political or economic realm, the regime is painted into a corner. It is in this situation that winners may turn against democracy, again citing the need to pursue further reform. A regime's lack of faith in its opponents to play within the rules of the game provides a large impetus to its antidemocratic behavior. Similarly, international and domestic agents' lack of faith in a regime's economic liberalization policy makes fears of a policy reversal a self-fulfilling prophesy. The irony, as I have outlined here, is that it is reformers' own inability to credibly commit to political and economic reform that can spawn this distrust and instability.

Domestic and international agents need to be reassured that liberalization is credible. Leaders would benefit from a way to guarantee their own commitment to reform (tying their own hands) and/or a credible signal that they are serious about reform. Either of these strategies would lower the level of distrust among elite political actors as well as provide a solid footing for economic reform.

In mature democracies, a common commitment and signaling strategy is the creation of institutions. Unfortunately, the option is not wholly credible in this particular political environment. Theories of "endogenous institutions" hold that domestic institutional arrangements can arise given the preferences of the relevant actors (Root 1994; North and Weingast 1989). These institutions bind actors to certain courses of action since their initiation and consequences reflect the mutual preferences of the actors themselves. Thus, a self-enforcing equilibrium is created. This option faces two major obstacles in new democracies.

First, given the vast uncertainty of the transitional period, information about the preferences of other actors is not widely known (Przeworski 1991, 87). Although this is not a strict requirement for demand-driven institutions to arise, North and Weingast (1989, 806) note that institutions must match "anticipated incentive problems" to be self-enforcing. Without knowledge of the basic preferences of actors, this task would prove to be troublesome. In some cases, it may not even be clear who the relevant political and/or economic actors are (Whitehead 1989). For example, will labor emerge as a powerful interest group to oppose reform, or will they remain marginalized? Will an "internationalist" coalition rise to power in the posttransitional period to push for further economic liberalization? Institutions that do not account for such groups are unlikely to be stable. Given this level of uncertainty, it is difficult to imagine the emergence of institutions to instantiate credible commitments.

Second, any commitment to these new domestic institutions would automatically be suspect. Unlike states in which institutions have survived for years and are only dissolved by lengthy political and legal processes, transitional states have recently gutted existing institutions. Again, the issue of reputation becomes important. Often, the distributional winners in a nascent democracy have used extra-legal means to achieve their goals (including overturning the previ ous regime). They also possess a power advantage in the domestic political process. These circumstances are especially devastating since reputation can be as important as institutions themselves in securing a credible commitment (North and Weingast 1989). In sum, even though domestic institutions may arise because of demand for credibility or to enhance efficiency, the commitment to these institutions themselves is lacking in the posttransitional environment.

So far I have only discussed the propensity of winners to undermine a transitional democracy. No doubt distributional losers play an important role in undermining democracy as well. The military, for example, is often placed in this category. It is not unusual for this group to move from the exalted position of supporting the autocratic regime with a free hand (and few budgetary constraints) to the less glorious position of competing for scarce resources while subjugated to civilian command (Aguero 1995). Of course, distributional losers such as the military enter the story as opposition groups that can be caught in the spiral of distrust with the leaders of the new regime. Distributional losers pose a direct threat of their own to the new regime, and the exclusion of these groups from this analysis is not intended to downplay their importance. Other work (Pevehouse 2000, chap. 4) suggests that IOs can induce losers to cooperate in the democratization process. In short, the hand-tying effect of joining IOs (discussed in the next section) can apply to winners and losers in the democratization process. Because the logic and reasoning behind why winners pose a threat to democracy are more counterintuitive, I have chosen to concentrate on this group in this chapter.

IOs and the Protection of Democracy

IOs can provide distributional winners a device to commit to reform efforts by simultaneously signaling a commitment to reform while setting in place mechanisms to increase the cost of antiregime behavior by tying their own hands. These mechanisms arise from conditionality imposed by the organization for new members and the reputational impact of joining an IO. The acceptance of conditionality is a credible signal to outside actors and domestic agents that the regime is serious about reform, since monitoring and enforcement is controlled by a third party. In addition, the costs associated with membership (fulfilling the initial conditions as well as traditional costs of membership) lend credibility to the commitment to the IO. The conditions also raise the costs of limiting reform since any reversal will bring an end to the benefits of the IO.[13] Finally, in membership in an IO can create expectation about the behavior of the regime (whether there are conditions or not), which, if violated, can create audience costs for the government.

Membership and/or assistance from some IOs is conditional upon domestic liberalization. The EU requires all members to be liberal, free-market democracies as does the Council of Europe (Schmitter 1996). These requirements are highly publicized and rigorously enforced. Turkey has been continually frustrated by the EU's refusal of admission, which has come on the grounds of that state's questionable record of democracy (Whitehead 1993, 159–61). This phenomenon is not limited to Europe: The Southern Cone Common Market (MERCOSUR) also contains a clause in its founding treaty (the Treaty of Asuncion) that requires all members to have a democratic polity (Schiff and Winters 1997). This clause has been a sticking point to Chile's full entry into the common market (*Economist* 1996).

Conditionality, however, is not a black and white issue. Some IOs are vague as to their conditions of membership. Although the NATO preamble contains references to democracy, one of its founding members was one of Europe's most infamous dictatorships (Portugal), and military coups in member states never resulted in major changes within NATO or in pressure to end authoritarian rule (Greece and Turkey). NAFTA is another example of imprecise conditionality. While there is not a clear cause within the NAFTA agreement calling for democracy, observers have often pointed out that the U.S. criterion for NAFTA expansion includes democracy.

In addition, some organizations condition their aid, although not membership in the organization. The World Bank and the IMF condition their loans and assistance on certain policy reforms, yet these conditions often have little to do with democratization.[14] As I will discuss later, despite conditions on assistance from "open" organizations, they will have little power to secure democracy (see note 19).

This conditionality imposed by the IO is not the only source of credibility enhancement for winners who utilize these institutions for this purpose. Joining an IO can entail costly measures that assist in making the action credible. Fulfilling the initial condition of membership can require policy changes and financial outlays that are certainly not trivial. Often, economic or political reform must take place before accession to the organization. Thus, joining IOs is anything but "cheap talk." In addition, membership in many IOs requires either the creation of additional bureaucracy, membership dues (to fulfill the IO's budget obligations), or even economic policy coordination. Such costs can be a clear signal of the state's commitment to the organization and its conditions.

This credibility is perceived by international and domestic forces alike, helping to escape the conundrum of "incredible" economic and political reforms. Economists point to IO membership as an important signal to both domestic and international economic actors (Rodrik 1989a, 1989b). Recently, Fernandez-Arias and Spiegel (1998, 229) have shown how regional trade institutions and organizations "can serve as credibility-enhancing mechanisms that induce additional foreign capital inflows into Southern partner nations." Thus, the problem of capital flight, balance of payment problems, and domestic financial crises from incredible reforms can be mitigated by these institutions.

IOs can also help to break the cycle of political distrust by providing external guarantees to groups concerned with the effects of democratization. By providing an external monitoring and enforcement mechanism for reform, societal groups know they have more latitude to cooperate with one another. That is, the risks of being cheated on in a Prisoner's Dilemma–like situation are lower if a third party can help identify cheating as well as threaten punishment for defection (Schelling 1960). Moreover, conditions imposed by IOs often require specific policies that may ease tensions among competing political groups. For example, the EU requires a commitment to respect property rights and compensation for property taken by the state. As Whitehead (1996, 271) has argued, this commitment has "offered critical external guarantees to the business and propertied classes of southern Europe."

Reneging on the conditions of the IO are even more costly to the regime. This potential cost serves as a deterrent to winners who would undermine liberal reform. At best, violating conditions of membership or agreement will lead to a suspension of specific benefits. At worst, a violation can bring expulsion from the organization. Given these potential costs, there is a strong incentive to work within the rules of the system rather than to work against them (Hyde-Price 1994, 246).

Enforcement of these conditions is an important part of the picture. The credibility aspect of the conditions is enhanced by the fact that a third party becomes the monitoring and enforcement mechanism (Schelling 1960; North 1990). Empirically, IOs do inflict punishment on those who break conditions of agreements. For example, the EU suspended the Greek association agreement in 1967 after the colonels came to power (Whitehead 1993, 154).[15] A potential coup in Paraguay was deterred thanks to the involvement of MERCOSUR ministers, who threatened expulsion to that state if the coup moved forward (*Economist* 1996).

Even if the conditionality policy of the IO is unclear (for example, NATO) or there is a possibility of nonenforcement by the organization, reneging on international agreements brings reputation and audience costs on the regime. Making international agreements places a state's relatively new reputation on the line. Any reversal, backsliding, or abrogation of its obligations of a treaty, even if it does not bring sanction from the organization, creates reputation costs for the state. In the economic realm, the lack of a reputation for keeping agreements can shake investor confidence, which can undermine efforts at economic change (Calvo 1986).[16]

Thus, international organizations can serve as a device to signal a commitment to democratic reform, especially if they are joined in the immediate posttransitional environment. By making international commitments to tie their own hands, winners send a costly signal to both domestic and international observers. But are there some international organizations that may serve this purpose better than others? For example, a nascent democracy joining the Warsaw Pact will probably receive much less benefit in terms of signaling and credibility than will a similar state that successfully joins the EU. As I alluded to in the introduction, we should probably expect "democratic" IOs to be tapped for this function. There are several reasons for this conclusion.

First, democracy-related conditions are likely to be set only in IOs where the vast majority of the members are already democracies. From a logistical standpoint, approving democratic conditions on membership would be much easier in an IO with five democracies than an IO with two democracies, two semidemocracies, and one autocracy. Thus, if a regime feels there will be few conditions on membership, it has little reason to join these organizations.

Second, from a signaling perspective, it does little good for a new democracy to join an IO made up of mostly autocratic states. If democrats within a state are attempting to send a signal to domestic and international observers, they are best served in attempting to join the most democratic international organization possible. Joining other organizations at this time only costs the young democracy scarce resources and brings it little reputational benefit.

Third, more homogenously democratic IOs are more likely to enforce the conditions imposed on membership. Knowing this, leaders attempting to tie their own hands will tap homogenously democratic IOs. Why are democratic IOs more likely to enforce conditions? Briefly, the transparency of democracies lessens the likelihood that any one state in the organization will shirk its enforcement of the conditions (on democracy and transparency, see Fearon 1994; Gaubatz 1996).[17] In addition, it is hypothesized that democracies maintain a promising advantage vis-à-vis one another (Lipson 1999) and also are less likely to renege on commitments (Leeds 1999). Finally, because enforcing the conditions can be costly (in terms of actual monetary outlays or opportunity costs), wealthier states are more likely to enforce them. Although the evidence of the democratizing effects of wealth is controversial (Geddes 1998), there is little doubt that democracies are more affluent than their autocratic counterparts (Londregan and Poole 1996; Przeworski et al. 1996).

Thus, one strategy for leaders in young democracies to secure democracy is to tie their own hands while sending a costly signal to international and domestic observers that they are serious about political and/or economic reform. One mechanism to accomplish this goal is international organizations. I now turn to an empirical test of this proposition.

Testing the Argument

If the preceding argument is correct, we should witness states that have recently undergone a transition to democracy joining democratic international organizations. To test this hypothesis, I estimate Model 1 on a time-series cross-sectional sample of all nation-states from 1950 to 1992.[18]

$$\text{JoinDemIO}_{it} = \alpha_0 + \beta_1 \text{DemTrans}_{it-1} + \beta_2 \text{GDP}_{it}$$

$$+ \beta_3 \text{RegConflict}_{it} + \beta_4 \text{NIO}_{it} + \beta_5 \text{NDemIO}_{it} + \beta_6 \text{Year}_{it}$$

$$+ \beta_7 \text{Hegemony}_t + \beta_7 \text{Democracy}_{it} + \mu_{it}. \quad (1)$$

The dependent variable in this model, labeled JoinDemIO_{it}, measures the probability that state i will join a democratic international organization in year t. It is coded as a 1 when this occurs and as 0 otherwise. I define a "democratic" IO as an organization in which the average level of democracy among the members is above a certain threshold (defined subsequently). I code the level of democracy in IOs in the following manner. First, I constructed a data set of IO membership using the list of IOs found in Banks and Mueller 1998 and Banks for various years.[19] I then computed the average level of democracy of all members *except* state i in the organization.[20]

I use the Polity98 data to determine the level of democracy in each member state.[21] I utilize Polity's autocracy and democracy scores, which are aggregates of several characteristics of each state, to come up with 0 to 10 scales of levels of autocracy and democracy in each country. I take each state's democracy score minus its autocracy score ($\text{DEMOC}_{it} - \text{AUTOC}_{it}$) to create a single, continuous measure of democracy (see Oneal and Russett 1996; Mansfield and Snyder 1995). The resulting measure runs from -10 (complete autocracy) to $+10$ (complete democracy). Using this single measure of democracy, scholars set "cutpoints" for labeling the regime type. I describe a regime as democratic if it is at or above a $+6$, while any regime at or below -6 is labeled an autocracy.[22] Thus, if the average level of democracy in an institutional organization is at or above $+6$, it is considered to be a democratic IO. If a state becomes a member of an organization with this characteristic in year t, the dependent variable is coded as 1. If the state joins no new IOs or any IOs with levels of democracy below $+6$, the variable is coded 0.

The first independent variable is the key variable of interest. DemTrans_{it} measures whether state i completed a transition to democracy in year $t - 1$. I code this variable utilizing the Polity98 data.

Again, I use the $+6$ cutoff to determine whether a state is a democracy. Any state that moves from below $+6$ to that level or above is coded as making a transition to democracy.

The second independent variable taps the economic size of the state in question, in each year. The variable, GDP_{it}, measures the gross domestic product (GDP) of each state at time t. Empirical work on the determinants of IO membership has found that higher levels of GDP are associated with a higher number of memberships in IOs (Jacobson, Reisinger, and Matthews 1986, 149). Moreover, if democracy and wealth are correlated (Lipset 1959; Bollen 1979; Jackman 1973),[23] we would like to hold the level of wealth constant if our independent variable of focus is democratization. I expect economically larger states to be associated with a higher likelihood of joining a democratic international organization. These data are gathered from Summers et al. 1995 as well as World Bank 1998.[24]

To control for the possibility that states do join regional conflicts to settle disputes, or do so in the aftermath of them, we must include a measure of conflict. $RegConflict_{it}$ measures the presence of the threats or uses of force involving state i's region at time t.[25] Fortna (1998) has argued that international institutions can be essential to enforce ceasefire agreements in conflicts. Thus, security concerns may motivate states to join IOs. One classic example is the formation of the EU. Although the Cold War peace in Europe may have many determinants, it is clear that much of the motivation behind the original formation of the EU was security concerns (see Schiff and Winters 1997; Wallace 1994). Finally, it should also be noted that current research on preferential trade agreements (PTAs) has found little relationship between military hostilities and the formation of or membership in these types of IOs (compare Mansfield, Milner, and Rosendorff 1998; Mansfield and Pevehouse 1999).

The next independent variable, labeled NIO_{it}, measures the number of IOs of which state i is a member. This variable is included since a state that is already enmeshed in many IOs will have less opportunity to join new ones. Thus, we expect this variable to be negative in sign—the more memberships a state has in IOs, the less the probability of joining new ones. This variable is computed using IO membership from the sample previously discussed.

A related control variable is $NDemIO_{it}$, which measures the number of democratic IOs of which state i is a member. Again, the argument is that states with many memberships in these organizations can reach a saturation point. In addition, because joining these organizations serves as a hand-tying and/or signaling device for new democracies, there may be little reason to expect a state to join multiple democratic IOs, although this is certainly a possibility. The intuition is that, if these are indeed costly signals, especially in economic terms, we should expect leaders to join as few IOs as possible to accomplish their desired goals.

Next, I include the year under observation as a control variable. Shanks, Jacobson, and Kaplan (1996) have shown that there has been a steady rise in IOs over time. Although the number of IOs has increased, there is a large amount of turnover in those IOs—that is, existing institutions die and new ones are created. Still, it is important to control for any secular trends in the number of IGOs, since democracy has also been on the rise over the period of observation. We want to be sure that any relationship between democratization and joining IOs is not a spurious one.[26]

I also include Hegemony$_i$ to control for systemic factors that may influence the likelihood of a state's involvement in a democratic IO. Work by Mansfield (1998) has found that membership in PTAs is influenced by these systemic factors. As power becomes more diffuse in the international system, states are more likely to take measures to make sure that a decline in systemic leadership will not erode their current gains. Although this idea is often applied to the economic arena, one can imagine a similar security side to the argument as well. As the leading state in the system declines, regional allies begin forming their own arrangements to guarantee their security, since they can no longer count on the hegemon to do so. Here, hegemony is measured as the proportion of trade in the international system controlled by the largest trading state (which is the United States for this period of analysis). This variable is measured each year and is identified for each state in year t.

Democracy$_{it}$ measures the level of democracy in state i in year t. It is measured using the continuous (Autocracy-Democracy) scale from the Polity98 data. Other empirical studies have shown that democracies tend to join international institutions at a higher rate than do nondemocracies (Russett, Oneal, and Davis 1998; Shanks, Jacobson, and Kaplan 1996). To control for the possibility that it is not democracies that have undergone a transition but rather existing democracies that are joining democratic IOs, it is essential to include this variable. I expect a positive coefficient estimate, since democracies are more likely to be involved in democratic IOs, ceteris paribus. Finally, μ_{it} is a stochastic error term.

Estimates of the Model

Model 1 is estimated using logistic regression. In addition to the seven independent variables described in the previous section, I include a measure of the length of time between joining democratic IOs (the dependent variable) to control for any temporal dependence in the data. Work by Nathaniel Beck, Jonathan Katz, and Richard Tucker has shown that in time-series cross-sectional data such as that used here, the presence of duration dependence can influence the estimates of the parameters and standard errors (Beck and Katz 1997; Beck, Katz, and Tucker 1998). To correct for this possibility, I include the aforementioned measure of time between joining democratic IOs and a natural cubic spline function with one knot in Model 1.[27]

TABLE 1. Determinants of Membership in Democratic International Organizations, 1950–92

	(1)	(2)	(3)
DemTrans$_{it-1}$	0.833*	0.888*	—
	(1.66)	(1.81)	
DemTrans$_{it-1 \to t-3}$	—	—	1.096***
			(2.96)
GDP$_{it}$	3.89×10^{-12}***	—	3.73×10^{-12}**
	(2.75)		(2.59)
RegConflict$_{it}$	0.079***	0.082***	0.100***
	(3.11)	(3.27)	(4.01)
NIO$_{it}$	−0.225**	−0.189*	−0.263***
	(−2.19)	(−1.93)	(−2.68)
NDemIO$_{it}$	0.555***	0.528***	0.602***
	(5.13)	(5.11)	(5.83)
Year$_{it}$	−0.060**	−0.060**	−0.064***
	(−2.44)	(−2.44)	(−2.85)
Hegemony$_t$	−27.094**	−28.661**	−33.664***
	(−2.09)	(−2.12)	(−2.84)
Democracy$_{it}$	0.067***	0.080***	0.065***
	(2.91)	(3.37)	(2.72)
Constant	118.039**	118.288**	127.205***
	(2.39)	(2.39)	(2.80)
N	4,350	4,762	4,314
Log-likelihood	−471.37	−477.86	−457.13
Chi-square	317.99***	327.48***	308.93***

Note: Figures in parentheses are asymptotic z-statistics computed using Huber/White/sandwich standard errors. Models include a counter for the number of years between joining democratic IOs that is used as a base for a natural cubic spline function with one knot.

  * $p < .10$; ** $p < .05$; *** $p < .01$.

Column 1 of table 1 presents the estimates of Model 1.[28] Note that our key independent variable of interest, DemTrans$_{it-1}$, is of the predicted sign and is statistically significant. Thus, a state is more likely to join a democratic IO if it has recently undergone a democratic transition. Ceteris paribus, such a change will increase the probability of that state joining such an organization by nearly two and a half times (125 percent). This is substantial evidence for the hypothesis that domestic political agents hope to utilize membership in democratic IOs to help lock in democracy.

Most of the remainder of the control variables are of the expected sign, and all are statistically significant. The estimate of GDP$_{it}$ indicates that economically larger states tend to join IOs, a result consistent with prior research. RegConflict$_{it}$ is positive and statistically significant, which supports the traditional neoliberal ideas of institutions as focal points for conflict resolution. That is, states in regions with more interstate conflict tend to join institutions at a higher rate. The total number of IO memberships is inversely related to the probability of joining a democratic IO, but the number of existing memberships in democratic IOs is positively related to joining more. It would appear that joining democratic IOs is somewhat contagious, while there may be a saturation point for overall membership in IOs.

Hegemony$_t$, as expected, is negatively related to joining democratic IOs. As the leading state in the system becomes less of a force in international politics, the need to turn to international institutions appears to rise. Finally, the higher the level of democracy in a state, the more likely it is to attempt to join a democratic IO.

To check the robustness of these results, I reestimate Model 1 excluding GDP$_{it}$. As mentioned in note 24, I filled in missing GDP data from various other sources, although a fair number of cases (almost 10 percent) are still missing GDP data. To ensure that these findings are not an artifact of the missing GDP data, I exclude this term from the model. Note that the estimates of the model are nearly identical with or without the GDP term. Thus, we can be confident that the results are not a statistical artifact.

Of course, some might argue that there is no natural time unit to the theory. That is, there is no reason to think that democracies will attempt to join IOs only in the first year after they have completed a transition to democracy. After all, problems in democratic consolidation can arise for some time after the initial transition. To consider this possibility, I reestimate Model 1 with a newly coded DemTrans variable, which is coded as 1 if state i underwent a democratic transition in either of the last three years—that is, in $t-1$, $t-2$, or $t-3$.[29]

The results of this new model are shown in column 3 of table 1. Again, there is strong evidence that newly democratized states join democratic international organizations very soon after the completion of transition. When the DemTrans independent variable measures transitions over a three-year period, the strength of the relationship grows. Notice now that if a state has transitioned in the past three years the odds of joining a democratic IO increase by almost 200 percent. Again, the remainder of the control variables are virtually identical in sign and significance to the previous model. We can now be more certain that this association between democratization and joining democratic IOs is not an artifact of the model specification (in terms of lag structure).

This test has provided some initial empirical evidence that a major determinant of a state's decision to join international organizations lies in the domestic political realm. The results also point to the importance of traditional ideas concerning the need for institutions to mitigate conflict. Clearly both are important when discussing a regime's decision to take the costly step of joining an international organization. While further statistical tests should be performed to assess the impact of democratization on overall IO membership, this first cut has provided support for my argument that domestic politics can be a driving force for the accession to international organizations.

Discussion and Conclusion

What implications does this have for neoliberalism, comparative political economy, and, more important, U.S. foreign policy? For neoliberals, who have emphasized the international coordination and cooperation benefits of IOs, explaining why states join institutions and organizations in the first place may have little to do with international outcomes. Although institutions may matter for interstate cooperation, if the impetus for joining these structures lies in domestic politics, what impact might this have on institutions' effects on cooperation among nations? Or is cooperation through institutions simply a by-product of domestic politics? More theoretical and empirical work must be undertaken before neoliberals or their realist counterparts can confidently address these questions.

Comparative political economists have increasingly recognized the impact of external factors (free trade, capital mobility, foreign direct investment, and so forth) on domestic political institutions and coalitions. Milner and Keohane (1996, 16) argue that "international-ization" means that "the interests on which domestic political coalitions rest will be increasingly shaped by international economic forces." This chapter suggested that this process is a two-way street. To protect their own domestic institutions and coalitions, leaders may turn to international forces such as IOs. As I have argued, in many cases this can be a regime's best option for tying its own hands while signaling a credible commitment to new domestic institutions.

Finally, in terms of U.S. foreign policy, the goal of democratic enlargement has taken many forms since the end of the Cold War. A key facet of this policy has been to enlarge existing international organizations to include young democracies in order to protect their fledgling regimes. As this chapter has argued, these states will be very willing participants. The irony, however, is that the easier it is for states to join democratic IOs, the fewer benefits they confer on the new members. With fewer conditions on membership, the hand-tying and signaling effects of these institutions will be weakened. Thus, they may be less useful in helping young democratic regimes make credible commitments to democracy.

In addition, the issue of enforcement should not be taken for granted. Each time a state breaks the conditions of membership in an IO (whether political or economic), it is essential that some sort of punishment be meted out. If not, the credibility of the conditions is eroded. I have argued that the more homogenously democratic an IO is, the more likely it will be to enforce these conditions. Enforcement, however, is never automatic. Members of IOs must be willing and able to punish condition violators, since in the long run inaction will only hurt nascent democracies' chances for survival.

International organizations are no magic bullet for nascent democracies. A host of factors determines whether these states survive as democracies or revert toward autocracy. Nonetheless, I have argued that several of these factors hinge on the lack of a young regime's ability to make credible commitments to political and/or economic reform. In these cases, IOs can play a role in strengthening democracy and democratic reform.

Notes

I would like to thank all of the participants in the conference "The Interaction of Domestic and International Institutions" for their insightful comments. I would also like to thank Dan Drezner, Dan Reiter, Ed Mansfield, Don Sylvan, David Bearce, Tim Frye, and Elizabeth Erickson Pevehouse for additional comments and advice.

1. The dependent variable for this study will be international organizations rather than international institutions. IOs make up a subset of all institutions, broadly defined. On the differences between IOs, institutions, and regimes, see Hasenclever, Mayer, and Rittberger 1996.

2. These costs can arise from a variety of sources (discussed later), but on the political front they include public opposition to joining the organization or potential fights over ratification. Economically, costs arise from the creation of a new bureaucracy to deal with the IO or from policy coordination required by the organization (i.e., reducing taxes, liberalizing trade, etc.).

3. This is akin to the ratification stage of the two-level games argument put forth by Putnam (1988). The argument has been made more poignantly by Milner (1997), who argues that the paucity of international cooperation can be understood in terms of concerns over the distribution of these gains in domestic politics.

4. The one slight difference between Milner's hypotheses and my own is that her work concentrates largely on industrialized states, while most of my discussion of democratizing states will deal with lesser-developed states. While our general hypotheses on the conditions under which states are likely to form PTAs should apply to both sets of states, in practice there may be differences because of varying levels of economic and political development.

5. I should note that there is a small, but growing, debate on whether governmental type affects alliance involvement, although that debate centers around the question of who allies with whom, not what effect the alliance itself might have on any of the member states. On this debate, see Walt 1987; Siverson and Emmons 1991.

6. An alternative explanation, not explored here, is simple human greed. Tempted by the ability to bias the system in their favor, either economically or politically, new leaders freeze or even reverse liberalization and reform. Oftentimes, this can result in concentrated rents in the economic realm (Hellman 1998) or biased institutions in the political realm.

7. Other credibility problems exist, especially in the realm of economic reform. The others, however, are less acute for transitional regimes. For a discussion of additional credibility problems in economic liberalization, see Rodrik 1989b.

8. Although winning groups may remain winning groups, there is often high turnover in leadership of these groups in the posttransition environment. See Whitehead 1989, 79.

9. Hellman (1998), for example, outlines how partial liberalization can create concentrated rents when trade liberalization is not accompanied by price liberalization.

10. One could cite the findings of Londregan and Poole (1990, 175) that coups tend to beget coups as evidence of this problem. They find that, once a coup occurs, "it has a much harder time avoiding further coups." For a further explication of these dynamics, see Finer 1962.

11. As I will discuss, the distributional losers (especially the military) are

often willing to ally with one another if they do not believe the regime is credibly committed to reform.

12. For example, limiting imports while continuing to encourage the export sector is a common practice to correct balance of payment problems. Of course, the imposition of tariffs, whether in the form of explicit limits, quotas, or nontariff barriers, can damage the regime's commitment to liberal economic reform, leaving it no better off in the long run.

13. I use the term "conditions" or "conditionality" to apply to democracy requirements by an IO or any terms of joining an organization. This includes the terms of any economic arrangement to which a state joins. For example, a condition of a regional free-trade agreement is that terms of trade are liberalized in the domestic market. Although many of my condition and enforcement examples will center on political requirements, the argument applies equally to economic agreements to liberalize and their enforcement.

14. I have chosen to exclude the World Bank and the IMF from this analysis, mostly because of the case-by-case conditionality enacted by these organizations. It is likely that these organizations do impact democratization efforts, especially in the case of liberal economic reform (Schmitter 1996, 30), although there is certainly no consensus on this matter. Since membership in these organizations is open and almost every country is a member, adding it to this analysis would have little bearing on the results (given my operational weighting of IOs, discussed later). Still, the signaling effects of IMF and World Bank programs can be substantial (see Rodrik 1997). Given the tremendous literature on these institutions, I have chosen to concentrate on joining regional economic and political organizations.

15. The fact that Greece left rather than being expelled was simply a technicality. The resolution to expel Greece was on the table when the military colonels defiantly declared they no longer wished to be a part of the organization.

16. As important as the international audience costs are domestic audience costs that leaders incur when they renege on international agreements. These domestic audience costs often flow from a poor international reputation and can lead to a loss of face for new leaders (Fearon 1994, 581). This domestic loss of face can have electoral ramifications for those in power in a democracy (Fearon 1994). Note that there may or may not be a loss of international reputation. Still, the domestic political audience is likely to be attuned to these issues since association with a highly democratic IO is an early chance to break with the vestiges of an authoritarian past (Pridham 1994, 26–27). I discuss this further in Pevehouse 2000.

17. These ideas are more fully explained in Pevehouse 2000, chapters 3 and 4.

18. Polity III (Jaggers and Gurr 1995) and Polity98 (Marshall 1999) exclude some states that the Correlates of War project considers the members of the international system. I have excluded these states as well.

19. I exclude a small number of IOs because of their lack of regular meetings or lack of organizational structure. Also, organizations that are open to any state are excluded since their membership, by definition, is not conditional (Keohane 1990).

20. This is essential since, if state i is included, it is possible that an organization would become democratic because of a transition to democracy in that state. Thus, we would be measuring the same phenomenon on both sides of the equation—a surefire, but highly incorrect, way to achieve a significant relationship among variables.

21. Polity98 (Marshall 1998) is an updated version of the Polity III data (Jaggers and Gurr 1996).

22. This is a slight change from common practice, which defines the cutoffs for democracy and autocracy at $+7/-7$. As I show in chapter 2 of Pevehouse 2000, the $+6/-6$ cutoffs correlate more highly with other data sets measuring democracy and democratic transitions.

23. Of course, this correlation may or may not be causal. On this issue see Londregan and Poole 1996 and Przeworski et al. 1996.

24. Where Summers and Heston data are missing, I fill in as much as possible from the World Bank data. All of the non-Summers and non-Heston data are converted to constant 1985 U.S. dollars. For those uncomfortable with combing economic data from various sources, I exclude this variable from the analysis in the next section.

25. State i may or may not be involved in the dispute, but the idea is that general instability in the region may move any neighbors or nearby states to form an IO. I follow the Correlates of War coding for region. See Singer and Small 1994. The militarized interstate disputes (MIDS) data are discussed in Jones, Bremer, and Singer 1996. The data are available at the Peace Science Society International web site: <http://pss.la.psu.edu/MID_DATA.HTM>.

26. For example, a general trend of more democratic IOs and more democracies could create a relationship that is spurious. The analogy in the time-series world would be cointegrating vectors of time-series data.

27. I do not report the estimate of these two additional terms to conserve on space. In all models, they are highly significant. I also tried including the time variable with both two and three knots, but in both cases the additional knots were not statistically significant.

28. Beck and Turner (1996) also show that traditional standard error estimates in time-series cross-sectional data are usually underestimated. They suggest the use of White/Huber/sandwich standard errors. Thus, the z-statistics presented in table 1 are computed utilizing these standard error estimates.

29. I chose a three-year period since most transitional governments fail relatively early in their tenure (Power and Gasiorowski 1997), although Pevehouse 2000 shows that their rate of failure still rises over time, but at a much slower rate.

Giving the Unrecognized Their Due: Regional Actors, International Institutions, and Multilateral Economic Cooperation in Northeast Asia

Jean-Marc F. Blanchard

There has been a surge of interest in the way domestic and international variables act together to produce outcomes (Evans, Jacobson, and Putnam 1993; Putnam 1988). The Tumen River Area Development Programme (TRADP), a multinational economic development initiative for the Tumen River area at the tri-juncture of the Chinese, Russian, and North Korean borders, represents an important but poorly known case resulting from the interaction of domestic and international factors. It presents a puzzle for extant approaches in two ways. First, the TRADP has made meaningful progress since it appeared on the international agenda in 1990.[1] This progress has occurred despite the fact that decision makers in the participating state capitals have given it only modest levels of political, financial, and legal support.[2] Second, Moscow backs the project because it wants to exploit the resources of the Russian Far East, improve the area's economy and infrastructure, and tap into Asia-Pacific money, markets, and economic institutions. In addition, it wants to facilitate control over the restive Russian Far East and gain political clout in the Asia-Pacific (Korkunov 1994, 38–42; Christoffersen 1994–95, 516–17; Ivanov 1995; Institute of Far Eastern Studies 1995, 41–42; Toloraya 1996; Portyakov 1998, 58–59). Yet it is Russia that has served as one of the primary obstacles to the continued advancement of the TRADP.

To get out of this analytical morass, we must go beyond the state centrism and unitary actor assumption of existing approaches.[3] Specifically, we must consider the role of nonstate actors like the United Nations Development Programme (UNDP) and subnational actors like the Province of Jilin in China and Primorskii Kray (territory) in Russia. My case study shows that Jilin and Primorskii played important roles in the dynamics of the TRADP. Specifically, Jilin acted as a policy initiator, facilitator, and implementor by supporting multilateral economic cooperation with studies, publicity, the construction of infrastructure geared to regional economic interactions, and participation in TRADP promotional activities. Primorskii, on the other hand, took advantage of its role as a policy implementor to establish real limits to the development of the TRADP. It not only challenged the Sino-Russian 1991 boundary agreement but also placed obstacles such as visa restrictions in the way of Chinese who wanted to transact business with the Russians. My case study further reveals that the UNDP acted as a policy facilitator and implementor by providing expert advice, facilitating negotiations and discussions, and contributing funds.

Overall, my analysis provides evidence for the argument that contracting and persuasion represent important channels of influence between international and domestic institutions. My work makes a novel theoretical contribution by specifying the conditions under which subnational actors and international institutions may play a prominent role in multilateral economic cooperation. It highlights that a facilitating domestic structure and borderland status can create the space and/or incentives for subnational actors and international institutions to get involved in foreign affairs. My work, then, tackles the question posed in the introduction to this book about the conditions that produce variation in the interaction of domestic and international institutions. This theoretical contribution differentiates my work from other detailed studies of the TRADP that take into account subnational actors (Burns 1994; Christoffersen 1994–95, 1996a).[4]

This chapter is divided into four sections. The first section specifies how subnational actors and international institutions can matter, particularly how they can fuel international economic cooperation. It also offers a theoretical framework to explain *when* such entities are likely to assume heightened salience. Filling in this theoretical framework, the second section describes the international context in Northeast Asia as well as the domestic context in both China and Russia. The third section presents the case study. It details how Jilin and the UNDP acted as policy initiators, facilitators, and implementors for the TRADP. It also examines Russia's involvement in the TRADP to explain why that country impeded its progress. A close analysis reveals that the key policy obstructionist was Primorskii, a borderland. The final section offers my interpretation of the case and a discussion of the implications of my findings for international relations theorists.

Theoretical Thoughts on Subnational Actors and International Institutions

As noted in the introduction to this volume, two-level game studies of the interaction of domestic and international institutions are flawed because they are state centric, assume the state is a unitary actor, and take an overly narrow view of international institutions. To rectify these shortcomings, it is necessary to go beyond the usual cast of domestic actors (for example, bureaucracies and societal interest groups) to paint a comprehensive portrait of the forces impinging upon a given state's foreign security and economic policies and relationships. In particular, it may be appropriate to study the activities of subnational actors such as states, provinces, or local governments.[5] To illustrate, in the 1960s, educational and cultural agreements between Quebec and France spurred political conflicts between France and Canada (Soldatos 1990, 49). It also may be necessary to place greater stress on international institutions, though international relations specialists often fail to do this (Karns and Mingst 1987, 457; Milner 1998, 779). After all, such institutions can change policy concepts, legitimize particular policies, and bring new participants into debates about national policy (Jacobson and Oksenberg 1990).

How Do Subnational Actors and International
Institutions Matter?

Subnational entities and international institutions, as agents, can affect policy-making in five ways: (1) interest and policy formulation; (2) agenda setting; (3) agreement development, amendment, and ratification; (4) coalition building; and (5) implementation (Keohane and Nye 1974, 45–46; Jacobson 1984; Karns and Mingst 1987, 460–67; Kahler 1993, 376–77; Risse-Kappen, ed., 1995, 283; Martin and Simmons 1998, 742–47).[6] Many of these influence mechanisms closely relate to the policy initiator and ratifier roles highlighted in the introduction to this volume.[7]

First, subnational actors and international institutions can shape understandings of the national interests through the production of expert knowledge, the shifting of the relative priority of issues, and the declaration or affirmation of international norms.[8] According to one analysis, the Economic Commission for Latin America provided a foundation for regional economic integration in the area by articulating interest in the idea of integration to solve the region's economic development problems and by providing an intellectual basis for integration (Gregg 1968, 313–18).

Second, they can influence the international or domestic foreign policy agenda. In 1963, Swiss authorities in Basel put the idea of regional development of the Upper Rhine region (at the tri-juncture of the Swiss, French, and German borders) on the international agenda by establishing the Regio Basiliensis, a regional planning advocacy organization that generated analyses of regional development and promoted networking among interested parties (Scott 1989, 144, 150–51).

Third, they can affect the game of international agreement development, amendment, and ratification. The German Länder, for instance, through the forum of the Bundesrat, "deliberate on the whole range of EC [European Community] policy issues presented to the Council of Ministers . . . [and] adopt resolutions on specific problems of European policy." In addition, the German federal government must "take into account in the Brussels negotiations the Bundesrat's position or . . . include it in its policy decisions" (Nass 1989, 176–78). Finally, the German Bundesbank clearly was a veto player in the negotiations surrounding the European Monetary Union and the creation of a European Central Bank (Cameron 1995).

Fourth, they can build coalitions with other domestic or international actors. In 1961, for instance, American and Canadian weather bureau officials joined together to defeat the U.S. Department of State's position on control of World Weather Watch. In the late 1960s, a U.S. Department of Defense official worked with his Japanese counterpart to write messages that would trigger the desired response in the U.S. bureaucracy regarding the return of Okinawa to Japanese control (Keohane and Nye 1974, 47–48). Soviet arms control experts worked closely with their counterparts in the United States to legitimize certain nuclear doctrines (Adler 1992, 133–39).

Fifth, they can have a significant role in the implementation of international accords or a nation's foreign policy. In 1996, for example, the governor of Okinawa prefecture in Japan obstructed the implementation of the terms of the U.S.-Japanese Security Treaty when he refused to renew the land leases underlying American bases on Okinawa. Furthermore, he injected strains into the relationship by supporting a referendum calling for a change in the Status of Forces Agreement governing the legal treatment of American soldiers stationed on Okinawa (Mochizuki 1996, 4–6; Miyagi 1996; Eldridge 1997). In the 1980s, Canadian provinces and American states regularly passed legislation that favored domestic over foreign producers and investors, thereby contravening the letter and spirit of GATT, to which their respective national governments were parties (Duchacek 1990, 11).

Focusing on multilateral economic cooperation, the preceding discussion implies that subnational actors and international institutions can improve the prospects for multilateral cooperation in a number of specific ways. For instance, by providing information on the international political, economic, or social environment, these entities can alert decision makers to the need for action. Alternatively, they can educate policy makers about the benefits of a multilateral as opposed to a unilateral policy solution. Furthermore, they can increase the likelihood of multilateral economic cooperation by building coalitions with other domestic or international actors and, as a result, expand the range of international agreements that are acceptable domestically.[9] Finally, they can nurture cooperation by passing legislation or expending funds to support such activities.

The preceding discussion, however, also suggests that subnational actors and international institutions have the capacity to diminish the chances for multilateral economic cooperation. One obvious way they can do so is by hindering the implementation of an international accord, for instance, by establishing protectionist barriers when an international agreement calls for liberalization measures. In addition, they can form coalitions that present an insurmountable barrier to the ratification of a multinational agreement and hence international negotiations before they have concluded. Moreover, such entities can put items on the international agenda that inject friction into the relationship of the parties attempting to finalize or implement a multilateral agreement.

When Do Subnational Actors and International
Institutions Matter?

Although the preceding discussion shows how subnational actors and international institutions can influence the prospects for multilateral economic cooperation, it does not inform us when they matter. There are a number of authors who have tried to specify when subnational actors and international institutions matter (Karns and Mingst 1987, 458–60; Soldatos 1990, 44–48). These theorists, though, tend to offer too many explanatory variables, fail to apply these variables to particular cases in a systematic fashion, and do not draw extensively on the extant international relations literature. Drawing upon this literature,

I emphasize two domestic contextual variables[10] that increase the chances for subnational and nonstate actors to play a meaningful role in the dynamics of multilateral cooperation: a facilitating domestic structure and subnational unit characteristics.[11] Domestic structure will empower subnational units and international institutions when there is a federal state structure, when political ideologies stress decentralization, or when the center has little material leverage over subnational units. Subnational units are more likely to shape transborder cooperation when they are borderlands. Borderland status gives such actors not only an incentive to become involved in such ventures but due to their location, an important implementation role as well.

Domestic structure is stressed in two-level game studies (Putnam 1988, 448–50; Moravcsik 1993, 24–27), recent examinations of transnational relations (Risse Kappen 1995a, 6), analyses of foreign economic policy (Eichengreen 1992; Evangelista 1997), and peacemaking after war (Ripsman 2002). Domestic structure is important because it determines the actors that get to play a role in policy initiation, ratification, and implementation (Milner 1997, 18). It also can provide opportunities for subnational units to act outside the boundaries of the state and to form coalitions with other subnational units or nonstate actors (Keohane and Nye 1974, 48). Finally, it mediates between the international environment (whether international security threats or pressures from nongovernmental institutions) and the domestic realm, determining in part how and if such influences are felt.

Although domestic structure is extensively used as a variable in the international relations literature, there is no commonly accepted definition of the term. For Milner (1997, 37–42), domestic structure consists of the political system (for example, presidential versus parliamentary), the number of political parties (for example, two party or multiparty), and norms such as party discipline. Thomas Risse-Kappen (1995a, 20–23) highlights the political institutions of the state (for example, centralized or fragmented), societal structures (for example, extent of societal cleavages), and policy networks that link the two. Norrin Ripsman (2002, chap. 3) argues that domestic structure is determined by the political system, the number of parties in the majority, the frequency of elections, the concentration of executive power, decision-making procedures, and the normative environment. What is important for our purposes is that these, as well as other, definitions emphasize a mix of formal and informal factors in their conceptualizations of domestic structure.

Informal factors are especially salient in the case of subnational units, since, as Ivo Duchacek (1970, 277) notes, there is an "extra-constitutional reality" that researchers need to consider. This extraconstitutional reality, though, goes beyond norms and decision-making procedures. It also relates to political relationships (for example, does the center have financial or political leverage over the subnational unit or vice versa?), political ideologies (for example, does the party in power favor centralization or decentralization?), and roles envisioned for the state (for example, should economic planning be centralized?) (ibid., 279, 311, 324–29). This extraconstitutional reality is reflected in the fact that subnational units in the United States had the ability to ban investments in South Africa, restrict foreign investment, and discriminate against foreign suppliers because it was not worth the political cost to reassert control. It had nothing to do with constitutional rights (Fry 1990, 280–81).

Generally speaking, a decentralized domestic structure, either de jure or de facto, empowers subnational actors because it often gives them the ability to interact with a variety of entities outside the state. In addition, it provides them with opportunities to build coalitions with other groups inside the state. Furthermore, it frequently vests subnational actors with the authority to initiate policies different from those desired or supported by the center. Moreover, it permits subnational actors to implement policies without heavy supervision or regulation. Finally, it affords them some leverage over the center since the center may need them as a partner against other domestic actors.

Subnational units have a variety of political, economic, and social characteristics, though one of the most important for understanding the potential for a subnational unit to get involved in international issues is whether it is a borderland.[12] Borderland status means that foreign ideas, institutions, and economic and cultural systems continuously buffet the subnational unit, albeit in different degrees, depending, for instance, on domestic structure and the international threat environment.[13] Borderlands often are alienated from their national center due to factors ranging from geographic distance to a history as a buffer zone along the interstate borderline (Martinez 1994, 6–12).

Representing the front line of a state, borderlands are deeply affected by cross-border migration, labor, pollution, investment, drug trafficking, and military-security issues. Hence, leaders of borderlands, particularly elected leaders, have a strong incentive to influence the foreign policy of their state (Martinez 1986, 2; Duchacek

1986, 11–12). In involving themselves in the external affairs of their state, borderland officials will be sensitive to any initiative that alters the distribution of material benefits or political power. Subnational elites will seek to maximize any increase in revenues and control the allocation of those resources so as to secure their political power. On the other hand, they will tend to oppose any policy that reduces their resource base or diminishes their relative power. At the very least, they will minimize the costs associated with such initiatives.

Borderlands will have an especially important role in relations with a neighboring state or states when they have the right to control access or play a role in the implementation of an international accord.[14] For instance, the Province of Ontario in Canada has a significant role in the regulation of the flows of goods and people crossing the U.S.-Canadian border because it is in charge of fourteen international bridges linking the two countries. Furthermore, Canadian provinces have certain jurisdictional rights over energy resources within their borders, which, in effect, gives them the right to grant access to foreign investors and purchasers (Feldman and Feldman 1990).

In sum, I expect that subnational units and international institutions will assume prominent roles as initiators, ratifiers, facilitators, and implementors when, in addition to complex interdependence, there is a facilitating domestic structure and when, in the case of a subnational unit, it is a borderland. In the next section, I seek to establish whether China and Russia had facilitating domestic structures.[15]

The International and Domestic Context

Increasing cross-border contacts since the 1980s evidence the complex interdependence of the Northeast Asian region. The end of the Cold War and the adoption of market- and/or export-oriented economic doctrines have led to a remarkable surge in trade, investment, and cross-border exchanges contacts in the region (Zhang 1995, chap. 2; Moon 1995, 36–40). The growth in intraregional interdependence is reflected in the Sino-Russian economic relationship. China went from being Russia's seventeenth largest trading partner in 1985 to its second largest by 1993 (Moltz 1995, 157).[16] Furthermore, since the early 1990s, there have been an expanded number of official and unofficial contacts among Chinese and Russian government officials as well as a rising number of scientific, educational, and cultural exchanges between the two countries.

The growth of trade and other contacts between China and Russia is further demonstrated by the opening of consulates and trade offices, the growth in Sino-Russian joint ventures, increasing Chinese investment in the Russian Far East, and the escalating importance of China as an export market for the Russian Far East, particularly Primorskii and Khabarovskii (Kim 1994, 1074; Minakir 1994, 191; Anderson 1997, 32–33; Moltz 1997, 190). The opening of the Sino-Russian border also has resulted in the presence of approximately fifty thousand to one hundred thousand Chinese in the Russian Far East on a daily basis. Many of these individuals are contract workers employed in construction or seasonal agricultural work or shuttle traders (Kim 1994, 1064–69; Portyakov 1996, 135–37).

From the founding of the People's Republic of China in 1949 until the commencement of the Cultural Revolution in 1966, the Chinese polity had a hierarchical structure as a result of the Chinese Communist Party's (CCP) tremendous power. In this hierarchical structure, bureaucrats, party functionaries, and others embraced the CCP line (once known) and implemented it zealously. The Cultural Revolution changed all that by undermining the legitimacy of the CCP and weakening the resources at its disposal (Goldstein 1991). Conscious of the need to rebuild the country after the tumult of the Cultural Revolution and to rebuild the authority of the CCP, Deng Xiaoping successfully pushed for major economic reforms after he took the reins of power (Harding 1987, chaps. 5–6; Lieberthal 1995, chap. 5). It is important that the CCP also reduced its use of ideology and coercive devices such as purges to control party and government officials (Harding 1987, chap. 7; Lieberthal 1992, 9).

These changes coupled with the relative weakness of the post-Mao leadership and the complexity and technical nature of domestic and international economic affairs, which generated a need for expertise and quick reaction, have created a more polyarchic polity, albeit one that is fundamentally authoritarian. Multiple voices, multiple command channels, and the lack of a clear division of authority among government ministries—and between government ministries and the provinces, which have the rank of a government ministry—only intensified the need for coalition building and bargaining (Zhao 1991; Lieberthal 1992, 8).

Provinces were one of the beneficiaries of Deng's economic reform program. Deng and his supporters empowered provincial leaders by giving them the authority to approve capital projects, to retain foreign currency, to control certain enterprises, and to offer tax deals to foreign ventures (Harding 1987, 167). The decentralization of budgetary authority for revenue collection and expenditures and other economic powers to the provinces gave them the ability to earn their own funds and thus made them less sensitive to demands emanating from the center (Lieberthal 1992, 8; Lieberthal 1995, 172–74, 249–50). The empowerment of the provinces was more than an economic move. It was a move to build political support to circumvent opposition to Deng's economic reform program in the center (Shirk 1993, chap. 9; Cheung 1998, 5). Provincial leaders also obtained power under the new regime because of their role in the implementation of the center's dictates. To ensure that provinces implement its policies, the center often makes an effort to get the consensus of provincial officials (Lieberthal 1992, 21). This is critical since "the provincial government is often given the discretion to decide on the details and schedule of implementation" (Cheung 1998, 10). Furthermore, provinces have input into the policy process through their participation in national economic work congresses and national planning conferences (ibid., 10). Finally, the center gives provincial leaders power so they can manage their provinces, a number of which approach the size of the large countries (Lieberthal 1995, 164–66).

In sum, the polyarchic nature of the polity, the economic and political reform ideologies of the center, the increased fiscal autonomy of the provinces, and the role of subnational actors—here provinces—as gatekeepers for the implementation of policy have given subnational actors such as Jilin considerable autonomy to act differently from the center's wishes. Moreover, Jilin itself was privileged because Chinese leaders placed it at the center of their multilateral cooperative plans for the Tumen, one of many regional economic circles that China conceived of for the Asia-Pacific (Christoffersen 1996a, 269–70).[17]

Russia's domestic structure also has changed drastically in the last decade. In the Soviet Union, power was "strictly controlled by the center and lay in the hands of the Communist Party" (Lynne and Novikov 1997, 189). Consequently, "republican and local governments were little more than organs of the center, which dominated the political-economic organization of the country" (ibid., 190). The dissolution of the Soviet Union in 1991, however, ended this pattern and saw the emergence of a democratic successor nation, the Russian Federation. Moreover, Russia abandoned its Marxist-Leninist economic practices (for example, state ownership and central planning) in favor of economic ideologies emphasizing private ownership, free markets, competition, the price mechanism, and reduced state expenditures (Remington 1999, 13–15).

In December 1993, the Russian people approved a new constitution that gave the president substantial powers, such as the right to appoint the prime minister, to rule by decree, and to dissolve Parliament (ibid., 46–50, 52–57). This constitution also made subnational units important players in the political dynamics transpiring in the center. It did so because it created a two-chamber assembly composed of the Duma (lower house) and the Federation Council (upper house), which were made up of representatives from Russia's administrative units such as republics and krays. Under the constitution, the Federation Council has the authority to reject legislation passed by the Duma and must vote on certain bills (for example, legislation passed by the Duma, amended by the president, and subsequently accepted by the Duma). Furthermore, the Federation Council is important because it is responsible for approving higher court nominees, decrees on martial law, and "any actions altering the boundaries of territorial units in Russia." In addition, it must consider legislation concerning taxes, treaties, budget, and financial policy (ibid., 50–51).

Despite this authority, provincial governors generally were beholden to the president from 1991 until 1996. First, after the August 1991 and October 1993 coups, Russian president Boris Yeltsin asserted the constitutional right to appoint and dismiss provincial governors, though the pre-1993 parliament tried to end this right. Second, he decreed in August 1991 that the president had the right to put a special representative in each region (Valliant 1997, 3–4; Kirkow 1998, 54–55; Remington 1999, 64). Third, the constitution authorized the president to suspend the acts of regional executives if they contradicted the constitution or international treaties on human and civil rights and to arbitrate between federal and regional bodies (Kirkow 1998, 4).

Weighing these facts, Peter Kirkow (ibid., 46) concludes that Russia has an "asymmetric federalism" that strongly favors the center. Yet this conclusion oversimplifies a complicated political reality. It is significant that the political struggles between the president and Parliament resulted in pandering to the provinces, particularly during the critical years of 1993 (when there was a national referendum on Yeltsin's policies, a violent struggle with Parliament, and a vote on the new Russian constitution) and 1996, a presidential election year (Valliant 1997, 6–9; Remington 1999, 56). The desire for provincial support in 1996 manifested itself in a series of bilateral agreements between center and local units beginning in 1995.[18] In addition, the center tolerated the proliferation of subnational charters that established broad areas of regional, federal, and joint jurisdiction and attempted to shield the regions from federal meddling (Lynne and Novikov 1997, 199–201).

Equally important was the shift to a system of elected regional governors in 1996, which changed the incentive structures for these officials (Kirkow 1998, 46, 52). Simply stated, it became more important for governors to represent the region in the center than to represent the center in the regions (Lynne and Novikov 1997, 202). Related to this, the space created for societal interest groups by the democratization of Russia has allowed for the formation of a Union of Governors from the krays and oblasts (provinces) that lobbies Parliament and the government, thereby bypassing the president (Kirkow 1998, 4; Remington 1999, 145). Furthermore, the center lost some control over the provinces because of its diminishing financial resources, though the economic crisis in Russia made aid from the center more vital than ever.

Access or ties to the president also afford provincial leaders the ability to oppose the government or the special representatives of the president. The governor of Primorskii, Evgenii Nazdratenko, for instance, used his connections with individuals close to Yeltsin to obtain the dismissal of the presidential representative in the region, who was critical of Nazdratenko and the questionable business activities of him and his cronies.[19] Nazdratenko also exploited his close ties with the heads of federal institutions in Primorskii—for example, the commanders of the regional secret service, border guards, and the Pacific Fleet—to distort the center's economic reform measures to serve his and his allies' political and economic ends (Kirkow 1998, 122–26).

Although the Russian president is relatively powerful and preeminent in foreign and military affairs, this analysis of Russia's domestic structure shows that its subnational units have the ability to affect its international relations. This capability results from the 1993 constitution (which gives subnational units a place in the Federation Council), bilateral agreements between the center and subnational units, the coalition-building activities of the president and the government, the center's weakened economic levers, and new electoral dynamics. The president and government are not oblivious to the importance of such actors. This is evidenced by the fact that the deputy heads of the local governments in the five relevant border areas were included as full members of the Russian delegation to the commission responsible for the demarcation of the Sino-Russian border pursuant to the 1991 boundary treaty (Kireev 1997, 17).

The TRADP

Proponents of the TRADP argue that countries in the Tumen River delta and surrounding areas should exploit, collectively, their comparative economic advantages to improve the Tumen River Economic Development Area (TREDA) and its associated hinterlands.[20] Specifically, they have highlighted the potential for the TRADP to combine Japanese and South Korean capital, managerial know-how, and technology with cheap Chinese and North Korean labor; Russian, Mongolian, and Chinese natural resources; and Chinese light industrial and Japanese and South Korean heavy industrial capacities. Tumen advocates contend that a multilateral economic venture can slash export costs by creating a land bridge into the interior of Northeast Asia and Europe as well as a point of transit through the Sea of Japan to Japan, the two Koreas, and the rest of the world.

Jilin had strong economic incentives to push for regional economic integration. Around the turn of the century, the Tumen River provided Jilin with access to not only the Siberian coast but also the Sea of Japan, from which it could reach markets in Japan and Korea. The Treaty of Beijing, signed by the Chinese and the Russians in 1860, terminated this access by granting Russia the entire Siberian coast, including the last fifteen kilometers (approximately ten miles) of the Tumen River, and by joining the Russian and Korean borders. Despite this loss of direct access, the Chinese still retained navigation rights on the river. The Soviet-Japanese conflict, though, led to the blocking of the river in 1938, and the Sino-Soviet conflict precluded any Chinese use of the river (Blanchard 1998a, chap. 4). By 1992, the Soviets had agreed to restore Chinese navigation rights. And between 1992 and 1997, the Russians agreed to transfer land to the Chinese so that they had direct access to the river.

Jilin's historical lack of access to the sea was problematic from an economic standpoint since it forced the province to use the overloaded port of Dalian in the Province of Liaoning as well as the overtaxed railway system leading to Dalian. Moreover, Jilin's lack of access to the sea precluded it from participating in China's Coastal Development Strategy with all the attendant economic benefits and privileges. Jilin's problems were compounded by the fact that it had become a center for inefficient, state-run heavy and extractive industries (Olson and Morgan 1992, 59, 69; Cotton 1996, 1087–93).

Given these obstacles to realizing its full economic potential, it is not surprising that "personalities and institutions in Jilin have been at the forefront of advancing the notion of Tumen regional cooperation" (Cotton 1996, 1094). Indeed, as early as 1988, the provincial government argued for a special economic zone around Hunchun. Moreover, research generated in the province played an important role in the central government's decision to seek to renegotiate China's navigation rights on the Tumen. In addition, academics and policy analysts from Jilin played a significant role in the convening of the first conference on Northeast Asian economic cooperation that took place in Changchun city in Jilin in July 1990 (ibid.). Finally, Jilin had discussions with the UNDP before the project was marketed to the other states that eventually opted to participate in the TRADP.[21] In fact, the Chinese consciously brought the UNDP onto the scene (Christoffersen 1996a, 272).

At the July 1990 conference, participants put the possibility of multinational development of the Tumen River basin on the international agenda for the first time. The next year, at a conference in Ulan Bator, Mongolia, the UNDP gave priority to the development of the Tumen River delta area. At a subsequent meeting in Pyongyang in October 1991, the UNDP proposed a two-stage development program for the Tumen area. The first stage entailed development of a small delta zone (the Tumen River Economic Zone, or TREZ) that would connect Rajin, Hunchun, and Posyet, while the second envisioned the development of a larger delta zone (the TREDA) that would include Chongjin, Yanji, Vladivostok, and Nakhodka/Vostochny. At this meeting, the participating countries also set up the Programme Management Committee (PMC).

Jilin was crucial to policy initiation, but the UNDP was vital to policy facilitation. The UNDP's contribution goes far beyond that of being a passive instrument of states and also that of the standard characterization of international institutions as policy initiators. For example, the UNDP acted to legitimize the Tumen project as a worthwhile objective by embracing China's proposal for the coordinated development of the Northeast Asian region. The subsequent discussion reveals that the UNDP influenced the course of the TRADP through its involvement in interest and policy formulation, agenda setting, agreement development, negotiation, ratification, and project implementation.

The UNDP affected interest and policy formulation by providing the initial seed capital (approximately $3.5 million) needed to pay for the cost of producing preliminary reports for the Tumen initiative. These studies were important in four ways. First, they identified the issues that needed to be addressed to bring the Tumen project to fruition. Second, they illuminated how the TRADP fit into the larger scheme of Northeast Asian economic cooperation. Third, they supplied knowledge about the feasibility of projects proposed for area ports, land transport, environmental protection, international trade, and investment promotion. Fourth, they provided information on the benefits that could be obtained through multinational cooperation.[22] Even now, the UNDP continues to influence interest and policy formulation by funding or arranging for Tumen studies. For example, the Tumen secretariat recently ordered a transportation study that will highlight the area's potential transport growth, detail the advantages of various ports in the region, and fill information gaps about the Tumen area's air, shipping, road, and rail endowments (<www.tradp.org/htmls/recproj.htm>). It is important to realize that without the UNDP there would not have been any money for many (and perhaps any) of these studies, since the World Bank, specialized UN agencies, and economic heavyweights like Japan did not have the mandate or interest to fund such studies.[23]

The UNDP also occupied the role of agenda setter. Profiting from its longtime presence in almost all the states in the region (the exception was Russia), its perceived neutrality, and its ability to meet with different government ministries, the UNDP went from capital to capital during the conceptualization phase of the program to promote the Tumen initiative.[24] Moreover, the UNDP met with Japanese officials and representatives at the U.S. Department of State to ensure that they had no objections to the project.[25] In this way, the UNDP ensured that these two powerful players in the political and economic dynamics of Northeast Asia did not keep the TRADP off the region's agenda. Finally, the UNDP helped to push forward those who were ambivalent about the project by creating a sense of excitement, emphasizing the project's benefits, and supporting the appropriateness of the Tumen project's timing.[26] According to one account, the UNDP sent Russian president Boris Yeltsin a letter to encourage Russia to participate in the project, highlighting the investment gains that Russia would derive from the project (Kouriatchev 1993, 10–11, 23).

In February 1992, the PMC held its first official meeting in Seoul. The PMC II, held nine months later in Beijing, witnessed the signing by China, Russia, North Korea, South Korea, and Mongolia of the Tumen River Area Development Programme Document, which officially launched the TRADP. In New York in December 1995 government representatives from China, Russia, North Korea, South Korea, and Mongolia formally signed international agreements establishing the Consultative Commission for the Development of the Tumen River Economic Development Area and Northeast Asia and the Tumen River Area Development Coordinating Committee. These agreements provided a legal basis for the Tumen secretariat to manage cooperation as well as created the institutional infrastructure for the TRADP.

Jilin engaged in policy entrepreneurship throughout this period. Exploiting a State Council of China decision in February 1992 to designate Hunchun an open border city, the Jilin provincial government gave Hunchun provincial-level authority for economic management, which meant that its economic and social development plans and border trade plans were delinked from provincial plans. The purpose of both actions was to facilitate the development of the TRADP. Hunchun quickly took advantage of its new authority to sign a number of agreements with Primorskii that would facilitate the development of transportation and communication facilities within the TREDA.

In addition to building the infrastructure needed for the TRADP, Jilin officials actively promoted and publicized the project. In April 1995, for instance, at the fourth international fair in Beijing, Jilin governor Gao Yan promoted investment in the development of the Tumenjiang and stated that the development of the Tumen Jiang area was the leading project in Jilin's opening to the outside world. In July, a delegation of Chinese central government and provincial officials and UN officials swept through Hong Kong to drum up interest in the TRADP. In October, China's Ministry of Foreign Trade and Economic Cooperation, the Jilin provincial government, the Yanbian prefectural government, and the United Nations Industrial and Development Organization (UNIDO) held an international investment and business forum in Yanji that, according to press reports, attracted almost $940 million in planned investment.[27]

In February 1996, the Tumen secretariat began operations in Beijing; Jilin was still a policy driver. The provincial government announced that it planned to complete the construction of a link with the Trans-Siberian railway and to make additional progress on building a highway between Changchun and Hunchun. In April, Ding

Shisheng, deputy secretary-general of the Jilin provincial govern-ment and director of the office in charge of the development of the Tumen River area, noted that China planned to strengthen coopera-tion with Russia in developing the Tumen by opening international train service from the capital of Jilin to Vladivostok, via Hunchun and Yanji, after the joining of the Chinese and Russian railways. In March, Ding appealed to the Eighth National People's Congress for more favorable policies for the Tumen project.

In September, the Tumen secretariat collaborated with North Korea, the UNDP, and UNIDO to run a TRADP-related investment fair in Rajin-Sonbong in North Korea. The next month, the Jilin provincial government acted to liberalize the economic environment further when it gave approval to Hunchun to open the long-closed Fangchuan area, except where army units were stationed, to assist the progress of the TRADP. It also celebrated the completion of the railway linking Tumen and Hunchun with Changlingzi, where the Chinese and Russian parts of the Tumen-Makhalino railway, which gives China access to the Russian ports of Zarubino and Posyet, meet. In the beginning of the following year, China again took the lead role in moving the TRADP forward when the State Council ap-proved the opening of a border road linking Hunchun with North Korea's Rajin-Sonbong.

In November 1997, at a meeting in Beijing, the relevant countries agreed to continue joint development of the Tumen area, signed TRADP documents for Phase II (implementation), considered a Northeast Asian Development Bank and the creation of an invest-ment support center that would promote investment in the TREDA, elevated the economic importance of tourism in the TREDA, and discussed environmental protection issues. More recently, the TRADP held an investment forum in Primorskii in May 1998 and si-multaneous investment forums in China and North Korea in Sep-tember. In June 1999, the UNDP funded and cohosted the Confer-ence on Economic Cooperation in Northeast Asia in Mongolia, which was attended by representatives from governments participat-ing in the TRADP, private sector and think tank representatives, and officials from other international institutions. After the conference, the TRADP Consultative Commission and the Coordination Com-mittee met and considered various proposals for furthering the de-velopment of the Tumen area. For instance, they considered the es-tablishment of a Tumen regional investor service (TRIS) network, consisting of centers in the relevant countries, which would maintain a database of potential investment projects, match investors with investment opportunities, facilitate the permit issuance and project clearance process, and help investors resolve project implementation problems (<www.tradp.org/htmls/trisnet.htm>).

My case study shows clearly that Jilin has played an important role in the initiation and development of the TRADP. First, it produced studies and analyses that highlighted the benefits to be gained from such a project, thereby playing a role in interest and policy formation as well as agenda setting. Second, it adopted economic liberalization and reform measures to support the program, which contributed to the implementation of the TRADP. Third, it actively promoted the project, thereby assuming additional agenda-setting and implementation functions. Fourth, it spent funds for the infrastructure needed for the TRADP and thus facilitated implementation of the venture. Fifth, it lobbied the center to provide funds and favorable policy measures, once again taking on responsibilities in interest and policy formulation, agenda setting, and implementation.

My case study also demonstrates that the UNDP was an important policy initiator, facilitator, and implementor. The agency affected agreement development, negotiation, and ratification in a number of different ways. For example, it served as the chair at a number of Tumen meetings, creating a perceived neutral environment in which past and current enemies such as North and South Korea, Russia and China, and China and South Korea could meet to work out TRADP agreements. In addition, UNDP officials and consultants reduced transaction costs by shuttling among the various states to relay ideas and suggestions and to help resolve difficult issues.[28] Furthermore, it oversaw the development of key Tumen agreements such as the 1995 accords that created the institutional and legal infrastructure for the program.[29]

The UNDP also has been significant because of its role in policy implementation. It improved the investment climate in the region by coordinating the publication of an investment guide in 1996 and sponsoring project workshops and investment fairs (Pomfret 1998, 84). It also collaborated with UNIDO to help identify, screen, and profile investment projects; prepare publicity and promotional tools such as investment videos; and dispatch promotional missions abroad (Tumen Secretariat 1997, 5).[30] In 1998, it provided almost two hundred thousand dollars to fund TRADP promotion tours, to train Mongolia how to encourage foreign investment, and to identify and promote investment opportunities in Primorskii (<www.tradp.org/

htmls/recproj.htm>). Furthermore, it has aided in the staffing of the TRADP. It hired the first TRADP program manager and helped identify the individual (David Husband)—previously a UNDP consultant for the Mekong River Commission in Vietnam—who serves as the acting director of the Tumen secretariat.[31] Finally, it acts to smooth relations, reduce misunderstandings, and promote a regional mindset (Pomfret 1998, 84).

In sum, the TRADP's birth and accomplishments to date are due to a decade of policy advocacy by Jilin and the UNDP and to the cooperation of all the major actors in the region. Despite this cooperation, not all the proposed policies have been implemented; the region has not experienced the economic takeoff hoped by TRADP's proponents. To explain this puzzle, we must look more closely at Russia's actions vis-à-vis the project.

After the end of the Cold War in East Asia, there were multiple reasons to expect the Russian Far East to embrace the TRADP as much as would Jilin. For instance, during the Cold War, the region was defense oriented, tightly controlled, and isolated, and hence unable to exploit fully its endowments (Stephan 1994, chaps. 21–25; Petro and Rubinstein 1997, 20–21, 26–27, 193–94; Blanchard 1998a, 211–12, chap. 8). These endowments included natural resources such as timber, water, diamonds, tin, gold, tungsten, and coal, as well as considerable scientific and technical expertise (Minakir 1994, chap. 2, 125–28; Kovrigin 1997; Dorian 1997). Soviet leader Mikhail Gorbachev and Russian president Yeltsin's economic and political reforms and the opening of the Sino-Russian border in 1992 reconnected the region to the outside world and gave it a chance to exploit its assets. Trade became more significant for Primorskii in its capacity as an exporter/ importer but particularly in its role as a transport and transit center. Given the size of Primorskii's market and its wealth of much coveted consumer goods, it is not surprising that China quickly became Primorskii's most important international economic partner (Minakir 1994, 156–59, 174–75; Christoffersen 1996a, 278; Lukin 1998, 822).

By 1993, however, the Sino-Russian relationship along the border had begun to sour. First, the Russians began to complain about the goods that they received from Chinese private traders, which included shoddy and fake items as well as contaminated food (Christoffersen 1996a, 279; Moltz 1997, 187). Second, the Russians started to complain that the Chinese were investing too little, draining Russia of its precious natural resources, and taking advantage of the Russians, who putatively were inexperienced in capitalist ways (Lukin 1998, 823–24).

One of the most important sources of friction, though, was the influx of Chinese for trade and work. According to Russian newspapers, between three hundred thousand and one million Chinese settled in the Russian Far East in the early 1990s, though these papers probably exaggerated the true extent of Chinese settlement (Portyakov 1996, 136).[32] Fearful Russians in Primorskii and other areas accused China of using economic cooperation to settle its surplus population into Russia to resolve Chinese "problems of unemployment and overpopulation" and to establish "the groundwork for future Chinese efforts to claim those Russian territories that Beijing held as previously belonging to China" (Lukin 1998, 824).

Reacting to and in some cases fueling these sentiments, Primorskii began in mid-1993 to institute restrictions on Chinese travel into Russia and on Chinese ownership and leasing of Russian property, and it imposed a daily resident tax and product inspection requirements (Christoffersen 1996a, 283; Anderson 1997, 29; Moltz 1997, 193; Lukin 1998, 826). Throughout 1994 and even when Chinese president Jiang Zemin was visiting with Yeltsin in Moscow, Primorskii used border guards, interior ministry troops, and military forces to round up illegal foreign, particularly Chinese, residents for deportation or a monetary penalty. Altogether, these restrictions reduced cooperation and caused bilateral trade to plummet (Christoffersen 1996a, 284–85, 287; Moltz 1997, 190; Rozman 1997a, 19; Lukin 1998, 826). Christoffersen (1996a, 282) observes that Primorskii saw the border as a "dike holding back millions of Chinese" and hence was in constant conflict with Moscow over how open the border should be.

In 1995, Nazdratenko added to the mix of problems bedeviling the Sino-Russian relationship when he chose to challenge the Sino-Russian border treaty of 1991. Nazdratenko said he would not give up any land to the Chinese because the three hundred hectares of land in the Khasan area to be transferred pursuant to the terms of treaty included the graves of Russian soldiers and was prime hunting and agricultural grounds. In fact, he called for the repudiation of the 1991 treaty, claiming, on top of his other charges, that the transfer of land would allow China to gain access to the sea and to build a major port on the Tumen River. This port, in turn, allegedly would kill Russian ports such as Vladivostok and Nakhodka and the area's economy and would weaken Russia's overall position in the Far East. Nazdratenko threatened to resign and called for a national referendum on the 1991 agreement (Hyer 1996, 93; Zinberg 1996, 81; Anderson 1997, 28–29; Lukin 1998, 826–28).

To press his case, Nazdratenko recruited regional representatives from the Joint Border Demarcation Committee (set up to determine the status of river islands), "arranged for Cossak units to be placed on disputed sections of the border and encouraged regional and federal Duma intervention" (Anderson 1997, 44). Although the Russian foreign ministry generally was unreceptive to his demands, Nazdratenko's activities resulted in delays in the border demarcation process, a shift in the amount of land to be transferred back to China so no graves would be transferred, and the termination of discussions about the joint economic development of certain river islands (ibid., 45). His actions also spurred the Chinese to make a complaint to the Russian government prior to Yeltsin's 1996 visit to Beijing and led Yeltsin to warn that Nazdratenko was threatening the entire Sino-Russian eastern border settlement (Zinberg 1996, 80–81).

Unfortunately for the development of the TRADP, Primorskii's maltreatment of the Chinese as well as its strenuous efforts to block the transfer of territory to China disrupted progress on the Tumen project (Christoffersen 1996a, 290; Anderson 1997, 29). Indeed, representatives from the Russian foreign ministry as well as researchers affiliated with Russian government think tanks have acknowledged that Primorskii's behavior has constrained the progress of this multilateral economic cooperation venture (Tomikhin 1997, 94; Portyakov 1998). The TRADP case shows what a subnational actor, empowered by a facilitating domestic political structure and motivated by its borderland status, can do to disrupt multilateral economic cooperation. In theoretical terms, Primorskii was important not because of its role in interest and policy formulation, coalition building, or agreement development, amendment, and ratification, but because it could obstruct the implementation of the Tumen program.

Why did Primorskii take measures that directly and indirectly hindered the advancement of the TRADP, despite Moscow's favorable attitude toward the project and Primorskii's dire need for foreign trade and investment? There are five prominent reasons. First, Primorskii elites saw obstructionism, interference with Sino-Russian bilateral relations, and policies that diverged from Moscow's as political levers to extract from Moscow additional economic benefits such as increased subsidies, reduced taxes and tariffs, higher export quotas, a greater share of customs duties, and more control of local natural resources (Kirkow and Hanson 1994, 73–81; Christoffersen 1994–95, 527–28; Alexseev and Troyakova 1999, 222–24, 228). Second, Nazdratenko's main political supporters—industrial managers, defense officials, local financiers, and entrepreneurs in whose companies the local government often has a controlling share interest—were worried that TRADP-related liberalization, foreign investment, and reform measures would erode their economic and political position (Kirkow and Hanson 1994, 82–83; Christoffersen 1994–95, 520–21; Burns 1995, 20–22; Rozman 1997b, 545–50; Alexseev and Troyakova 1999, 232–34). Third, Nazdratenko saw hostility to the Chinese as a means to exploit the public's sense of vulnerability to Chinese economic, demographic, and political pressures and thus to bolster his political standing (Zinberg 1996, 84; Rozman 1998, 100). Fourth, there was a real fear that the Tumen project would compete with the major ports in Primorskii as well as major Russian rail lines such as the Baikal-Amur and Trans-Siberian railways (Zabrovskaya 1995, 35–36). Fifth, patriotism and anti-Chinese racism supported opposition to multinational economic initatives like the TRADP (Stephan 1994, 293–300).

Conclusion

The TRADP represents the first substantive multilateral economic venture in Northeast Asia since the end of the Cold War. Admittedly, its achievements are limited. It does not have the institutional richness or depth of the EU or the accomplishments of the EU or even the Association of Southeast Asian Nations. Nevertheless, it has aided the development of the region around the Tumen River delta. Furthermore, it has facilitated the cooperation of one-time adversaries in the area such as Russia and China, North Korea and South Korea, and China and South Korea. Finally, it provides a rare opportunity for dialogue among TRADP participants that does not exist in the bilateral realm, given the state of relations between various TRADP participants such as North and South Korea (<www.tradp.org/htmls/0609conf.htm>).

This chapter demonstrates that in order to understand the dynamics of the TRADP—that is, its successful initiation and constrained implementation—it is critical to take into account domestic as well as international variables. This chapter reveals, however, that a traditional state-centric view or unitary actor assumption cannot provide adequate grounds for understanding the TRADP.[33] Specifically, we need to recognize the importance of subnational actors such as regional or provincial governments as well as international institutions to explain the initiation and development of the project and its current (relative) stagnation. Jilin, for instance, fueled the initiation and implementation of the TRADP with studies, liberalization measures, and infrastructure spending, while Primorskii obstructed its implementation by limiting cross-border interactions and raising territorial issues.

This study makes a theoretical contribution to the discipline of international relations by stipulating the conditions that create the space for such actors to affect international relations. Specifically, it confirms that domestic structure conditions when subnational entities and international institutions will be relevant. Furthermore, it highlights that a situation of complex interdependence increases the opportunities for such actors to play a consequential role in foreign affairs. Finally, it shows the relevance of borderland status in the case of subnational entities.

In addition, this chapter makes a direct contribution to the literature emphasizing domestic structure by enriching our knowledge about the factors that shape this important domestic variable. First, my discussion of China's domestic structure supports previous observations that regime type (for example, democracy or nondemocracy) does not tell us much about whether a domestic structure will intensify the importance of domestic or international pressures (Evangelista 1995; Milner 1998, 775). Second, it lends additional credence to arguments stressing the importance of informal factors for understanding domestic structure (Ripsman 2002). Specifically, the analysis of the Russian and Chinese cases underscores the significance of extraconstitutional realities such as economic ideologies of decentralization, the relative balance of capabilities between the center and its subnational units, and political logrolling between the center and its subnational units. Overall, my analysis of domestic structure suggests limits to the argument that subnational actors assume special significance when there is a *democratic federal* system such as in the United States, Australia, or Switzerland (Duchacek 1990, 2).

Summarizing a 1990 edited work on subnational actors, Hans Michelmann (1990, 313) observes, "no country-chapter author concludes that the international activities of his federation's component units [that is, a subnational actor] seriously threaten the foreign-policy prerogatives of the national government." This is hard to debate, yet it would be a mistake to conclude from this that subnational actors are irrelevant to the course of world politics. What this chapter demonstrates is that, when certain international and domestic variables are present, subnational actors and international institutions can indeed make a difference, in both the realms of multilateral economic cooperation as well as high politics.[34]

Notes

I would like to thank Daniel Drezner, Dimitris Stevis, the participants in the conference "The Interaction of Domestic and International Institutions"; and Norrin M. Ripsman for their helpful comments and suggestions.

1. This progress has in no way been spectacular, though the TRADP has gone much further and lasted much longer than cynics and critics expected in the early 1990s.

2. Beijing has always evidenced the most enthusiasm for the project, though its support has moderated in recent years (Blanchard 2000).

3. For elaboration on these limitations with existing theory, see the introduction to this volume as well as Caporaso 1997 and Milner 1998.

4. These accounts also fail to do justice to the role of the UNDP.

5. I define a subnational actor to be a subunit of a territorial state that has a territorially defined limit, its own areas of jurisdiction, and its own political institutions.

6. On nonstate actors as instruments of foreign policy, see Karns and Mingst 1987, 467–69, and Raustiala 1997, 726–31. These authors note inter alia that such entities give states information about policy options, enhance their ability to monitor the activities of other states, provide transparency about the policy process, facilitate logrolling activities, and shape international public opinion.

7. My listing certainly is not exhaustive of the potential channels through which subnational units and international institutions contribute to the dynamic of international relations. Nevertheless, these paths of influence represent some of the more significant ones.

8. These effects also are highlighted in the international regime literature (Keohane 1997, 29–30), though regimes obviously work their effects passively, i.e., unless they are coupled with an international organization.

9. Leonard Schoppa (1993), who studied when American pressure on Japan was successful in producing Japanese economic policy changes, implies this possibility. Schoppa found that the Americans achieved success when they brought new groups into the policy process and thereby enlarged the universe of international bargains that Japanese negotiators could strike.

10. For an argument on the importance of considering context when studying the relationship between trade and conflict, see Blanchard and Ripsman 2001.

11. There are other permissive factors, such as the presence of complex interdependence among countries (Keohane and Nye 1989). As noted in the introduction, complex interdependence produces an incentive for international coordination or cooperation. It also creates the space for subnational

actors and international institutions to play a more consequential role in international affairs. Specifically, it empowers such entities by allowing them to provide expert knowledge, serve as coalition partners, set the agenda, shape the content of and prospects for an international agreement, and affect the implementation of international accords (Keohane and Nye 1974, 42–43, 61; Haas 1992a, 12–16; Adler and Haas 1992, 373). In addition, in a world of complex interdependence, central authorities cannot exploit the international threat situation, since it is by definition low, to privilege themselves against subnational actors.

12. A borderland is an area "whose economic and social life is directly and significantly affected by proximity to an international boundary" (Asiwaju 1994, 58).

13. When two states have hostile relations, they tend to close their border and constrain or prevent cross-border interactions. Thus, borderlands may have more interactions with distant countries than with their geographically proximate neighbors. Hence, it is very important a priori that an environment of complex interdependence exists for cross-border flows and interactions to matter. I thank Dimitris Stevis for highlighting this point.

14. Stephen Krasner (1995b, 268–69, 272–75) emphasizes the importance of the power to grant access.

15. There is no need to conduct an analysis of whether the subnational units under consideration herein are borderlands since they incontrovertibly are. Critics might argue that historic tensions along the Sino-Russian border mean that complex interdependence does not truly exist between the two countries. In actuality, though, each country sees the other as nonthreatening. Furthermore, force lacks utility as an instrument of statecraft in the bilateral relationship. This situation is the result of shared geostrategic interests, the conventional military balance, and each side's possession of nuclear weapons (Andersen 1997, 15–20; Bilveer 1998, 495–99). Finally, as detailed later, there has been substantial development along other dimensions of the complex interdependence spectrum.

16. Admittedly, Sino-Russian economic interdependence is asymmetric, with China being a more important economic partner to Russia than Russia is to China. Nevertheless, economic relations with Russia are very important for the development of China's relatively backward Northeast, the People's Liberation Army's (PLA) military modernization, and China's refurbishment of Soviet-era industrial plants. Moreover, the Chinese view border trade, a major portion of contemporary Sino-Russian economic interactions, as a way to develop border areas, promote specialization, and open new markets (Yu Lixing 1993). I am grateful to Daniel Drezner for raising this issue. On the measurement of economic interdependence, see Blanchard and Ripsman 1996 and Blanchard and Ripsman 2001.

17. Nevertheless, the autonomy afforded by China's domestic structure is bounded, given that the center appoints all top provincial officials, controls

the key coercive organs (e.g., military and state security agencies), maintains many levels of control over foreign economic activities, and can send specialized work teams to investigate the activities of provincial leaders (Lieberthal 1995, 317–19).

18. Gaye Christoffersen (1996a, 289) notes that many of these arguments waived restrictions on the regions' use of foreign exchange and ability to sign foreign agreements and suggests that they set a precedent for the weakening of central control over foreign trade and investment.

19. Reports suggest that Nazdratenko had close ties to Yeltsin himself, having stayed at Yeltsin's dacha and being one of several dozen informal presidential advisors (Kirkow 1998, 138–39).

20. Except as noted, this section draws upon Blanchard 1996, Blanchard 1998b, and Blanchard 2000.

21. Interview with Roy Morey, former UNDP resident representative in Beijing, 7 October 1999.

22. Interviews with Benjamin Brown, former deputy chief of the country division of the UNDP, 29 September 1999; and Roy Morey, 7 October 1999. This also is noted in Kouriatchev 1993, 9–10, and Pomfret 1996, 135–36.

23. Interview with Benjamin Brown, 29 September 1999.

24. Interviews with Dr. Nay Htun, UN assistant secretary-general and UNDP assistant administrator, 6 October 1999; and Roy Morey, 7 October 1999.

25. Interview with Roy Morey, 7 October 1999.

26. Interview with Benjamin Brown, 29 September 1999.

27. This was later revised to $600 million (Tumen Secretariat 1997, 5).

28. Interview with Dr. Nay Htun, 6 October 1999.

29. Ibid.

30. Dr. Nay Htun stated that it was the UNDP that asked UNIDO to become involved in the Tumen investment fair process (ibid.).

31. Interview with Roy Morey, 7 October 1999.

32. The true concern for the Russians probably is the fact that the population of Northeast China is approximately 110 million while the population of the Russian Far East, which consists of ten administrative subdivisions and represents 36.4 percent of Russian territory, does not top 8 million (Portyakov 1996, 132, 136, 140 n. 1).

33. In another work, I consider the interests of China's center (i.e., Beijing) to understand why it was the most enthusiastic supporter of the TRADP among all the national governments participating in the project (Blanchard 2000).

34. For a similar point, see Cameron 1995, 76–77.

Part 2. Coercion

Tying Hands without a Rope: Rational Domestic Response to International Institutional Constraints

Eric Reinhardt

How do international institutions interact with domestic politics to affect states' policy choices? One familiar way is through the device of "blame shifting" or "tying the hands" of national leaders. Imagine a leader who wants to impose unpopular economic reforms but whose plans are resisted by the legislature. What happens if an international institution such as the IMF or the WTO prescribes liberalization? The leader may be able to claim that the institution is tying his hands, with the hope of avoiding the political backlash following reforms. In short, by serving as a commitment device for reformist leaders facing domestic opposition, an international institution makes possible policies like liberalization that may not otherwise occur. Institutional constraints as varied as IMF conditionality (Cottarelli and Giannini 1998); fixed exchange rate regimes such as the European Monetary System (EMS) (Agénor 1994; Giavazzi and Pagano 1994; Martin and Simmons 1998, 748); regional trade agreements such as the NAFTA and EU (Ibarra 1995, 59; Gould 1992, 21; Whalley 1996, 15–16; Smith 1997, 183); and WTO investigations (Francois 1999, 5–6) are all said to affect state policy-making for this reason.

Yet tying hands may not be so easy. Namely, most international institutions provide no rope; they lack enforcement power. If the domestic opposition is rational, it will know a reformist leader has an incentive to misrepresent the extent of the institutional constraint, and it will discredit the "tied hands" rationale for reform. This observation explains why the policy prescriptions of the IMF (Killick 1995, 55; Rodrik 1995, 25; Fairman and Ross 1996, 31–34; Bird and Rowlands 1997, 980–84; Rodrik 1996, 31; Dhonte 1997, 7; Ball 1999, 1837); the EMS (Weber 1991; Sandholtz 1993, 35; Frieden 1994, 27; Velasco 1997; Bleaney and Mizen 1997); and regional trade agreements (Ibarra 1995, 59) are often ignored or at least yield fewer economic gains due to the fear of policy reversal. Domestic opponents of reformist leaders have good reason to view the rhetoric of tied hands with suspicion, as they often do. For instance, in reaction to the British government's attempt to close some shipyards by deferring to a European Commission action, a member of Parliament (MP) said,

> The Minister has sought to blame [the Commission] for the decision, but has also sought to argue in the House that it was the right decision. Will he clarify whether ... he urged the [continued support of the shipyards] or simply accepted [the Commission's] decision—or even welcomed it? (Smith 1997, 179)

How can an international institution help a leader implement reforms if the opposition is aware of the difficulty of enforcement?

Of course, there may be genuine external constraints on a country's policy, such as retaliatory threats from other states or the behavior of private market actors. But these constraints may well apply regardless of the institution's involvement. What additional leverage, if any, do the institution's prescriptions provide? How valid is the venerable view that international institutions facilitate domestic commitment? Can leaders tie their hands without ropes?

To answer this question, I develop a game theoretic model focusing on policy-making by an agent with monopoly agenda control (for example, a chief executive, president) and a principal with veto power (for example, a legislature, congress) in the context of an institution with uncertain enforcement capability. The imagined setting is a WTO investigation of a trade dispute. The president of the defendant state seeks to lower existing trade barriers, against the wishes of a protectionist congress, and he has private information about the probability that the WTO will rule for the plaintiff. A ruling against the defendant, if issued, will make foreign retaliation more probable unless liberalization occurs, but litigation imposes transaction costs on the president.

Surprisingly, the model indicates that leaders can indeed tie their hands without ex post ropes, despite rational opposition. Presidents who know that the WTO is unlikely to rule against their country's protectionist policy can nevertheless elicit significant liberalizing concessions from their congress. This is true even in the absence of costs for exiting or reversing a decision to comply with the institution.[1] The catch is that the benefits of tying hands when enforcement is not likely are matched one for one by losses when enforcement *is* forthcoming. The domestic commitment function of international institutions adds nothing to the overall level of liberalization, contrary to the expectations of many institutionalist theorists (Keohane 1984; Axelrod and Keohane 1985). Moreover, all the benefits of tying hands via a WTO ruling are realized before a ruling is issued, in the form of early settlements. Once a ruling is issued and sanctions for noncompliance are either realized or not, a leader who does not face sanctions is unable to extract significant reform from the opposition. Ironically, a leader attempting to tie his hands with an international institution can only do so in cases in which the institution does not issue prescriptions.

The model yields a number of other counterintuitive findings. Remarkably, for instance, the institution only works as a commitment device if the transaction costs of utilizing it are sufficiently high. This contradicts the conventional view that institutions promote cooperation by doing precisely the opposite, that is, lowering transaction costs. It follows that, since less developed countries (LDCs) face higher opportunity costs when litigating WTO disputes, leaders of LDCs will be more able to tie their hands using the WTO than will those of advanced industrial states. In addition, comparing my model to one without a domestic veto player suggests some testable differences between unified and divided governments. For instance, WTO cases against advanced industrial states (that is, states facing lower transaction costs for litigating) with unified governments should be more likely to go to a ruling than those with divided governments. Yet defendants with unified and divided governments should be equally likely to concede in cases ending after rulings are issued.

The remainder of this chapter develops the formal model and some key results and testable propositions, in a few cases sketching supportive, though preliminary, empirical findings. These results add up to a picture of how international institutions interact with domestic politics that differs substantially from the received wisdom(s). International institutions do indeed affect policy-making by changing the incentives for domestic actors, but not in ways imagined by functional-institutionalist logic. The conclusion discusses some of these broader implications for theory and for optimal institutional design.

The Model

How, if at all, can leaders tie their hands using international institutional constraints if domestic audiences are rational and aware of the limited enforceability of such constraints? Since this is a rationalist critique, I will use a rationalist method, that is, a game theoretic signaling model, to explore its limitations. The empirical referent for this model is dispute settlement under GATT or its successor, the WTO. Like institutions governing exchange rate regimes, multilateral lending terms, and regional trade blocs, GATT/WTO dispute adjudication lacks enforcement power but potentially conditions the behavior of other states and private market actors. Thus the model's key insights should apply to other institutions as well.

Some Background

The essence of GATT or WTO dispute settlement is as follows. A plaintiff state identifies another country's objectionable trade practice, for example, an excessive subsidy or import barrier. Any policy that "nullifies or impairs" commitments made in the various GATT treaties is potential grounds for a formal complaint, though only states, not private parties, have legal standing in this body. If the defendant does not settle the issue to the plaintiff's satisfaction, ultimately a GATT or WTO ad hoc court, known as a panel, is called upon to issue a ruling. Panels are composed of independent legal experts. Rulings specify the extent of violation of GATT law by the defendant and may suggest corrective measures. The court lacks a bailiff, or enforcement power, yet at any point the plaintiff may retaliate unilaterally (often without GATT/WTO approval, however). Over six hundred complaints have been filed since 1948.[2]

Two features of the process, which I embed in the model to follow, are worth noting. First, chief executives, or more precisely their delegated negotiators, enjoy an informational advantage over legislators with respect to GATT/WTO litigation. The executive possesses a larger and usually better trained legal and economic staff, which conducts the actual litigation. In many countries legislators have few informational resources at their disposal on any issue, let alone foreign trade (Milner 1997, 21, 84). Of course, affected firms might be relied upon to inform legislators (ibid., 21), but even for large businesses, buying legal advice for GATT/WTO litigation is often prohibitively costly, and collective action problems may diminish the willingness of individual firms to contribute to such costly public goods when an entire domestic industry is affected. Also, opposing interest groups may provide contrary advice to legislators, thereby diminishing their joint informative value (ibid., 239). Furthermore, the executive in many countries has repeated litigation experience with GATT/WTO, while this is not generally true of groups advising legislators on industry-specific cases. Dispute proceedings of GATT/WTO occur behind closed doors, without private party access.[3] Finally, the lack of stare decisis, and the fact that the majority of disputes end prior to rulings being issued, means that outsiders have little observable basis for refining their own estimates of legal merits across cases. For these reasons, executives are much better informed than legislators about their GATT/WTO litigation's prospects.

Second, litigating these disputes is costly. The transaction costs include the time spent by the support bureaucracy researching cases, preparing briefs, meeting with representatives of the affected domestic industries and the other disputant(s), filing documents to conform with domestic trade law, and appearing before the WTO. The opportunities forsaken may be significant, since each case litigated is another one neglected, poorly argued, or aborted prior to filing. Disputes often last for years, especially now that the WTO has added up to twenty-nine months of additional legal steps such as appeal and arbitration. From the perspective of the plaintiff, or a defendant seeking to tie his own hands using an adverse ruling, litigation is particularly costly because it locks in the protectionist status quo for that much longer (Reinhardt 1999, 10–15; Horn and Mavroidis 1999, 15–17; South Centre 1999, 24). (And the WTO makes no provision for retroactive compensation.)

The transaction costs of GATT/WTO litigation hit LDCs the hardest (Reinhardt 1999, 16; Hoekman and Mavroidis 1999; Horn and Mavroidis 1999). LDCs typically have no or few personnel dedicated to WTO dispute negotiation, and even less frequently are those personnel permanently stationed in Geneva. Even India, presumably one of the best prepared LDCs, had no dedicated staff at home or abroad to negotiate WTO disputes as of late 1997 (*India Today,* November 10, 1997, 52). Michalopoulos's (1998) exhaustive count estimates that up to 60 percent of developing members in 1997 had insufficient representation to even participate in regularly scheduled WTO activities, let alone disputes. In 1999, thirty LDC members had no WTO delegation at all. A matter as small as real estate costs, which are exorbitant in Geneva, has deterred some LDCs, especially since Switzerland's promised housing subsidies for LDC representatives have never been delivered (*Independent,* July 18, 1999, 13). Furthermore, since LDCs have participated in significantly fewer disputes, they have less GATT/WTO litigation experience and higher startup costs in preparing new cases. As a Colombian representative put it, "The problem is not a lack of information but too much of it" (ibid.). In part due to such hurdles, Ecuador, Guatemala, Honduras, and Mexico let the United States take the lead in their (meritorious) complaint against the EU's banana import regime. The nominal figures on WTO litigation costs are relatively low: the average case, by one estimate, costs about two hundred thousand dollars, once filed. But the problem goes deeper: LDCs are "less sophisticated buyers of legal advice" and are less able to "manage and absorb legal advice by virtue of a well-developed institutional structure" (Trade and Development Centre 1999, 45). As the Malaysian trade minister has noted, without adequately trained in-house staff, LDCs lack the ability to proactively identify and pursue the best cases (*Business Times (Malaysia),* April 30, 1997, 20). To resolve such difficulties, the WTO has ostensibly increased technical assistance but in practice rules out aid to the many members who fail to pay their dues, that is, precisely those states that need it the most (Michalopoulos 1998; South Centre 1999, 23–24). That many LDCs have put increases in legal aid at the top of their priorities for the Millenium Round testifies to the high transaction costs of dispute settlement in the existing regime (WTO 1999).

Model Setup

With these two features in mind, I will now proceed to the model. The model contains two players, the defendant state's chief executive (which I will call the president, or P), who has monopoly agenda control, and the median legislator (labeled congress, or C), who has a veto role only. Since I am exploring the potential for tying hands, I will focus on the special case in which the president prefers to liberalize and the median legislator, or congress, prefers to maintain a protectionist status quo. In this model, a nonstrategic WTO panel issues a ruling when called upon, and a foreign state threatens exogenously probabilistic retaliation, conditioned on the type of ruling issued, if the defendant fails to sufficiently liberalize.

   The sequence of action is as follows (see fig. 1). First, nature selects the president's type ρ, $\rho \in \{\rho_{lo}, \rho_{hi}\}$, where $\text{Prob}(\rho = \rho_{hi}) = \pi$, $\rho_{lo}, \rho_{hi}, \pi \in [0,1]$, and $\rho_{lo} < \rho_{hi}$. The type ρ reflects the president's private information about the probability of an adverse ruling by the WTO. Type ρ_{lo} is more likely to win its WTO litigation than is type ρ_{hi}, but keep in mind that the president wants to lose, that is, have WTO condemn his state's protectionist policy,[4] so ρ_{hi} is P's "strong" type

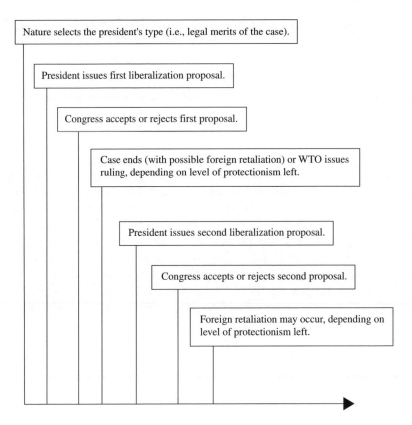

Fig. 1. Sequence of play in the model

and ρ_{lo} is P's "weak" type. Denote the WTO's ultimate ruling decision as $r, r \in \{0,1\}$, where $r = 1$ is a ruling against the defendant. Thus $\rho = \text{Prob}(r = 1)$.

Second, the president makes a proposal, $p_1 \in [0,1]$, where higher values reflect greater protectionism. The president most prefers a policy of 0.

Third, having observed the president's proposal, the congress updates its beliefs about the president's type. The congress's posterior belief is μ, where $\mu = \text{Prob}(\rho = \rho_{hi})$. The congress then chooses $a_1 \in \{0,1\}$, where $a_1 = 1$, to accept the proposal and $a_1 = 0$ to reject it in favor of the protectionist status quo, 1.

The case is more likely to go before the WTO panel if the initial proposal outcome is more protectionist. Specifically, the probability of a ruling, given the actions of P and C beforehand is proportional to the level of protectionism in place, that is, p_1 if $a_1 = 1$ and 1 otherwise. If the case does not go to the WTO, the probability that the plaintiff unilaterally retaliates is likewise p_1 if $a_1 = 1$ or 1 otherwise, after which the game ends. If retaliation occurs, its level in a dispute ending before a ruling is $s \in [0,1)$.

Fourth, if a ruling r has been issued (where $r = 1$ if the ruling supports the plaintiff), the president again makes a proposal, $p_2 \in [0,1]$. Fifth, now with no updating of beliefs since P's private information is obsolete, the congress rejects or accepts the proposal, $a_2 \in \{0,1\}$. The foreign state retaliates at this point with a probability equal to the level of protectionism in the resulting policy (that is, p_2 if $a_2 = 1$ or 1 otherwise). The level of retaliation, if it occurs, is s_0 if the ruling supports the defendant and s_1 otherwise.[5] I constrain $s_1 > 1$ and $s_0 \in [0,1)$.

Now turn to the utilities. The president prefers less protectionism (lower accepted proposals), while the congress prefers more. Both, however, suffer equally from retaliation, if it occurs. To simplify matters, I will assume linear, or risk-neutral, utility functions. In addition, the president, but not the congress, suffers a transaction cost $\lambda > 0$ when compelled to litigate his country's defense. Expressed formally, the president's utility once the dispute has gone to the ruling stage but before the ruling is realized is

$$U_p(\rho) = -[a_2 p_2 + (1 - a_2)] - \lambda + a_2 [\rho(-s_1 p_2) \\ + (1 - \rho)(-s_0 p_2)] + (1 - a_2) [-s_1 \rho - s_0 (1 - \rho)]. \quad (1)$$

If the above expression is g, the president's utility prior to the first proposal is

$$U_p(\rho) = a_1[p_1 g + (1 - p_1)(-p_1 + p_1 s)] + (1 - a_1)g. \quad (2)$$

The congress's utility once a dispute has gone to the panel but before the ruling is issued is

$$U_c = [a_2 p_2 + (1 - a_2)] + (1 - a_2) [\mu[-s_1 \rho_{hi} - s_0 (1 - \rho_{hi})] \\ + (1 - \mu) [-s_1 \rho_{lo} - s_0 (1 - \rho_{lo})]] + a_2 [\mu[\rho_{hi} (-s_1 p_2) \\ + (1 - \rho_{hi})(-s_0 p_2)] + (1 - \mu) [\rho_{lo} (-s_1 p_2) \\ + (1 - \rho_{lo})(-s_0 p_2)]]. \quad (3)$$

If this is h, then C's utility from the start is

$$U_c = a_1[p_1 h + (1 - p_1)(p_1 - p_1 s)] + (1 - a_1)h. \tag{4}$$

Results

By constraining $s_1 > 1$ and $s_0 < 1$, as we will see, I am assuming that the WTO's decision conditions the level of retaliation the plaintiff is willing to enact if the defendant fails to liberalize. That WTO approval might make sanctions from other states more likely (or more extensive) is certainly plausible (Martin 1992, 45). This may, however, seem like building the desired results—enforcement of adverse rulings[6]—automatically into the model. Yet it is not: the key is that rulings against the defendant are themselves not automatic at all. Recall that the president has two types, which respectively expect a high and low probability of an adverse ruling. Naturally, if adverse rulings are effectively enforced, we should expect the president who anticipates such a ruling with very high probability to have great bargaining power relative to the congress. Such presidents can tie their hands because they do have ropes, and thus they are uninteresting cases. The real question is whether the presidential type who expects the WTO to rule against the plaintiff can nevertheless convince the congress to accept a significantly liberalizing policy. If I demonstrate this, I will have confirmed that tying hands without an ex post rope is possible in equilibrium.[7] By "ex post" I mean after the president learns his private information but before any action occurs.

Hence, the objective is to show that an equilibrium exists in which the congress is unable to fully distinguish the weak type of president ($\rho = \rho_{lo}$) from the strong type ($\rho = \rho_{hi}$), based on the initial proposal p_1. In such a "pooling" equilibrium, the weak type benefits from the congress's belief that the president might be the strong type (meaning an adverse ruling is likely), even though he knows that the WTO will probably not rule against the status quo. Remarkably, such an equilibrium does exist for certain parameter values. The remainder of the section characterizes this equilibrium and walks through the existence proof and the intuition behind it. It then explores comparative statics concerning the consequences of tying hands and the effects of transaction costs. It also investigates alternative variants of the model to generate claims about the welfare effects of the institution and the differences in compliance rates between unified and divided governments.

A Pooling Equilibrium

Consider the following program for the players. Both types of president propose p_1^*, where

$$p_1^* = \frac{(1 - s_0)}{(1 - s)} \left[\pi(1 - \rho_{hi}) + (1 - \pi)(1 - \rho_{lo}) \right]. \tag{5}$$

If a ruling occurs, both types propose $p_2^* = 0$. The congress accepts ($a_1 = 1$) the initial proposal if and only if $p_1 \geq p_1^*$. The congress does not alter its beliefs about the probability that the president is type ρ_{hi}, no matter what initial proposal P makes; hence $\mu = \pi$ for all $p_1 \in [0,1]$. If a ruling against the defendant is issued (that is, $r = 1$), the congress accepts ($a_2 = 1$) any proposal p_2; if the WTO decides against the plaintiff, however, the congress rejects any subsequent proposal p_2.

In plain language, this program of action calls for the president to issue the same initial compromise proposal regardless of how he expects the WTO to rule, which the congress always accepts. The resulting policy does not entirely eliminate the protectionism, so there is a chance the plaintiff immediately retaliates and also a chance the plaintiff pushes for a WTO ruling. If the case goes to a ruling, then the president proposes full liberalization, and the congress accepts that proposal or rejects it entirely, depending on whether the ruling supported the plaintiff or the defendant, respectively.

This set of strategies and beliefs constitutes an equilibrium if certain conditions are satisfied.[8] The proof follows; I will turn to the meaning of the conditions afterward.

Start by working backward. A ruling r has been issued, and the president has made his second proposal p_2. Simplifying from (3), the congress has utility

$$a_2 p_2 + 1 - a_2 + a_2 \left[-s_1 p_2 r - s_0 p_2 (1 - r) \right]$$

$$+ (1 - a)\left[-s_1 r - s_0 (1 - r) \right]. \tag{6}$$

If $r = 1$, then (6) becomes $(1 - s_1)(1 + a_2 p_2 - a_2)$, which, given $s_1 > 1$, is maximized by $a_2 = 1$. If $r = 0$, then (6) equals $(1 - s_0)(1 + a_2 p_2 - a_2)$, which, given $s_0 < 1$, is maximized by $a_2 = 0$. The congress thus has a dominant strategy to accept any proposal after an adverse ruling and to reject any proposal after a supportive ruling, due to the way the ruling conditions the retaliation by the plaintiff. Thus if $r = 1$, then a_2

$= 1$, and simplifying from (1), the president receives utility $-p_2 - \lambda$ $- s_1 p_2$, which is maximized when $p_2 = 0$. If $r = 0$, then $a_2 = 0$, and the president receives utility $-1 - \lambda - s_0$. The congress is going to reject any proposal he makes, so choosing $p_2 = 0$ is a best response.

Now back up to the preruling stage. Simplifying from (4) and (3) with the expectations for p_2 and a_2, the congress receives

$$p_1[(1 - s_0) [\mu(1 - \rho_{hi}) + (1 - \mu)(1 - \rho_{lo})] + (1 - p_1)(p_1 - sp_1) \quad (7)$$

if it accepts p_1 and

$$(1 - s_0)[\mu(1 - \rho_{hi}) + (1 - \mu)(1 - \rho_{lo})] \quad (8)$$

if it rejects the proposal. Hence the congress accepts iff (7) $\geq$ (8), which when solving for p_1 yields the following *acceptance condition:*

$$p_1 \geq \frac{(1 - s_0)}{(1 - s)} [\mu (1 - \rho_{hi}) + (1 - \mu)(1 - \rho_{lo})], \quad (9)$$

or $p_1 = 1$, whichever is less.

Next consider the initial proposals the president can rationally make. If p_1 is accepted, the president receives utility

$$p_1(-1 - \lambda - s_0 + \rho + \rho s_0) + (1 - p_1)(-p_1 - sp_1), \quad (10)$$

and if his proposal is rejected, he gets

$$-1 - \lambda - s_0 + \rho - \rho s_0. \quad (11)$$

The president thus prefers to make a proposal that will be accepted iff (10) $\geq$ (11), which simplifies to the following *proposal condition:*

$$p_1 \leq \frac{1 + \lambda + s_0 - \rho - \rho s_0}{1 + s}, \quad (12)$$

or $p_1 = 1$, whichever is less.

We have yet to ascertain that the acceptance and proposal conditions can be compatible. Can p_1 be lower than the ceiling defined by (12) yet higher than the floor identified by (9)? Remember that each presidential type has a different constraint, replacing ρ in (12) with ρ_{lo} or ρ_{hi} as appropriate. For the pooling equilibrium to exist, both types' proposal conditions must obtain. Since $\rho_{hi} > \rho_{lo}$, type ρ_{hi}'s proposal condition is the more severe constraint. Hence both presidential types' proposal conditions are compatible with the congress's acceptance condition iff

$$\frac{1 + \lambda + s_0 - \rho_{hi} - \rho_{hi}s_0}{1 + s} \geq \frac{(1 - s_0)}{(1 - s)} \; [\mu(1 - \rho_{hi}) + (1 - \mu)(1 - \rho_{lo})], \tag{13}$$

which reduces to

$$\mu^* \geq \frac{-\lambda - \rho_{lo} + \rho_{hi} + s_0 (\rho_{lo} + \rho_{hi} - 2) + s(2 + \lambda - \rho_{lo} - \rho_{hi} + s_0\rho_{lo} - s_0\rho_{hi})}{(1 + s)(s_0 - 1)(\rho_{lo} - \rho_{hi})}. \tag{14}$$

Because this candidate equilibrium calls for $\mu = \pi$ regardless of the initial proposal, if π satisfies constraint (14), then, from (9), the congress accepts a proposal as low as p_1^* and both the president's types prefer to make the accepted proposal p_1^* over any other. In the postruling subgame, elimination of dominated strategies suffices to rationalize the use of the candidate equilibrium's strategies there. And, because both presidential types propose identical p_1's, the congress's updated beliefs are consistent. Thus the candidate strategies and beliefs constitute an equilibrium.

Here is the intuition. Both players know that a ruling against their country will effectively force the congress to agree to complete liberalization: WTO's call for sanctions is enough to guarantee foreign retaliation that is more costly to the congress than are the benefits of maintaining the status quo. Conversely, a supportive judgment rules out a deterring level of retaliation. The uncertainty concerns how the WTO will rule, and the president is much better informed about the panel's decision making than is the congress. Retaliation is, of course, possible in the absence of a WTO ruling. Accordingly, prior to a ruling, the congress has an incentive to agree to partial liberalization to the extent that its net expectation about the likely ruling direction times the levels of retaliation anticipated for each kind of ruling exceeds the likely level of preruling retaliation.

Unfortunately, the president's initial proposal conveys no information about his expectations for an adverse ruling by the WTO. If it did, the congress would demand and receive less liberalization in the initial proposal in cases unlikely to yield adverse rulings, and it would be willing to accept even greater liberalization in cases known to be most likely to yield adverse rulings. Thus, a president who expects an adverse ruling would prefer to reveal his private information. The other type of president seeks to free ride on him after all. What might differentiate the two is that the "strong" president has heavy incentives to await a ruling, since he knows with high probability it will work in his favor. Yet—and here is the key to my result—even the strong president is leery of awaiting a ruling, due to the transaction costs of litigating. Transaction costs raise the level of protectionism the strong president is willing to accept as an early settlement, thereby giving him enough common interests with the "weak" president to leave the congress uncertain as to which kind of president it faces. The outcome is an accepted early settlement proposal that reflects hedged bets; that is, it is not as liberal as the strong president would like but is more liberal than the one the congress would demand if it knew it faced the weak president.

Consider the following numerical example. Imagine $s_0 = 0.1, s = 0.3, \rho_{lo} = 0.25, \rho_{hi} = 0.75, \lambda = 0.5, \pi = 0.65$, and $s_1 > 1$. These values mean that the retaliation expected for a given level of protectionism is quite low after a supportive ruling and somewhat higher before a ruling is issued; the strong and weak presidential types know an adverse ruling is 75 percent and 25 percent probable, respectively; the congress believes the president is somewhat more likely to be strong than weak; and the transaction costs of litigation carry half the weight of the trade policy itself in the president's utility function. From (5), $p_1^* = 0.546$. From (7) and (8), the congress receives a utility of 0.383 for accepting p_1^* and 0.383 for rejecting it: the congress is indifferent. From (12), presidential type ρ_{hi}'s proposal ceiling is 0.596, higher than p_1^*. The transaction costs (λ) raise the proposal ceiling in this case on a nearly one-for-one basis.[9] From (10) and (11), types ρ_{hi} and ρ_{lo} receive, respectively, utilities of -0.746 and -1.046 for proposing p_1^* (which will be accepted) and -0.775 and -1.325 for a lower, alternative p_1 (which will be rejected). Thus even the strong type benefits from proposing p_1^*, due to the high transaction costs of litigation.

What happens if the equilibrium condition, (14), is not satisfied? In the extreme,[10] the strong presidential type's proposal ceiling is lower than the floor set by the minimum acceptable proposal for the congress. That is, the transaction costs of litigating are low enough and the prospect of losing at the WTO is high enough that the president has more to gain if the congress rejects his proposal than if he proposes what would be acceptable to the congress. If this is true, the president who expects an adverse ruling will propose something unacceptable, for example, $p_1 = 0$, whereas the weaker presidential type still benefits by meeting the congress's acceptance condition, which is now ratcheted up because the congress knows the president is the weak type, that is, $\mu = 0$. The result is thus fully separating behavior, undermining the ability of the president to get any significant concessions from the congress when an adverse WTO ruling is not expected.

How sensitive is the existence of the pooling equilibrium to refinements on out-of-equilibrium beliefs? If the congress observes an initial proposal different from p_1^*, the equilibrium calls for it to believe that both types were equally likely to deviate in that fashion. Is this plausible? Start with an easy case, out-of-equilibrium proposals higher than p_1^*. Regardless of the congress's beliefs, neither type has an incentive to issue such a proposal, since a strictly superior and still acceptable offer is available in the form of p_1^*. The harder question concerns proposals lower than p_1^*. If the congress believed such proposals would more likely come from a strong type (ρ_{hi}), it would accept a proposal as low as $(1 - s_0)(1 - \rho_{hi})/(1 - s)$, derived from (9). Type ρ_{hi} strictly prefers lower accepted proposals to higher accepted proposals and thus would certainly deviate. But the weak type, ρ_{lo}, also strictly prefers such proposals[11] and would deviate as well—after all, it would be capitalizing even more than in equilibrium on the congress's beliefs that the president expects an adverse ruling. That any alternative belief causing the strong type to deviate causes the weak type to deviate in the same way means that my pooling equilibrium satisfies the quite stringent "divinity" refinement (Kreps 1989, 39; Fudenberg and Tirole 1991, 448–56). Hence, the existence of the pooling equilibrium does not depend on implausible out-of-equilibrium beliefs.

Tying Hands without an ex post Rope Is Possible

The potential for tying hands without a rope is measured in this model by the president's ability to get significant liberalization approved even when he knows an adverse ruling is unlikely. Liberalization is significant in this sense only if it exceeds what the president could get in the complete information game, that is, if the congress had identical information about the WTO panel's likely judgment. By this definition, the pooling equilibrium demonstrates that tying hands without a rope is indeed possible, despite rational opposition. (The possibility, before the fact, that such a rope might exist is, however, essential.)

What gives the institution influence even when it is unlikely to rule against the defendant? First, the congress must know that the WTO's ruling will affect the plaintiff's likelihood or level of retaliation and also that an adverse ruling in particular will result in retaliation high enough to deter any protectionism. If not, then the congress has no incentive to ever capitulate. For tying hands to work, there must be some probability of enforcement, however small, to condition the congress's expectations in those cases when enforcement is not actually forthcoming. Second, the congress must not possess accurate knowledge of the case's merits, that is, the probability that the WTO will rule for the plaintiff. Otherwise, the congress will know when an adverse ruling is not likely, and the president will be unable to get significant concessions in that case. Third, the transaction costs of litigation must be sufficiently high. A strong president's proposal condition—above which the president will prefer to wait for a ruling—will be too demanding if the process of eliciting a ruling is costless. Transaction costs give the strong president enough common interests with the congress to desire to settle the issue prior to a ruling, thereby allowing a weak president to take advantage of the congress's belief that the president might be strong even when the congress observes an initial proposal it can accept.

It is important to note what this result does not depend upon. Namely, the model includes no costs for reversing a decision to comply. The standard argument about tying hands, after all, goes like this. If the president is somehow able to impose liberalization when the congress's guard is down, doing so through the medium of an international institution may prevent reversal because the institution adds costs for reneging on the commitment. The problem with this logic is that it assumes away the difficulty of imposing the policy in the first place. My model focuses on the initial decision to liberalize (or comply more generally), a harder case. It demonstrates that, contrary to the conventional wisdom, an institution need not add to the costs of policy reversal to facilitate commitment in the face of domestic opposition.

We can quantify the benefits arising from the tying hands function of the institution. The baseline is a complete information game, in which the congress has the same knowledge as the president about the chances of an adverse ruling. In such a game, assuming that the same parameter conditions apply as before, if an adverse ruling is likely, the congress's acceptance condition (9) becomes $[(1 - s_0)/(1 - s)]$ $(1 - \rho_{hi})$, and if unlikely, $[(1 - s_0)/(1 - s)] (1 - \rho_{lo})$, which the president proposes as appropriate. Thus, the weak president's accepted proposal under private information contains $[(1 - s_0)/(1 - s)](\rho_{hi} - \rho_{lo}) \pi$ less protection than what he would be able to get accepted with complete information. (In the numerical example used earlier, this computes to a drop of 0.418 out of 1, or 42 percent off an original 100 percent tariff, a hefty quantity.) That is, the institution increases liberalization despite its relative lack of enforcement power to an extent proportional to the probability that the institution was expected to *have* enforcement power.

There is a downside, however. The institution's ability to encourage liberalization even when enforcement is unlikely comes at the expense of the institution's ability to encourage liberalization when enforcement does turn out to be forthcoming. A president who knows the WTO will rule against the status quo will be unable to elicit as deep concessions from the congress as would be possible if the congress knew what the president knew. What keeps such a president from taking advantage of his knowledge is the cost of litigating through the WTO. Like "crying wolf," tying hands without a rope comes at the price of lesser credibility even when a rope exists. This function of the institution adds nothing to the net expected level of liberalization.

In addition, the benefits of tying hands without a rope are not evenly distributed across time in a dispute. Recall that plaintiffs will sometimes ask for a ruling even when partially liberalizing pleas are accepted by the congress. If this occurs, all benefits for the weak president are lost. After a ruling, a president's private information is irrelevant: the congress's subsequent action is contingent on the ruling itself, not on the president's expectations about the ruling direction. The irony is thus that, when it lacks enforcement power, an institution can only bolster domestic commitment before it intervenes. There can be no tying of hands without enforcement in cases that fail to be settled before the institution offers its prescriptions.

The Effect of Transaction Costs

Surprisingly, for the institution to facilitate domestic commitment when enforcement is unlikely, transaction costs of utilizing the institution must be sufficiently high. For instance, the derivative of (12) with respect to λ is $1/(1 + s)$: that is, the upper limit on the set of agreements the president would prefer to no agreement increases as the transaction costs of litigation go up. Transaction costs thus have the power to create common ground between even the strong type of president and the congress, regardless of the congress's prior beliefs about the president's type. Such common ground is essential for the weak president to credibly pool or to capitalize on the congress's fear of an adverse ruling. Put another way, equilibrium condition (14) indicates that, as λ goes up, the prior probability of the strong presidential type, ρ_{hi}, can go down proportionally, and the pooling equilibrium—and therefore the potential for tying hands—can still exist. Remarkably, from the institution's standpoint, high transaction costs are desirable: they make possible significant liberalization even when enforcement is not forthcoming.

However, this counterintuitive assertion requires some caveats. First, transaction costs exert a threshold effect; above a certain point, defined by the λ necessary to satisfy condition (14), higher values do not improve the potential for tying hands. Second, raising λ does not affect the congress's acceptance condition or, accordingly, the type of initial proposal issued: p_1^* does not depend on (5). In other words, increasing transaction costs, or decreasing them for that matter, has no effect on the overall level of liberalization approved. All it does is redistribute the congress's concessions from strong types to weak types by enabling the pooling equilibrium. Third, while a president who expects a supportive ruling is more able to elicit concessions if transaction costs are high enough to make pooling possible, the expected utility of even this weak type is diminished by higher transaction costs. The benefits of a better p_1 are outweighed by the added loss (from the transaction costs) in the event the dispute goes to a ruling.

The findings concerning transaction costs yield a number of testable hypotheses. Namely, "improvements" that reduce the transaction costs of utilizing an international institution will decrease that institution's ability to induce liberalization, or reform more generally, in cases when enforcement is unlikely. For instance, many observers argue that the WTO has reduced the transaction costs of dispute settlement in comparison to GATT, yet (at least when dealing with countries besides the United States and the EU) foreign retaliation for noncompliance is extraordinarily rare (Petersmann 1997, 202–5; Sevilla 1998, 7–11; Ruggiero 1998; Reinhardt 1999). Counter to the conventional wisdom, this model suggests that the WTO will be less efficacious than GATT in disputes where retaliation is unlikely (for example, when the plaintiff's legal case is weak), to the extent that the WTO has indeed reduced transaction costs.

As noted earlier, LDCs arguably face much more significant transaction costs in litigating WTO disputes. If it is true that LDCs have the equivalent of higher λ's in the model, then they should on average possess greater ability to tie their hands in WTO disputes and should tend to liberalize more as defendants, at least when enforcement is not forthcoming (for example, in cases they are likely to win or when facing plaintiffs outside of the United States and the EU). This should be true even controlling for obvious factors such as asymmetrical trade dependence and relative market size.

What If the Government Is Unified?

This chapter's model assumes a division of opinion between executive and legislature. Such a division is perhaps most likely to occur when they represent different political parties, in divided government. What role might the international institution play when there is no domestic opposition, for example, when the government is unified? In particular, consider a variant of the model in which there is no congress and the president prefers to maintain the status quo.[12] In this variant, the president would liberalize after an adverse ruling and keep the status quo after a supportive judgment. Hence, his utility at the initial proposal stage would be $p_1[-\rho\lambda + (1 - \rho)(1 - \lambda - s_0)] + p_1 (1 - s)(1 - p_1)$, which is maximized by

$$\tilde{p}_1 = \frac{2 - s - s_0 - \lambda - \rho - \rho s_0}{2(1 - s)}. \tag{15}$$

In the numerical example used earlier, the presidential weak type would propose 0.589, and the strong type, 0.196. Weighted by π, these average to 0.334, whereas the expected p_1^* in the original model is 0.546, notably higher. It follows that a unified government (even one with a protectionist executive) may sometimes concede more as a defendant than would a divided government (even one with a liberalizing executive). To understand why, the key, again, is transaction costs. The unified government's equilibrium initial proposal, $\tilde{p}_1$ (15), is a decreasing function of λ, yet the divided government's offer of p_1^* (5) is not. The transaction cost parameter determines whether a unified government's initial proposal is lower or higher than a divided government's.

This line of reasoning suggests two testable hypotheses. First, recall that the likelihood of a ruling occurring in the model is proportional to the level of protectionism in the initial (accepted) proposal, for example $\tilde{p}_1$ or p_1^*. Accordingly, the probability of the dispute going to a ruling is higher in cases with unified government defendants ($\tilde{p}_1$) than in those with divided government defendants (p_1^*), if transaction costs are low, as they should be for advanced industrial states using the GATT or WTO dispute settlement regimes. Conversely, if transaction costs are high, as in the case of LDC defendants, the probability of a dispute going to a ruling is greater in cases against divided governments than in those against unified governments.

Second, regardless of differences prior to a ruling, both the original and the variant model, focusing on divided and unified government, respectively, prescribe identical equilibrium behavior once a ruling has been issued. Specifically, an adverse ruling evokes full compliance and a supportive ruling locks in the status quo. Thus, unified and divided governments should exhibit a similar level of concessions in disputes ending after rulings are issued.

How closely do these hypotheses match the reality of GATT and WTO trade conflicts? Data are available to run preliminary tests. In particular, Reinhardt (1996, chap. 4) lists 256 GATT disputes conducted between 1948 and 1994, along with a dummy measure of divided government, a dummy reflecting whether GATT issued a ruling of any sort, and a three-category ordinal measure of the level of the defendant's liberalization reflected in the dispute outcome, relative to the status quo.[13] Reinhardt (1999) provides a dummy indicator of LDC status, as officially defined by GATT/WTO, in addition to a measure of relative GDP size.[14] Consider the first hypothesis. Table 1 shows the results of a probit regression of whether a ruling was issued, conditional upon a set of interactions between LDC and unified/divided government. There are no divided government LDC defendants in the sample; therefore, that cell is empty. That leaves two variables on the right-hand side: A dummy for LDC unified governments and one for advanced industrial unified governments (both referring to defendant states). Advanced industrial divided governments are the baseline category. If my hypothesis is correct, the coefficient for advanced industrial unified government should be positive and significant, which is exactly what turns up. Granted, this empirical finding is merely suggestive, but it is particularly striking insofar as it is a "new fact," that is, something we would not have looked for in the absence of this chapter's model.

Table 2 shows results bearing upon the second hypothesis, concerning just those disputes ending after rulings have been issued. The dependent variable is the level of liberalization (higher is better). The right-hand side includes a dummy for divided government, as well as

GDP ratio as a control. I expect divided governments to concede at
the same rate as unified governments in disputes ending after rulings.
The results support the claim; that is, the null hypothesis that divided
government makes no difference cannot be rejected. If anything, our
intuition would be that divided governments concede less (Cowhey
1993, 302), and that they do not do so in this case again suggests that
the model provides useful insight.

Other Results

The model yields a number of other surprising conclusions. For instance, does the institution increase liberalization overall, relative to
a world in which no institution exists? The latter world can be represented by a variant of the model with *exactly the same probability of*

TABLE 1. Probit Estimates for Whether Ruling Was Issued,
GATT Disputes, 1948–94

Prob(Ruling)	Coefficient	Robust SE
Defendant is LDC with unified government	0.010	0.303
Defendant is advanced industrial state with unified government	0.422*	0.186
Constant	−0.221	0.160
Number of observations	256	
LL (restricted)	−177.15	
LL (unrestricted)	−173.98	
Pseudo-R^2	0.02	

*2-tailed $p < .05$.

TABLE 2. Ordered Probit Estimates of Liberalization, GATT Disputes with
Rulings, 1948–94

Level of Liberalization	Coefficient	Robust SE
Divided government dummy	−0.223	0.265
Ratio of plaintiff's GDP to sum of plaintiff's and defendant's	0.714*	0.296
Intercept 1	−0.174	0.185
Intercept 2	0.623	0.190
Number of observations	124	
LL (restricted)	−135.83	
LL (unrestricted)	−132.17	
Pseudo-R^2	0.03	

* 2-tailed $p < .05$.

foreign retaliation but without the ruling device and hence transaction costs and the president's private information. In such a variant, the president makes a proposal that the congress accepts or rejects, and afterward the same expectation of foreign retaliation obtains as in the original model, subsequent to a ruling. For any given policy p, then, both players' expectations about the probability and costs of retaliation are

$$-p[\pi \rho_{hi} s_1 + \pi(1 - \rho_{hi}) s_0 + (1 - \pi)\rho_{lo} s_1 + (1 - \pi)(1 - \rho_{lo}) s_0], \quad (16)$$

which we can abbreviate as $-pk$.

Congress accordingly accepts p only if $p - pk \geq 1 - k$, which is true iff $k \geq 1$, which in turn obtains (substituting the expression in (16) for k and simplifying) only when

$$\pi \geq \frac{1 + s_0(\rho_{lo} - 1) - s_1 \rho_{lo}}{(\rho_{lo} - \rho_{hi})(s_0 - s_1)}. \quad (17)$$

The president, strictly preferring lower accepted p's, proposes and gets approved $p = 0$ if condition (17) applies; the outcome is 1 otherwise. Recall that the original model never has an expected value of protectionism strictly equal to zero. Thus, amazingly, the institution actually decreases the president's ability to liberalize overall, compared to the counterfactual in which the institution does not exist if condition (17) holds.

Granted, this condition is generally more stringent than, say, the pooling equilibrium threshold (14): π would have to exceed 1.3, a disallowed value, for the institution to be counterproductive in the earlier numerical example, for instance. But the condition can obtain. The key is s_1, the maximum level of retaliation expected, which does not enter the calculations for p_1^* from the original model. Here, however, s_1 strictly lowers the π necessary to sustain the result, since the derivative of (17) with respect to s_1 is $(1 - s_0)/(\rho_{lo} - \rho_{hi})(s_0 - s_1)^2$, which is always negative. In other words, if the maximum plausible level of retaliation crosses a certain threshold, the institution may actually obstruct liberalization instead of facilitating it. The reason is subtle: the ruling mechanism provides information about the likelihood of retaliation, before the president's and congress's final opportunity to decide policy. In the worst case scenario after a ruling (that is, an adverse ruling with guaranteed retaliation), the congress can adjust its policy prior to suffering the consequences of recalcitrance.

Without such a preview, the congress has to factor the worst case scenario into its one-shot decision, thereby making it much more open to liberalizing—if the maximum expected retaliation is sufficiently high. In part, this may be an artifact of the finite, as opposed to infinitely repeated, game structure. However, it seems quite plausible to view one of the institution's main functions as staging interaction in an iterated format, as many scholars have observed (Axelrod and Keohane 1985, 234). Surprisingly, doing so can be counterproductive in some cases.

Consider a related point. As long as the institution exists, the maximum expected level of retaliation s_1 need not be higher than the minimum necessary to compel a protectionist legislature to liberalize. Exceeding that level only costs both parties, without improving the level of liberalization in equilibrium. Yet, in a dispute occurring outside the WTO or other institutional framework, as the earlier paragraph suggests, the higher the complainant's threatened maximum level of retaliation, the more concessions the defendant will make. Consequently, I expect retaliation threats to involve much greater sums, ceteris paribus, in ungoverned international trade disputes than in WTO conflicts.

The model also points to the importance of the levels of retaliation possible prior to a ruling and after a ruling supporting the defendant. Note that p_1^* is proportional to $(1 - s_0)/(1 - s)$. That is, the possibility of retaliation in the absence of a ruling *decreases* the equilibrium level of liberalization, and the possibility of retaliation even when WTO supports the defendant *increases* the likely liberalization by the defendant. The ideal world, from the standpoint of maximizing liberalization, is one in which plaintiffs are bound not to retaliate before a ruling yet are encouraged to retaliate (against sustained protectionism) even when the WTO approves the defendant's protectionism. The WTO embodies only half of this prescription, since it discourages retaliation in either circumstance.

A final hypothesis concerns the decision to litigate a defense in GATT/WTO disputes. The model predicts that, regardless of their beliefs about their case's merits, defendants are equally likely to litigate, as opposed to settling early. Intuition would suggest in contrast that defendants who expect to lose will be more likely to settle. This alternative is ruled out when the pooling equilibrium exists. Domestic politics is the explanation: executives may seek to tie their hands with an adverse WTO ruling, and in such cases they would like to litigate precisely when they expect to lose, not win. Yet that likely winners want to deceive the domestic opposition means that they act identically to likely losers, thereby nullifying the effects of a case's real merits on the decision to litigate a defense.

Implications

The previous results have a number of significant implications for international relations theory and institutional design. Traditional rationalist theories (for example, Martin and Simmons 1998, 748) suggest that institutions promote cooperation by allowing leaders to tie their hands. The results here support this argument, and indeed strengthen it, by showing how it can be true even when we acknowledge that a domestic opposition will view attempts to tie hands with suspicion.

However, my findings contradict much conventional wisdom in rationalist institutional theory. The benefits of tying hands occur in proportion to the ex ante probability of enforcement, even if enforcement is not forthcoming in a given case. There is no way to bootstrap a domestic commitment effect if enforcement is 100 percent absent. In addition, the benefits of tying hands (in terms of the institution's effect on policy) when enforcement turns out to be unlikely ex post are matched by losses when enforcement turns out to be likely ex post. That is, the possibility of leaders "crying wolf" diminishes their leverage when a wolf actually appears. Hence, even when noncompliance with EU regulations would result in significant costs for Britain, a British leader invoking such regulations may have little credibility at home, as revealed by one MP decrying the "hidden agenda that leads the British Government, in the most subservient way, to give in to every arbitrary and legally dubious whim on which [the European Commission] decides" (Smith 1997, 197). Tying hands does not have a net positive effect on the institution's influence over policy.

Furthermore, all the benefits of tying hands are realized *before* the institution makes its policy prescriptions in a given case. Surprisingly, to tie her hands, a leader cannot rely on a judgment by the international institution, or on any resulting retaliation; if such a judgment or retaliation occurs, she has lost her opportunity. An institutional prescription and the consequent foreign retaliation eliminate the uncertainty domestic opponents have about the probability of foreign retaliation, which is the only lever a leader has when an adverse ruling or retaliation is not very likely.

The model also sharply contradicts traditional institutionalist theory with respect to transaction costs. For example, Keohane (1983, 155–57) argues that by reducing the transaction costs of negotiating and otherwise interacting, institutions promote cooperation — which in the WTO disputes context means liberalization. My model, however, demonstrates that if the institution lowered transaction costs, it would eliminate all of its potential to influence state policy in cases in which the institution lacks enforcement power. For the WTO dispute settlement regime in particular, imposing high costs on those seeking to negotiate through the institution or to obtain the institution's information is precisely what permits reformist leaders to convince recalcitrant legislatures that the WTO will condemn the status quo when it actually might not or when foreign retaliation is not going to occur, which is certainly the majority of cases. High transaction costs can be good, from the institution's perspective. This result is particularly important because it points to the incompatibility of a number of mechanisms that are often regarded as reinforcing. If the institution reduces transaction costs, it may facilitate negotiation and reciprocity, but it will destroy the ability of leaders to tie their hands and impose reform against the wishes of a domestic opposition.

Likewise, the model suggests that information provision is not always beneficial, again in contrast to traditional theories of institutions (Keohane 1983, 159–61, 165). The logic is not so surprising, however. In particular, the institution is more able to influence state policy if the recalcitrant domestic opposition that it aims to constrain is unaware of the institution's lack of enforcement power and inability to sway foreign states to retaliate. The institution dilutes its tying hands potential by providing greater information about the intentions of other states or even the institution's own workings, in the case of adjudication systems like the WTO's.

Taken as a whole, the results here enforce a perspective on international institutions that is similar in many ways to conventional functional theories. It views institutions through their influence on strategic, rational actors at various levels of analysis. It lends support to an oft-cited hypothesis, that is, the domestic commitment effect of international institutions. Yet it goes well beyond the standard view. In particular, it points out inconsistencies in the deductive logic of functionalism, especially concerning the compatibility of different institutional functions and the role of transaction costs and information provision. The perspective is not merely critical, however, since the model points to a great number of testable propositions to which adequate attention has not been addressed. In that respect, I offer this model as a constructive attempt to identify more conditional hypotheses on how and when institutions "matter," as opposed to reiterating stale debates over whether institutions affect state policy at all.

I conclude this chapter by highlighting the model's implications for optimal institutional design. To maximize its influence on state policy when it nevertheless lacks enforcement power, an international institution should have the following characteristics. It should make it costly for states to elicit normative judgments from the regime. It should privilege sovereign state leaders with information and access to its proceedings, at the expense of domestic audiences and private actors. It should remove barriers to and even encourage unilateral retaliation when a member state fails to abide by its prescriptions, yet it should cap allowable retaliation just above the extent of the target state's violation. It should stridently ban unilateral retaliation without due process, for example, prior to the issuance of an institutional judgment, but it should not penalize unilateral retaliation against member states that fail to fully cooperate subsequent to an institutional judgment, even after a judgment that approves such failure.

How does the WTO score on these dimensions? By lowering some transaction costs, such as the unilateral veto over panel establishment and authorization of rulings (Sevilla 1998), the WTO may have ironically harmed its ability to induce liberalization. In other areas, however, the WTO has added to the costliness of litigation: for example, extending deadlines, imposing many new steps in the legal process, and adding vast quantities of complex new law to be sorted through (Reinhardt 1999, 12–17). The net effect on transaction costs may be a wash. The early WTO has been precisely optimal in terms of its lack of transparency to private parties and nonexecutive government actors in disputant countries. This is likely to change, however, since the United States has recently made increased transparency its key demand for reform of the regime.[15] The WTO is particularly flawed in its treatment of retaliation by plaintiffs. To be sure, unilateral action prior to a ruling is indeed discouraged, but the all-important potential for retaliation after a ruling for the plaintiff is hamstrung by new requirements to arbitrate the quantities involved. Arbitration, after all, splits the difference between the parties' demands, which is bound to leave any ultimate retaliation lower than what is necessary to compel liberalization by the plaintiff. The result is a case like the U.S.-EU banana dispute, in which after years of delay the WTO has approved sanctions of hundreds of millions of dollars less than the trade affected by the protection in question; the EU has so far evinced no intention to change its policy as a result.[16] The WTO's focus on "defendants' rights" therefore obstructs its mission to encourage liberalization of disputed policies (Reinhardt 1999).

One final question is this: *Should* leaders resort to the tied hands defense of unpopular reforms, attempting to shift the blame to international institutions? Rodrik (1997, 79–80), for example, argues that doing so results over the long run in costly political backlash against such institutions, spilling over to undermine even policies that are beneficial for the affected domestic groups. The model here implies a similar, though not so pessimistic, answer. In the short run, playing the international institutional constraint card may prove useful to a reformist leader. In the long run, the short-term gains will be offset by decreased credibility when such international constraints occasionally prove genuine. A wise leader recognizes the limits of such a strategy.

Notes

This research was supported in part by the University Research Committee of Emory University. I am grateful for comments from David Ahn, Marc Busch, Dan Drezner, Stephen Krasner, Helen Milner, John Pevehouse, Ken Schultz, Duncan Snidal, Alex Thompson, Suzanne Werner, and conference participants, with special thanks to Dan Drezner for organizing and editing the project.

1. Constraints applying only after the liberalizing policy has been implemented cannot explain why such a policy is chosen over the status quo in the first place. Why would a domestic opposition permit a leader to sign on to a regime whose prescriptions it opposes when that regime cannot easily be exited? Answering this puzzle requires more than the assumption of costs for exiting an institution.

2. See Reinhardt 1999, esp. 3–5; Komuro 1995; and Petersmann 1997 for a more precise description of GATT and WTO procedures and the differences between them. This synopsis obscures those differences, but it captures the key strategic elements of the process.

3. In a 1998 ruling the WTO opened the door to legal submissions by NGOs, but this has affected only one dispute so far (South Centre 1999, 17).

4. Rulings for the defendant do indeed occur in practice. GATT decided substantially for the plaintiff in no more than 85 of 129 rulings (65.9 percent) from 1948 through 1993 (Reinhardt 1998, 5).

5. Making the foreign state's behavior exogenous is the most significant shortcut in this model. Nevertheless, it seems quite reasonable to suppose

that the plaintiff will be (a) more likely to continue litigation the more protectionist is the defendant's initial stance and (b) more likely to retaliate the
more protectionist is the defendant's ultimate policy. (Note that the level of
retaliation, once initiated, is allowed to vary here.)

6. By "adverse," I mean a ruling against the defendant state's protectionist status quo (which is precisely what the president, but not the congress,
desires).

7. This chapter's use of the WTO ruling itself, rather than the enforcement such a ruling may yield, may strike some readers as inappropriate to
quantify "tying hands without a rope." It may concord better with intuition to
restructure the game so that the president has private information not over
the likely WTO ruling but over the probability of foreign retaliation contingent on the ruling. However, such a representation condenses to exactly the
same model: here, the president's private information about the likely ruling
is the critical basis for the congress's estimates about foreign retaliation.
Moreover, it stretches credulity to assume that the president has private information about the probability of foreign retaliation, since that information
is the property of foreign leaders conducting an adversarial dispute process.
This is why I adopt the model construction used here; the results are the
same.

8. I refer to perfect Bayesian equilibrium, which requires that both players choose best responses to each other's strategy and that the updating of
beliefs for the congress be consistent with these strategies in all game histo-
ries such a combination of strategies can generate. (The pooling equilibrium,
as it turns out, also satisfies relatively stringent conditions concerning plausible out-of-equilibrium beliefs. See subsequent discussion.)

9. Specifically, if (12) is z, then $\partial\lambda/\partial z = 0.769$ in this example.

10. There are a number of possibilities, depending on parameter values,
all of which rule out a pooling equilibrium involving a nontrivial (e.g., $p_1 <$
1) yet accepted proposal. What follows is an illustration of the extreme case
in which the strong president would have nothing to gain from an accepted
proposal, relative to what happens after a ruling, even if his private information were common knowledge.

11. Lower proposals, recall, are valued in themselves, plus they reduce the
chances of foreign retaliation and costly litigation. This is valid at least for
certain plausible parameter values that satisfy equilibrium condition (14).
Formally, the derivative of (10) with respect to p must be negative for lower
accepted proposals to be strictly preferred to higher ones, for either type.
This is true iff

$$p_1 < \frac{2 + s + s_0 + \lambda - \rho - s_0\rho}{2(1 + s)}.$$

The out-of-equilibrium proposals under consideration are necessarily lower
than the proposal condition (12), which is lower than the ceiling described by

the equation just given, for both types, as long as $\rho_{l_o} > (s - s_0 - \lambda)/(1 + s_0)$. This in turn is satisfied for any value of ρ_{l_o} as long as $\lambda + s_0 > s$.

12. We are assuming that the president's country is the defendant in a dispute that has already been filed. Thus, if the president is the only decision maker, it seems plausible to infer that he is responsible for, and prefers to keep, the protectionism giving rise to the dispute in the first place.

13. Unfortunately, data on the merits of the case—the property operationalized as ρ in the model—are not presently available.

14. The data set used for all analyses in this chapter is available at <http://userwww.service.emory.edu/~erein/>.

15. *Journal of Commerce,* April 26, 1999, 3A; Barshefsky 1999.

16. *Journal of Commerce,* April 20, 1999, 3A.

Tying Hands and Washing Hands:
The U.S. Congress and Multilateral Humanitarian Intervention

Kenneth A. Schultz

Among the new issues that national governments and international institutions have grappled with in the post–Cold War period is armed humanitarian intervention, or the deployment of military force primarily for the purposes of protecting citizens of a target state from widespread violations of human rights (see, for example, Murphy 1996, 11–12). While such missions are not unprecedented historically, they have been greatly facilitated in recent years by a number of developments. The end of the superpower rivalry freed the UN and regional security institutions from their Cold War fetters, creating opportunities for them to play a more active role. Advances in communications technology have made distant tragedies seem more immediate to publics in the developed world, feeding a "humanitarian impulse." And, while norms of sovereignty and nonintervention have long been ignored by powerful states (Krasner 1999), the idea that the international community should intervene in a country for the good of its own people has gained greater legitimacy (Finnemore 1996a). As a result, the last decade has witnessed a large number of military interventions designed to stop humanitarian catastrophes due to civil war (for example, Bosnia and Liberia), state collapse (for example, Somalia), or oppressive government (for example, Haiti and Kosovo). In all of these instances, international organizations such as the UN and regional security such as NATO, the Organization of American States, and the Organization of African Unity have played a role in bestowing legitimacy on the operations and in organizing a collective response.

In the United States, these new developments at the international level have become enmeshed with a long-standing struggle at the domestic level: the dispute between Congress and the president over war powers. In each of the cases of armed humanitarian intervention involving the United States—particularly Somalia, Haiti, Bosnia, and Kosovo—the debate over which branch controls the deployment of American troops has occupied politicians almost as much as the debate over the merits of the intervention itself. This debate alone is not new, as the struggle over war powers has been a constant feature of American foreign policy. What is new is the interjection of a new set of actors into the mix—international organizations such as the UN and NATO and, through them, other states with influence in these bodies. The missions in Somalia, Haiti, and Bosnia were preauthorized by the UN Security Council; the Bosnia and Kosovo operations were approved by NATO. By contrast, none of these missions was fully preauthorized by Congress, and indeed most met strong opposition there. In the case of Kosovo, the Senate, but not the House, voted to authorize the air campaign the night before it began. In the case of Somalia, the president received some ex post authorization, but the different resolutions of the House and Senate were never reconciled, and the whole matter of authorization fell by the wayside once large-scale casualties occurred.

These events are put in perspective in table 1, which lists all of the major operations involving U.S. troops from 1950 to 1999, based on a list compiled by the Congressional Research Service (CRS) (Grimmett 1999).[1] For each mission, the table indicates whether there was congressional authorization and/or opposition. In cases in which Congress authorized the mission, the entry indicates whether the authorization came before the mission started (pre) or after it was already under way (post). Opposition to an operation can, of course, take many forms and be of different degrees. There are few, if any, cases in which no member of Congress opposed the use of force. For the purposes of the table, a higher threshold was used to determine opposition: majority support in at least one house for a resolution to cut off funding, deauthorize, or declare opposition to the mission or a majority vote against a resolution to authorize the mission, if such a measure came to a vote. Finally, the last column of the table indicates whether the mission was approved by an international organization such as the UN or NATO.

The cases in this table obviously vary quite a bit in terms of the mission's size, goals, duration, and danger to U.S. troops. As a result, it is important to be cautious in drawing conclusions. For our purposes, two patterns stand out. First, the largely humanitarian operations of the last decade met much more congressional opposition, and enjoyed less frequent congressional authorization, than did opera-

TABLE 1. Uses of U.S. Armed Forces Abroad, 1950–99

Years	Mission	Congress Authorized	Congress Opposed	International Organizations
1950–53	Korean War	no	no	UN
1954–55	Taiwan Straits	pre	no	no
1958	Lebanon	pre	no	no[a]
1961–62	Laos	no	no	no
1962	Thailand	no	no	no
1962	Quarantine of Cuba	pre[b]	no	no
1964–73	Vietnam War	pre	yes	no
1965	Dominican Republic	no	no	no[a]
1970	Cambodia	no	yes	no
1975	Mayaguez incident	no	no	no
1980	Iran hostage rescue	no	no	no
1982	Sinai multinational force	pre	no	no[c]
1982	Lebanon	post	no	UN
1983	Grenada	no	no	no
1986	Libya	no	no	no
1987–88	Persian Gulf (tanker reflagging)	no	no	no
1989–90	Panama	no	no	no
1990	Saudi Arabia (Desert Shield)	no	no	no
1991	Persian Gulf War	pre	no	UN
1992	Somalia (UNITAF)	post	no	UN
1993–94	Somalia (UNOSOM II)	no[d]	yes	UN
1993	Iraq (retaliation for Bush plot)	no	no	no
1993–	Iraq (no-fly zone enforcement)	pre[e]	no	UN
1993–	Macedonia	no	no	UN
1993–95	Bosnia (no-fly zone & safe havens)	no[d]	no	UN, NATO
1994	Rwanda	no	yes	UN
1994	Haiti	no	yes	UN
1996	Zaire	no	no	UN
1998	Afghanistan/Sudan	no	no	no
1998–	Iraq (WMD inspections)	pre[e]	no	UN
1995–	Bosnia (IFOR/SFOR)	no	yes	UN, NATO
1999	Kosovo (air strikes)	no[d]	yes	NATO
1999–	Kosovo (peacekeeping)	no[d]	no	UN, NATO

Note: The list of operations is based on a list of cases given in Grimmett 1999.

[a] In these cases, U.S. deployment was alongside, but neither part of nor authorized by, a UN mission.

[b] While not strictly authorized by Congress, the Cuban quarantine followed the spirit of a joint resolution passed on Oct. 3, 1962, which declared that the United States was determined "to prevent in Cuba the creation or use of an externally supported military capability capable of endangering the security of the United States" and to prevent, with force if necessary, the extension of Cuban influence in the hemisphere (Wormuth and Firmage 1989, 45).

[c] The Sinai mission grew from the Egypt-Israel peace treaty, which called for monitoring by a UN force; however, Soviet, Arab, and Third World opposition to the Camp David accords prevented the UN from assuming that role.

[d] Only the House voted in favor of authorizing U.S. participation in UNOSOM II. Only the Senate passed resolutions authorizing the missions in Bosnia (post) and Kosovo (pre). Prior to the air war, the House preauthorized a peacekeeping operation to Kosovo, but the mission envisioned at the time was much different than the one that followed the war.

[e] Authorization for these missions derives from the original authorization for the Persian Gulf War (PL 102-1), a fact that was reaffirmed in PL 102-190.

tions during the Cold War. Whether this is a post–Cold War effect, a
humanitarian intervention effect, or a Clinton effect is still too early
to determine. The second observation is that the frequency of IO involvement skyrocketed after 1990. Virtually every mission in this period had not just a multilateral cast but the explicit blessing of an international organization. As a result, there are very few cases in this
period in which the president used military force on his own—that is,
without authorization from either Congress or an international body.
Moreover, two of these cases—the June 1993 attack on Iraq and the
August 1998 attacks against Afghanistan and the Sudan—consisted
of cruise missile strikes that put no troops at risk and were over in a
matter of hours.

These patterns—the rise of congressional opposition and the increased reliance on international organizations—make U.S. involvement in armed humanitarian interventions an interesting setting in
which to explore the relationship between domestic and international institutions. Table 1 suggests that the president has found international organizations to be a useful ally in part to decrease and to
overcome the resistance of the national legislature. In this chapter, I
consider whether and how international organizations play this role.
In what ways does the involvement of IOs help the president deal
with Congress in this policy area?

I argue that working through international institutions magnifies
the considerable advantages that the president has long enjoyed over
Congress when it comes to the use of force—advantages that are primarily domestic, rather than international, in origin (see, for example,
Lindsay 1994, 1995; Hinckley 1994; Warburg 1989). For example,
members of Congress tend not to care as much about foreign policy
since their reelection is driven more by domestic, even local, concerns; collective action is harder for legislators than for the executive,
making it easier for the president to present Congress with faits ac-
complis; and the president has access to better information about
diplomatic and military conditions that will affect the success of the
mission. Many of these factors play an important role in the cases
considered here, and they do not depend upon the involvement of international institutions.

Working through international organizations can, however, magnify the president's advantages in this area, and IOs are thus part of
a multifaceted strategy to overcome, or render irrelevant, congressional resistance. In particular, organizing missions through interna-

tional bodies can increase public support—or at least diminish public opposition to a point at which the president has leeway to ignore it. Working through international organizations also creates a way for the president to commit himself to an operation, by increasing the costs of turning back. As we will see, by tying his own hands and signaling that he will go forward with an operation, regardless of congressional resistance, the president can induce legislators to shy away from efforts to deauthorize, defund, or otherwise limit the mission.

My strategy in developing this argument is first to consider how domestic institutional arrangements influence the incentives of legislators and the discretion of the president when it comes to using force. In the first section, I develop a simple formal model that captures the interaction between the president and a pivotal legislator who is inclined to oppose a deployment of forces. The model shows, in a very general way, some of the factors that tend to increase the president's ability to mute congressional opposition. In particular, it shows that the president can induce inaction on the part of Congress by making clear signals that he is willing to proceed with an operation in the face of congressional efforts to block him. By doing so, the president can put legislators in the politically risky position of having to put the breaks on an ongoing operation. I argue that legislators' motivation to avoid blame for failed policies—and dead soldiers— can lead them to sit on their hands under these conditions.

In the second section, I theorize that working through international organizations facilitates this policy of commitment by increasing both public support for an operation and the costs to the president of giving in to congressional resistance. The next three sections explore the predictions of the theory by looking at three cases of armed humanitarian intervention: the 1994 invasion of Haiti, the 1995 deployment of peacekeepers to Bosnia, and the brief 1994 humanitarian operation in Rwanda. The first two cases show how the use of international organizations helps to create a momentum toward deployment that members of Congress are unwilling to try to stop. The third case shows how weak domestic and international commitments by the president can open the door for Congress to effectively block an operation. I conclude with a brief consideration of whether members of Congress have learned anything from their failure to resist the president and of the extent to which they have sought to change the rules of the game to increase their leverage in this area.

Congress, the President, and Armed Humanitarian Intervention

The struggle between Congress and the president over war powers has been the subject of numerous studies (Lindsay 1994, 1995; Warburg 1989; Wormuth and Firmage 1989; Hinckley 1994; Fisher 1995a), and there is no need to reiterate all the political and legal arguments that have surrounded this issue. There is little disagreement that the Constitution endows Congress with the ultimate authority to make war and that the framers envisioned that power as covering acts that have, for presidential convenience, been labeled "police actions" or "limited engagements" (see, especially, Fisher 1995a). Since at least 1945, however, the political reality has been very different, as the president has enjoyed strong discretion over decisions to use force. Though the reasons for this are numerous, there are two particular features of the U.S. political system that are worth highlighting in the context of armed humanitarian intervention. The first deals with the incentives of legislators; the second deals with the institutional prerogatives of the president.

For reelection-minded legislators, armed humanitarian interventions are high-risk, low-return policies. Taking bold stands on matters of foreign policy is not how most members of Congress count on being reelected. Except for a small handful of individuals who do stake out visible positions on foreign policy—often senators with presidential aspirations—most consider constituent service, pork-barrel politics, and position taking on domestic issues to be more politically potent (see, for example, Mayhew 1974; Arnold 1990). At the same time, there is a great deal of risk and uncertainty associated with military ventures. This uncertainty is not unique to decisions over the use of force, but it is more pressing in this context. Whereas the consequences of domestic policy choices are often unclear and unfold over a long time, decisions about the deployment of troops can have immediate and dramatic consequences. Thus, years after the passage of, say, a welfare reform bill, people will be arguing over its effects; decisions to use force, on the other hand, can have observable costs and benefits in the very near time—that is, before the next election.[2] As a result, while uncertainty over outcomes can embolden legislators to take strong policy stands on domestic issues, it can have the opposite effect when it comes to the use of force.

For most members of Congress, the politics surrounding humanitarian intervention are dominated by what Weaver (1986) calls "the politics of blame avoidance": There is very little electoral advantage in claiming credit for policy initiatives, but there is a danger of being blamed if things go badly. Indeed, Kull, Destler, and Ramsay (1997), in their study of public and elite views on intervention, find that members of Congress see much more danger than opportunity in voting for humanitarian operations:

> Politics is driven enormously by what'll get you in trouble; and members . . . think through "Where could it go wrong?" and "What trouble would I be in?" Now, if they don't vote enough for the UN, they're not going to hear [criticism] from anyone. But if they vote for the UN or vote for a peacekeeping operation and it ends up like Somalia, they know how the phones light up. And the phones did light up then, and they were mostly negative. (143)

Thus, members of Congress want to avoid blame that might arise from authorizing a mission that ends up going badly.

The desire to avoid blame for failures can cut both directions, however. Members of Congress also wish to avoid the charge that their actions undermined the country's foreign policy or, even worse, put U.S. soldiers at risk. Particularly once troops are deployed, a vote to deauthorize, defund, or otherwise constrain their mission has enormous political risks. We will see in the following cases that members of Congress are very reluctant to be seen as undercutting troops that are in the field (see also Hendrickson 1998; Auerswald and Cowhey 1997). Unless the operation is already causing casualties—as in Somalia—there is a strong tendency to "leave well enough alone," lest congressional action be blamed for any tragedy that might occur. In addition, the act of deploying troops puts the credibility of the United States, and any sponsoring organizations, on the line. Pulling the plug on an ongoing operation thus exposes a legislator to blame for any reputational costs thereby incurred. Thus, members of Congress face risks on both sides: In voting for an operation they risk blame for supporting a failed and costly mission; in voting against it they risk blame for causing the mission to fail.

These incentives toward inaction are compounded by a second key feature of the U.S. political system: the unilateral powers of the president to conduct foreign policy and to deploy troops. Like other policies considered in this volume and in the literature on two-level games (for example, Evans, Jacobson, and Putnam 1993), decisions to use force require ratification by the legislature: At the very least, Congress must supply funds for the operation. It is generally accepted, however, that the president can use his control over foreign policy to make international commitments and can use his authority as commander in chief to deploy troops—both without explicit preauthorization from Congress. Indeed, the 1973 War Powers Resolution, Congress's landmark attempt to reclaim its war powers after Vietnam, explicitly permits the president to put troops in potentially hostile situations for a period of at least sixty days before having to come to Congress for authorization.[3] Thus, rather than needing ratification before the policy can go forward, the policy initiator can start implementing the policy unilaterally and then dare the ratifier to pull the plug. Even if a majority in Congress prefers that the policy not go forward, the president's powers give the legislature few opportunities to block the policy preemptively. Opponents of the operation then face a choice between trying to veto, defund, or otherwise limit an ongoing policy—thereby risking blame if things go badly—or throwing up their hands in frustration. More often than not, they do the latter.

To understand the conditions that enhance presidential discretion, I present a simple formal model that captures the interaction between the president and Congress on a decision to deploy troops. In the real world, of course, multiple games are going on at the same time: between the president and Congress, between the Democrats and the Republicans, and between the leadership and the rank and file, not to mention the strategic interactions at the international level involving international institutions and target states. Focusing on the first of these interactions allows me to strip away some of this complexity to focus on the conditions under which legislators' reelection incentives and the president's unilateral powers interact to produce congressional inaction. In modeling the interaction between Congress and the president, of course, one has to be careful because the former is obviously not a unitary actor. Rather than have a model with 536 actors, however, I will focus on the problem of a pivotal legislator—that is, a legislator (or bloc of legislators) whose vote or votes determine whether a measure to block an operation passes.[4]

Sequence of Moves

The extensive form of the game is depicted in figure 1. The game begins with the president's decision of whether or not to commit the United States to an international operation in a way that would entail substantial costs for reneging. A strategy of commitment entails making public statements, such as televised addresses, ordering vis-

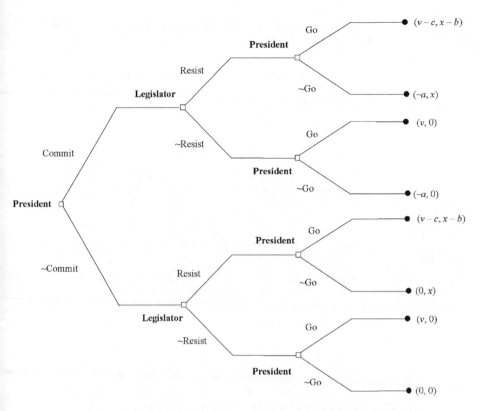

Fig. 1.   Presidential commitment and congressional inaction

ible troop movements, and/or obtaining the support of international actors and organizations. As Fearon (1994), Sartori (2002), and Guisinger and Smith (2000) have argued, such actions put the credibility of the president and the nation on the line, thereby exposing him to "audience costs" should he later back down from the commitment.[5] A decision not to commit does not prevent the president from undertaking an operation if he wants to, but it does decrease the costs of deciding not to do so. To give a concrete example, President Clinton made numerous commitments to deploy peacekeepers to Bosnia as part of a NATO force; he then argued, and many in Congress seem to have agreed, that he had to carry out these commitments to preserve U.S. credibility and leadership of the alliance. On the other hand, Clinton made few such commitments when deploying troops to aid in humanitarian assistance to Rwanda; the deployment was not widely touted or publicized, and the administration was careful to avoid entangling U.S. troops in the larger UN operation. Thus, there were fewer costs to pulling out of the operation.

After the president makes his move, the legislator must decide either to resist or not to resist the operation. Resistance can take a variety of forms, including the denial of funds or the imposition of stringent time limits. In reality, of course, legislators have additional choices, including authorizing the mission or voicing opposition without actually imposing burdens on the operation. To keep things simple, however, I will assume that the pivotal legislator is generally opposed to the mission and must decide whether to try to stop it. The president must then decide either to go forward with the operation or not to do so. Notice that the president can still continue the operation if Congress resists it; as we will see, congressional opposition makes the continuation of the operation more costly.

Payoffs

The president's expected value for the operation is given by v. I further assume that, if the operation goes forward after Congress tries to block it, the expected value is reduced by an additional cost, c. This cost reflects both the political costs that the president might incur for moving ahead in spite of an act by Congress to stop him and the possibility that the operation will be less successful if it is restricted with time limits or not properly funded. If the president does not go forward with the mission, he receives a payoff of zero if he did not undertake a costly commitment and a payoff of $-a$ if he did.

The legislator's payoff has two components: one that depends upon the position he took (if any) and one that depends upon the outcome of the operation. I assume that the legislator has some fixed motivation to take a position against the mission, a motivation that derives from personal, ideological, or partisan considerations. Thus, in the cases I consider, those who voted to block the missions tended to be conservative and Republican—ideologically predisposed to be against armed humanitarian operations and politically motivated to oppose Clinton. Liberals and Democrats tended to be more supportive, for exactly the opposite reasons. To capture such biases I let x denote the payoff to the pivotal legislator for voting against the mission; if the legislator chooses not to act, the payoff is zero because the legislator has effectively taken no position. Thus, legislators with high values of x are strongly motivated to take a position against the operation. In addition, the legislator faces some political risk if she or he votes to resist the operation and things go badly. I capture this risk by assuming that the legislator pays a cost, b, if the president goes forward with the operation after the legislator has voted to block it. This term combines the probability that the mission will go badly, the probability that some future opponent will attempt to use the legislator's vote against her or him, and the political costs of incurring that blame. Without being explicit about the magnitudes of these probabilities and costs, I simply assume (consistent with my reading of the cases and the literature) that this effect is negative in expectation.

Information and Beliefs

I assume that there is two-sided incomplete information: The legislator is unsure about how much the president values the mission, v, and the president is unsure about the strength of the pivotal legislator's opposition to the mission, x. I assume that v is drawn from a probability distribution over the real numbers and that x is drawn from the positive real numbers. The second assumption focuses our attention on cases in which the pivotal legislator is known to be against the mission, which seems appropriate for most cases. Let F denote the cumulative distribution function for v and G denote the cumulative distribution function for x.[6] These functions are common knowledge to both players.

Solution

The solution to the game is rather straightforward. We begin by positing an equilibrium of the following form. The president's strategy is described by two cutpoints in the continuum of possible types. The first cutpoint, which we denote v^*, separates those types that will make a costly commitment and those that will not; thus, when $v > v^*$, the president will make a costly commitment to the operation, and when $v \leq v^*$, he will not. The second cutpoint, which we denote v^{**}, separates those types that will go forward in the face of congressional resistance after making a costly commitment and those that will not. It is shown in the appendix to this chapter that $v^* \leq v^{**}$, meaning that the continuum of types is effectively divided into three ranges: those that do not make the commitment and will not go forward if Congress resists ($v < v^*$); those that make the commitment and go forward if and only if Congress does not resist ($v^{**} > v > v^*$); and those that make the commitment and go forward regardless of what Congress does ($v > v^{**}$). Under some conditions, the middle range does not exist.

Given this strategy, the pivotal legislator knows that the president will not go forward in the face of resistance if he did not make a commitment. Hence, because the legislator is inclined to oppose the mission (that is, $x > 0$), she or he will move to block it, safe in the knowledge that such a move will be successful. If the president does make a commitment, then the legislator's posterior probability that the president would go forward in the face of an attempted veto is

$$\Pr(v > v^{**} \mid \text{Commitment}) = \frac{1 - F(v^{**})}{1 - F(v^*)} \equiv q. \tag{1}$$

Clearly, the legislator will only move to block the mission if the expected payoff from doing so is greater than zero, the certain payoff for abstaining. Simple arithmetic shows that the legislator resists if

$$x > qb. \tag{2}$$

Thus, the more the legislator is opposed to the operation the more she or he wants to resist it, but how much opposed the legislator has to be depends upon how likely it is that the president will proceed anyway (q) and upon the potential blame that the legislator would incur if things go badly in this event (b).

The model has several implications about the conditions that foster congressional inaction. First, the legislator is less likely to resist when the president has made a costly commitment than when he has not. Moreover, while there is no guarantee that an increase in audience costs always leads to a lower probability of resistance, the overall relationship has this shape. In particular, I show in the appendix that the probability of resistance when $a > G(b)c$ is always less than the probability of resistance when $a < G(b)c$. Second, anything that increases the value of the operation to the president will also decrease the likelihood of resistance. If, for example, it was known that the value to the president increased from v to $v + z$, keeping the distribution of v constant, then the probability of resistance by Congress would go down. Both of these changes serve a common purpose: convincing the legislator that the president will go forward even if she or he tries to block him. Recall that, in trying to block the operation, all but the most extreme opponents (that is, all

legislators for which $x < b$) are gambling between their best outcome, in which the mission is successfully blocked, and their worst
outcome, in which the mission goes forward despite their attempts to
stop it. The more likely it is that the president will go forward in spite
of the legislator's attempts to limit the mission, the less attractive
that gamble becomes. In practice, there are a number of ways in
which the president can increase the costs of his commitments
and/or his value for the operation, thereby making congressional inaction more likely. I now argue that garnering the support of international organizations is an efficient way to do both.

How International Organizations Help the President

There are two primary benefits that the president enjoys when he or-
ganizes an intervention through an international organization. The
first is an increase in public support for the mission by adding legitimacy and a promise of burden sharing. This has the effect of increasing his expected value for the operation and may soften the opposition of members of Congress who are otherwise on the fence. The
second benefit is that making commitments to international organizations provides a way for the president to increase the costs of backing down in the face of congressional resistance. International organizations can help tie the president's hands, thereby dampening the
prospects that obstruction by Congress will have its desired end. I will
treat each of these features in turn.

Political Support

The blessing of international bodies serves to make the operation
more palatable to public opinion. Opinion polls routinely show that
the public is more supportive of military action when it is done mul-
tilaterally (see, for example, Sobel 1996; Kohut and Toth 1995; Kull
1996; Kull, Destler, and Ramsay 1997). There seem to be several mutually reinforcing reasons for this. First, multilateralism is a means of
burden sharing and works against the image of the United States as
the "world's policeman" (Kull 1996, 105). By enlisting the support of
other countries, the United States can undertake an operation with
fewer of its own troops and financial resources. In addition, IO involvement promises a partner to which the United States can hand
off the mission at some future date. Second, the blessing of the UN
and other international bodies can also enhance the legitimacy of the

operation in the eyes of internationalists who care about such things. As Abbott and Snidal (1998, 24–29) note, international organizations are seen as "community representatives" that speak for the broader interests. Their consent can serve both as a stamp of legitimacy and as a signal that the use of force will be interpreted by other countries as acceptable under community norms.

For isolationists, of course, UN sanction could act in the opposite direction: serving as a clear signal that the proposed operation should be avoided. Indeed, critics of humanitarian interventions have often played on suspicion of the UN and particularly the possibility that U.S. troops might be placed under foreign command. While this sentiment is real and at times politically potent (see, for example, Rosner 1995–96), there is no evidence to suggest that those who oppose missions due to the involvement of international organizations would otherwise support them. After all, such isolationists are likely to oppose humanitarian interventions regardless of the degree of multilateralism. I will show evidence to this effect when considering the Haiti case.

Commitment

The president can use his agenda control over foreign policy and his influence with international organizations to make commitments from which it would be costly to back down. As Fearon (1994) has argued, making public commitments to intervene can be seen by domestic actors as placing national honor and credibility on the line. Fearon argues that this audience cost effect gives state leaders a way to commit themselves to fighting, thereby increasing the credibility of their threats. Such actions as televised addresses and troop deployments can make backing down more costly and thus can tie the president's hands. Martin (1993a) has shown that making commitments to, and working to obtain the consent of, international organizations can magnify this effect. By getting the UN and/or NATO to support a mission, the president can put the credibility of those organizations, as well as U.S. influence within them, on the line. As we will see, a major factor pushing President Clinton toward action in Bosnia was the commitment he made to NATO to send U.S. forces either to extricate NATO troops or to serve as peacekeepers in the event of a peace deal. This commitment not only weighed heavily in his decision making but also permitted him to argue that there was a national interest at stake: the preservation of NATO and U.S. leadership of the alliance. In addition to tying the president's hands, such actions can also have an influence on members of Congress, who might be reluctant to undercut commitments made in the country's name. I will return to this issue when considering the Bosnia case.

The president can also use the blessing of international institutions as a legal and diplomatic veneer behind which to deploy troops, which is one of the most effective commitment mechanisms. As already noted, members of Congress are reluctant to be seen as undercutting troops who are already in harm's way. Every time there is talk about ending funding for a mission or imposing size or time limits, the administration marches generals up to the Hill to tell lawmakers how their actions are going to undermine morale and increase the risks of troops in the field. These arguments have tended to be quite persuasive.

The sections that follow examine three cases of U.S. intervention in the light of the model and arguments made here. Two of the cases—Haiti and Bosnia—show how working through international organizations can be part of a presidential strategy to overcome, or render impotent, congressional resistance to an operation. The third case, which looks at U.S. intervention and nonintervention in Rwanda, illustrates an alternative equilibrium outcome: one in which the president makes no strong commitments and opens the door for Congress to successfully restrain a military operation.

Haiti: Washing Hands

The intervention in Haiti is a good example of how Congress, or at least a persistent majority thereof, can wash its hands of a military venture and effectively allow the president and international organizations to call the shots. This is not to imply that Congress was silent on this matter. In the year between October 1993 and the deployment of troops in October 1994, members of the House and Senate cast fifteen votes directly related to the deployment of U.S. military forces in Haiti. The votes, and the debate surrounding them, indicated that a majority in both houses was, at a minimum, skeptical of an invasion and that many, both Republicans and Democrats, were thoroughly opposed to one. Moreover, almost all members went on record demanding that the president not go forward without congressional authorization. And yet, legislators repeatedly shied away from anything more than symbolic, nonbinding assertions of congressional prerogatives and costless position taking. Amendments and resolutions that would have forced a showdown with the president—for example, by denying funds in the absence of congressional authorization—were consistently defeated or blocked from coming to a vote. And after the president deployed troops without honoring congressional demands to have some say in the matter, Congress choose neither to authorize nor to limit the mission in any way.

A number of factors helped Clinton mute congressional resistance in this case, not all of them a product of working through international organizations. Obtaining UN authorization and support was part of a multifaceted strategy that created an inexorable momentum toward military action starting in the spring of 1994. With the president increasingly committed to removing Haiti's military government by force if necessary, members of Congress opposed to such an operation repeatedly found that there was no good time to take strong action to block it. Prior to the deployment, when international pressure was seen as the only way to get Haiti's rulers to step aside peacefully, centrists in Congress were persuaded not to limit the president's options prospectively for fear that such an action would undermine coercive diplomacy and bring about the very outcome they hoped to avoid. After the deployment, which unexpectedly took place peacefully and without loss of life, legislators decided that both authorizing the mission and acting to limit its scope or duration had political risks due to the ongoing danger to U.S. troops. In the end, inaction was preferable.

Once Clinton switched to a more forceful stance in April and May 1994, he took a number of actions that effectively committed him to a military operation in the event that diplomacy failed. The first action was a decision, announced on May 8, to stop automatically repatriating Haitian refugees. This move, combined with a tightening of economic sanctions, restarted the influx of Haiti "boat people" to American soil and created a situation that could not be tenable for long. The administration also ordered a rapid military buildup in the Caribbean and staged a mock seizure of Haitian airfields and ports (Doherty 1994c).

The next key step was to get UN backing for the use of force, which happened on July 31 with the passage of Security Council Resolution 940. The administration put a great deal of effort into securing that resolution, reportedly smoothing Russian assent by softening its attitude toward a Russian peacekeeping effort in Georgia and Tajikistan (Malone 1998, 106–7). Administration officials described the resolution as creating "momentum" toward an invasion by lending additional credibility to U.S. threats and by insulating the president from some of the political risk due to public opposition (Drew 1994, 428; Jehl 1994). Because the UN resolution called for a multinational force, the United States worked assiduously to round up what would amount to symbolic support from other countries, including a force of 266 soldiers from four small Caribbean countries (Harding 1994).

Though public support for the mission was never impressive, it mattered a great deal to the administration to have an international blessing. The reason becomes clear when we look at the effect of multilateralism on public opinion. Figure 2 shows the level of support for U.S. military action in Haiti. The figure reports responses for all opinion polls conducted in 1994 prior to the September 18 deployment.[7] At first glance, the responses display wide variation, ranging from 10 to 64 percent. As the figure shows, however, all four of the lowest scores came when the poll questions explicitly said that the U.S. would act unilaterally,[8] and all but one of the top thirteen scores came when the question mentioned participation by other countries.[9] Indeed, the only polls that showed majority support for sending U.S. troops were ones in which the operation was described as being multilateral. The polls clearly show that about 10 percent of respondents favored military action regardless of what other countries did, about 40 percent opposed it regardless of what other countries did, and 30–40 percent supported it conditional on other countries' participation. Thus, a multilateral approach meant the difference between majority opposition and plurality support.

At the same time, there is no evidence that UN involvement decreased support for the operation among some constituencies, especially Republicans. Indeed, two polls directly refute this hypothesis. A Time/CNN (1994) poll conducted on July 13–14 asked respondents whether they supported sending U.S. troops to Haiti with "no military assistance from any other country" and whether they supported sending troops "along with troops from other countries".[10] The beneficial effects of multilateralism are clear: Support for the mission rose from 17 percent to 51 percent when the contribution of other countries was added. The individual level data show that increased support for multilateralism did not depend upon the respondent's partisan loyalty: For both Republicans and Democrats, around 40 percent of the respondents who opposed a unilateral mission supported a multilateral one. On the other hand, only 3 percent of respondents said they would support a unilateral operation but oppose a multilateral one, a figure

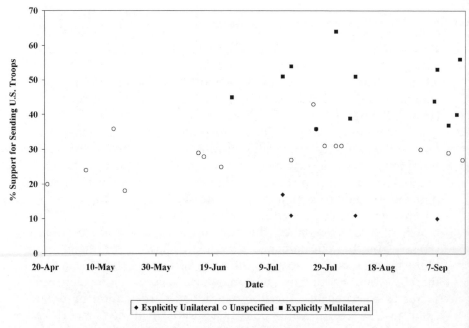

Fig. 2. Multilateralism and support for the Haiti operation, 1994

that also does not depend upon party identification. Thus, the increased support for multilateral missions that we see in the aggregate data does not seem to mask significant shifts in the other direction among more conservative constituencies.

Related evidence comes from a CBS News/New York Times (1994) poll conducted on August 2. Respondents were first asked whether they favored or opposed sending U.S. ground troops to Haiti. Those who answered "oppose" or "don't know" were then asked to consider their position if the troops were "part of a United Nations multilateral force." As usual, half of the respondents who initially opposed the mission said they would favor it once the UN was mentioned. Even more important, the poll permits us to test how news of the UN participation influenced those who initially had no opinion. Do those who are wavering either because of ambivalence or ignorance see UN involvement as a positive or negative signal? The answer is clear: While 44 percent of those who initially had no opinion came to support the sending of troops when told of UN involvement, only 8 percent switched to opposing it. In all, only five respondents out of 594 initially had no opinion and then opposed the mission once the UN was mentioned. As before, while support for the mission was lower among Republican respondents than among Democrats, the rates at which these two groups switched positions at the second question were not statistically different. Hence, UN participation turned very few people against an operation, and those who did change were not exclusively Republican.

Of course, public support for the operation was never strong, but in the field of foreign policy, in particular, the president can often act in the face of majority opposition (see, for example, Graham 1994, 195–97). The counterfactual to consider here is what the constraints on the president might have been had he been unable to marshal international support and instead had to go completely alone. We have seen that a unilateral operation would have been opposed by 80–90 percent of the public, a level of resistance that would have been harder to ignore.

With the president increasingly committed to an invasion in the event that the military rulers did not step down, members of Congress shied away from taking strong action to block him. On two occasions, the Senate rejected measures that would have prohibited the use of funds to send troops to Haiti unless the operation was authorized in advance by Congress or if its purpose was confined to the protection or evacuation of U.S. citizens. An amendment to the 1994 defense appropriations sponsored by Jesse Helms (R-NC) was soundly defeated on October 21, 1993, ten days after a boat full of lightly armed U.S. and Canadian troops was prevented from landing in Haiti to implement a UN-brokered deal. The vote on the measure was 19-81, with all Democrats and a majority of Republicans voting against it. In its place, the Senate voted overwhelmingly (98-2) to support a nonbinding, "sense of Congress" amendment declaring that U.S. armed forces should not be sent to Haiti unless Congress grants prior authorization or the president submits a report in advance of the operation summarizing the national security interests at stake, the justification for using armed forces, the exit strategy, and the likely costs. This weaker alternative was sponsored by the majority and minority leaders, George Mitchell (D-ME) and Robert Dole (R-KS), after negotiations with the White House (Towell 1993b). The House did not have explicit vote on this matter, but it effectively adopted the Senate's position when it accepted the conference report on the defense authorization bill on November 10.

In June 1994, as talk of a U.S.-led invasion increased, the Senate went through an almost exact replay of this maneuvering. In this case, Judd Gregg (R-NH) proposed an amendment to the 1995 defense authorization that borrowed the language of the Dole-Mitchell amendment but would have given it statutory power. Once again, this amendment was defeated, 34-65, and a nonbinding version offered by the leadership passed overwhelmingly, 93-4. The debate over the Gregg amendment revealed the cross-pressures that members of Congress can feel. Many Democrats have traditionally supported the War Powers Act and the effort to limit presidential war-making authority. In this instance, however, Democrats were motivated to vote against the Gregg amendment because they sympathized with the overall goals of the policy and/or wanted to support their president. Republicans, on the other hand, were generally opposed to the specific mission and were happy for an opportunity to embarrass Clinton, but many were also long-standing defenders of presidential prerogatives in such matters. Sen. John McCain (R-AZ), for example, said, "I cannot support any resolution which prospectively limits the power of the president as commander in chief" (Doherty 1994b, 1814). Lindsay (1995, 81) suggests that the increased support for the Gregg amendment as compared to the Helms amendment shows growing assertiveness by Congress as events progressed. However, it is important to note that Gregg's version, by adopting the language of the Dole-Mitchell amendment, was less restrictive than Helms's, since it gave the president the option of submitting a report rather than seeking congressional authorization. Gregg admitted as much in trying to convince skeptical colleagues to vote for his amendment, noting that it provided "a lot of flexibility for the president" (Doherty 1994b, 1814). It is clear that the more binding and more restrictive a proposal was, the less support it received in the Senate.

In this period, the House also failed to send a strong, or even consistent, message on the prospective invasion. On May 24, 1993, it voted 223-201 for a nonbinding resolution calling on the president not to invade Haiti without first certifying to Congress that "a clear and present danger to citizens of the United States or United States interests requires such action." Two weeks later, however, the exact same measure was defeated, 195-226, when thirty Democrats who had previously supported it changed their votes. The reason for the turnabout is unclear, but it followed a strong push by the administration to garner support for its policies (Greenhouse 1994, 3). At least one Florida congressman changed his vote after being convinced by Sen. Bob Graham of Florida, a strong supporter of intervention (Feldmann 1994, 3).

It is also noteworthy that, on June 4, Aristide suggested for the first time that he might support a "surgical action" led by the United States (Murphy 1996, 267).

The pace of congressional activity picked up after the UN Security Council adopted Resolution 940. Passed at the request of the United States, this resolution signaled that a military operation was quite likely unless Haiti's military rulers stepped down. Despite this clear indication, however, majorities in Congress continued to exhibit a preference for symbolic acts over costly ones that would have asserted institutional rights. On August 3, the Senate voted unanimously (100-0) to endorse a resolution offered by Dole asserting that UN approval "does not constitute authorization for the deployment of U.S. Armed Forces in Haiti under the Constitution of the United States or pursuant to the War Powers Resolution" (*Cong. Rec.* 1994, S10415). At a news conference the same day, Clinton said he agreed that UN approval was not the same as congressional approval, but he then went on to argue that the latter was unnecessary: "I would welcome the support of the Congress, and I hope that I will have that. Like my predecessors of both parties, I have not agreed that I was constitutionally mandated to get it" (Clinton 1994). Despite this rebuff, two days later the Senate tabled an amendment by Arlen Specter (R-PA) that reiterated Congress's constitutional authority to make war and would have prohibited Clinton from using armed forces in Haiti without prior approval by Congress. The 63-31 vote to table, and thereby effectively kill, Specter's amendment followed party lines, but one-third of Republicans voted with the majority.

By mid-September, it was clear that an invasion was imminent. In the days prior to the sending of the Carter delegation, opponents of the policy in both chambers attempted, and failed, to force a vote on the matter. An effort by McCain in the Senate to introduce an amendment opposing an invasion was blocked by Majority Leader Mitchell's parliamentary maneuvering (Doherty 1994d, 2578). In the House, David Skaggs (R-CO) drafted a nonbinding, concurrent resolution declaring that the president was required to get congressional authorization before deploying troops. Similarly, Reps. Gene Taylor (D-MS) and Christopher Cox (R-CA) tried to force an up-or-down vote by invoking parliamentary rules that allow members to bring a "privileged motion" to "protect the rights of this House collectively" (*Cong. Rec.* 1994, H9117). The Skaggs resolution never came to a vote, and while the Taylor-Cox effort could have forced a vote by September 19, it became moot when Haiti's leaders agreed on September 18 to step down, thus paving the way for a peaceful deployment the following day (Doherty 1994d, 2578).

While a number of factors played into this sequence of events, legislators hesitated in part because it was becoming increasingly clear that the president was resolved to move ahead with or without congressional support—a point that administration officials made quite explicitly (see, for example, Doherty 1994d). Given the president's domestic and international commitments, centrists who held the decisive votes on these measures clearly saw a political downside in voting to restrict such an invasion in advance. After all, an invasion would not be necessary if Haitian leaders were sufficiently convinced that it would happen. Thus, the president's allies warned that opponents' efforts to constrain the president might encourage the very outcome the latter were seeking to prevent. The clearest example of this came in July, when Dole proposed an amendment calling for a bipartisan commission on Haiti that was widely seen as an effort to slow the momentum toward an invasion. Dole was quickly put on the defensive, however, when Haiti's military leader, Lt. Gen. Raoul Cedras, endorsed the idea in a television interview. In the debate on the measure, Democrats harped on Cedras's comments and argued that congressional efforts to tie the president's hands would only encourage the junta to resist (for example, *Cong. Rec.* 1994, S8947). These arguments seem to have prevailed: While a majority of senators were against a military operation, they voted 57-42 to kill the proposal (Doherty 1994c). Such arguments were raised repeatedly by the president's allies in the debates leading up to the deployment. The politics of blame avoidance dictated that all but the fiercest opponents of the mission should avoid acts that were seen as undermining the president's diplomacy and thereby increasing the danger that troops would have to be sent.

A similar pattern continued after troops were deployed, as members of Congress continued to be reluctant to take all but the most symbolic steps to assert control over the policy. The main issue that arose in the wake of the deployment was whether Congress would authorize the president's actions in accordance with the War Powers Act and/or place a time limit on the mission. In the end, it did neither. Instead, the House and Senate passed identical measures (SJRes 229 and HJRes 416) stating that "the president should have sought and welcomed" congressional support before sending the troops and requiring him to make reports on the cost, scope, and projected timetable of the operation. The resolutions called for a "prompt and orderly withdrawal" of troops but otherwise placed no time limit on their presence in Haiti (Doherty 1994g, 2895). This measure passed the Senate by an overwhelming majority, 91-8. It passed the House by a somewhat less impressive margin, 258-167. The House had also considered and rejected two alternative measures. The Republican version, proposed by Minority Leader Robert Michel (R-IL) and Benjamin Gilman (R-NY), criticized Clinton for sending troops, called for a pullout "as soon as possible in a manner consistent with the safety of those forces," and provided for an up-or-down vote in January on whether to continue the mission. That version was defeated 205-225. The second alternative, proposed by Robert Torricelli (D-NJ), provided limited authorization for the deployment until March 1, 1995, and left open the possibility of extending the authorization indefinitely. This too was rejected, 27-398. Thus, the majority of the House chose neither to authorize the mission, even temporarily, nor to shut it down, preferring instead to leave control over policy in the hands of the president and the UN. Sen. Robert Byrd (D-WV) characterized the outcome as a "shrug of the shoulders in terms of any real assertion of the constitutional role of Congress" (Doherty 1994g, 2895).

Again, the strategy of blame avoidance accounts for this outcome, as members were hesitant to take action that could be seen as jeopardizing troops (Doherty 1994e, 1994f, 1994g). The president's ability to set the agenda by putting troops in harm's way made it difficult to oppose the mission once it was under way. As McCain, an ardent opponent of the mission prior to deployment, suggested, "Suppose you set a deadline of, say, Feb. 1. If something goes wrong Jan. 15—if there is some act of violence—the president could turn to Republicans and say it's their fault" (Doherty 1994f, 2816). The problem was magnified by good early results: The troops had gone in without loss of life, and the military dictators were on their way out. Given that congressional elections were only a month away, that positive signal in the short term not only increased the uncertainty but also had some political significance. Doherty (1994g, 2895) captures this dilemma well: "[W]ith midterm elections just a month away, most members simply did not want to vote for or against a mission that, for all its potential risk, has been largely successful."

Bosnia: Tying Hands

The 1995 deployment of U.S. peacekeeping troops to Bosnia is a particularly important episode because, unlike the Haiti invasion, it occurred during a period of Republican control of both chambers. Smith (1998) finds that party is a strong predictor of legislative voting on post–Cold War military operations: Those from the same party as the president tend to vote for his policies while those from the rival party tend to vote against them. This is evident from the previous case in the large number of party line votes and the efforts of the Democratic leadership to block early votes on the Haiti operation. The Bosnia case permits us to explore whether the lack of congressional assertion in that case was simply a product of the partisan composition of the legislature. As we will see, though, the outcome over Bosnia in 1995 looks a good deal like the outcome over Haiti in 1994. This similarity comes in spite of the fact that Republicans took office determined to reign in the UN and to assert congressional control over peacekeeping operations (about which I will say more later). The overall pattern thus suggests that the constraints on congressional action derive from the structure of the problem that legislators face rather than from the particular configuration of preferences at a given time.

As in the case of Haiti, a driving force behind events in the United States concerning Bosnia was the public and international commitments made by Clinton during the early days of his presidency. The so-called lift and strike proposal that Clinton offered shortly after coming into office included a commitment that twenty thousand U.S. troops would participate in a NATO mission to police any peace agreement or, if it became necessary, to evacuate UN peacekeepers from the country. While Clinton was not eager to see U.S. troops sent to Bosnia, the commitment was seen as important to help address European complaints that the United States was not willing to put its own soldiers at risk (for good discussions of Clinton's Bosnia policy, see Gow 1997; Drew 1994; Gompert 1996). Not long after the commitment was made, Clinton abandoned lift and strike, and the prospects for a peace deal, which had briefly seemed imminent, fell by the wayside. Nevertheless, the commitment came back to haunt Clinton two years later, when Serb advances threatened to make the UN situation in Bosnia untenable. With Britain and France threatening to pull their troops out of the country, the United States was faced with the prospect of having to deploy U.S. troops in a dangerous mission to help their evacuation—or to break its earlier commitment. Given that neither option was considered acceptable, the United States instead pushed for a sustained NATO bombing campaign in August 1995 and started the diplomatic process that lead to the Dayton peace talks (Gow 1997, 276–77).

Prior to this point, legislative activity on Bosnia had focused primarily on the question of lifting the arms embargo and not on the use of force by the United States. The relative quiet on this matter persisted in spite of the fact that U.S. planes were patrolling a UN-approved no-fly zone and engaged in air strikes to protect so-called safe havens on several occasions in 1994 and 1995. Although these actions clearly placed U.S. troops in hostile situations, neither Congress nor the president showed any interest in invoking the War Powers Resolution (Doherty 1994h; Hendrickson 1998, 248). The closest Congress came to doing so came in a measure introduced by Mitchell in May 1994 that gave retroactive authorization and approval to air strikes conducted in February and April of that year. The measure barely passed, 50-49, but most of the interest in it centered on its provisions regarding the arms embargo, as the Mitchell amendment was an administration-sponsored alternative to Dole's effort to unilaterally lift the embargo (Doherty 1994a, 1233). In any event, the underlying bill was never considered in the House.

The situation changed in October 1995, when a cease-fire and the prospect of peace talks signaled that the U.S. might have to make good on Clinton's commitment to contribute ground troops to a peacekeeping operation. In a major policy address, Clinton announced that he was determined not to break his word to NATO. He added that he would "want and welcome" congressional support for the mission, but he only promised consultations (Doherty 1995, 3158). Republicans, on the other hand, declared that the president would have to seek congressional authorization before the deployment, just as Bush had done before the Gulf War. "What we'll be seeking is a formal request for authorization from the president and a full-scale debate," said McCain, adding (in a statement that shows a stunning lack of foresight as well as ignorance of history), "It would be foolish of the president not to do that because they know we have too many ways to block it" (Doherty 1995, 3158). As it turns out, the president did not ask for preauthorization for the mission and Congress was unwilling to block it.

As in the case of Haiti, strong preemptive action on the part of Congress carried political risks. With peace negotiations under way at Dayton, a move to prevent U.S. troops from being sent to enforce any eventual agreement could have scuttled the entire process. If the United States refused to go, the logic went, NATO too would balk, and there would be no effective military presence to implement the peace. The administration and its congressional allies argued that if

Congress voted against sending peacekeepers the move would undermine the negotiations. Thus, when the House met on October 30, two days before peace talks started at Dayton, GOP leaders helped to turn aside an effort by conservatives to prospectively cut off funds for a peacekeeping operation. Instead, the House passed a nonbinding resolution warning the participants at Dayton not to count on U.S. troops in a peacekeeping mission and opposing any deployment without prior congressional authorization (Towell 1995a). Evidence from this episode suggests that House members feared being confronted with a fait accompli and thus hoped to get on the record as soon as possible. Indeed, HR 247 was brought up in expedited fashion, and only forty minutes were allocated to debate it. Representative Cox explained that urgency was required in light of the fact that an agreement could be reached at any time and a deployment would begin shortly thereafter: "It is important that we act tonight. Else we will abdicate" (*Cong. Rec.* 1995, H11400). In reality, of course, the measure was only a nonbinding sense of Congress resolution that did not come out for or against a deployment but merely stated the House's desire to have some say in the matter. As is typically the case with such resolutions, it passed overwhelmingly, 315-103.

Nevertheless, staunch opponents in the House chose not to wait long. On November 17, House members voted 243-171 for a bill that would have denied funds for the mission unless it was approved in advance by Congress. Democrats argued that the timing was poor, given that the peace talks at Dayton were nearing a successful conclusion, but the sponsor of the bill, Joel Hefley (R-CO), argued that immediate action was necessary because of the hand-tying effect: "The farther along we go down the road, the more difficult it will be to say no if we decide to say no" (Towell and Cassata 1995a, 3549). Without Senate concurrence, however, this move had no chance of becoming law, and the Senate had little appetite for the measure. Indeed, the Senate waited almost a month before considering the Hefley measure. William Cohen (R-ME), a moderate Republican, conceded that the hesitation was a product of blame avoidance:

> [W]e should be very candid about it, if we had taken so-called preemptive action to assert our constitutional authority, our control over the purse strings, saying, "No funds appropriated under this account may be expected for the deployment of ground forces in Bosnia," and the negotiations then failed, Congress did

not want to accept the blame for it. So we backed away and we waited. (*Cong. Rec.* 1995, S18428)

By the time the measure did come to vote in the Senate, a peace deal had been struck, the first contingents of U.S. troops were en route to help implement it, and the effort to block the mission quickly died. As Dole noted on November 30, "It is time for a reality check in Congress. If we would try to cut off funds, we would harm the men and women in the military who have already begun to arrive in Bosnia" (Towell 1995c, 3668). In the Senate, Hefley's bill was soundly defeated 22-77. In the House, the same language was reintroduced by Robert Dornan (R-CA). This time the bill was defeated 210-218, as forty-seven members switched from support to opposition; only nine members switched in the opposite direction.

Clinton kept his earlier promise of asking for congressional support, but there was a strong sense that Congress had little choice but to go along. After agreeing that a fund cutoff was undesirable, both chambers took a series of votes on whether to support the mission and/or the troops. The House, with its stronger conservative contingent, came out more forcefully than did the Senate, though it still fell far short of any real assertion of congressional authority. The House passed 287-141 a resolution supporting the troops but explicitly opposing Clinton's policy. The House measure (HRes 302) pointed out that the president's deployment decision came in spite of two attempts—HRes 247 and the Hefley bill—to secure prior congressional approval. Nevertheless, unlike similar amendments in the Haiti case, the measure did not call for a withdrawal or even require the president to make reports on the mission. A measure offered by Democrats that simply declared support for the troops without commenting on the policy was rejected 190-237.

In the Senate, the outcome was reversed, thanks in large part to Dole, who apparently had an eye toward his presidential run (Hendrickson 1998, 254). Dole helped to craft a bipartisan measure supporting the troops and permitting the president to fulfill his commitment for approximately one year. Interestingly, the measure (SJRes 44) explicitly noted that the president's decision had been taken in spite of reservations expressed by Congress but that the deployment was already under way and "preserving United States credibility is a strategic interest" (SJRes 44). The measure passed 69-30. An alternative that would have supported the troops but expressed opposition to Clinton's policy was defeated 47-52.

Tough rhetoric from the House notwithstanding, the Bosnia case did nothing to alter the institutional balance on war powers. Instead, it confirmed the president's ability to tie members' hands by forcing the pace of events, making commitments to international actors and institutions, deploying troops without authorization, and then daring Congress to take votes that could be interpreted as undercutting them. The importance of these factors is plainly evident in the debates, particularly in the Senate, over the various measures considered there. The comments of moderate Republicans, who held the decisive votes, demonstrate a strong sense that the president had used his commitment to NATO and his authority to deploy troops to railroad Congress into inaction. Cohen nicely summed up the futility of congressional resistance, given the president's commitment to proceed:

> Even if the House and the Senate were to vote overwhelmingly to disapprove the sending of American troops to Bosnia, the President has already indicated they are going in any event. "It is my prerogative. It is my power. I am going to keep the commitment I made to the NATO allies. . . ."
>
> So this entire debate on what we are going to pass in the way of a resolution has no ultimate, no practical, consequence in terms of preventing the troops from going there. (*Cong. Rec.* 1995, S18428)

Similarly, Rod Grams (R-MN), who voted to oppose the mission but not to cut off funds, complained that Clinton "has essentially dared Congress to break his ill-considered commitment of U.S. forces and thereby, he says, risk undermining the peace agreement, our international credibility and our relations with NATO allies" (*Cong. Rec.* 1995, S18451).

While rhetoric may be a poor guide of actual motivations, it also seems that many senators thought that the commitment to NATO not only tied the president's hands but their own as well. Unlike the UN, NATO is an organization that most members, on both sides of the aisle, see as vital to U.S. security. The president and his supporters argued that, even if there was no national interest at stake in Bosnia, there was such an interest in maintaining the cohesion of NATO and U.S. leadership within the alliance—an interest that would be jeopardized if Congress pulled the plug on the mission. This consideration would tend to decrease the value of successfully blocking U.S. participation and to motivate pivotal legislators to sit on their hands. Thus,

Slade Gorton (R-WA) justified his vote against cutting off funds and against opposing the mission:

> [I]t remains vital to the peace not only of Europe but to the rest of the world that NATO continue and that it be credible. As a consequence, even though NATO may have, as I believe it has done, made an erroneous and unwise commitment, and even though the President of the United States may have done and has done, in my view, an unwise thing in entering into this commitment, we now must honor it. (*Cong. Rec.* 1995, S18418)

Thus, the president can help overcome opposition to an unpopular mission by tying its fate to that of a popular organization, such as NATO.

Rwanda: A Negative Case

In both of the cases just discussed, the president was strongly motivated to go ahead with the mission and managed to overcome congressional resistance to do so. Of course, this is not the only equilibrium outcome predicted by the model. As we saw, when the president has low expected value for a mission, he has incentives to avoid costly commitments, and the prospects for congressional activism are greater. To explore whether this prediction is borne out, I briefly consider the case of U.S. intervention—and nonintervention—in Rwanda during the spring and summer of 1994.

On the one hand, the U.S. decision not to intervene in the genocide and civil war in Rwanda is a trivial nonevent for the purposes of this analysis. Had the administration really wanted to intervene militarily and had its hand been stayed by the prospect of congressional resistance, then it would be an important case in which Congress exercised power through its anticipated reaction: a very potent veto lay off the equilibrium path of play. However, this is not the case. There is no evidence that the administration wanted to act to stop the genocide and was prevented from doing so. Indeed, the tragedy in Rwanda came just as the administration was putting the finishing touches on Presidential Decision Directive 25, which called for the government to cast a skeptical eye on peacekeeping operations in the wake of Somalia. At the same time, the administration was preoccupied with events in Haiti, where more compelling national interests were at stake. According to a *Washington Post* reconstruction of events in April,

"Everyone involved—the president, [National Security Advisor Anthony] Lake, Assistant Secretary of State for African Affairs George E. Moose, officials at the Pentagon's Africa department—agreed from the beginning that Rwanda simply did not meet any test for direct U.S. military intervention" (Lippman 1994a; see also Power 2001; Prunier 1998, 274; Des Forges 1999, 623–25). Thus, while it is true that there was no appetite in Congress for intervention, that the president similarly lacked any desire to intervene makes the ultimate outcome uninteresting from our perspective.

On the other hand, other elements of this story support the model's predictions. While the United States stood idly by during the early months of the genocide and civil war, it did send over two thousand troops to help with the delivery of humanitarian assistance, in an operation dubbed Support Hope. Most of the troops operated in Zaire, but 220 of them helped to secure the airport in the Rwandan capital, Kigali. What is interesting about this episode is that congressional action did help to bring the operation to a premature end. Consistent with the model, however, the action took place in the midst of clear signals that the administration was not committed to the operation and had no interest in pressing ahead in the face of congressional resistance.

Though Clinton sent the troops with some fanfare, declaring the disaster in Rwanda "the world's worst humanitarian crisis in a generation," the U.S. commitment was quite small and never lived up even to the modest expectations the administration set for it (see, for example, Lippman 1994a; Smith 1994). Moreover, while the operation helped to support a UN peacekeeping operation, administration officials took pains to emphasize that the U.S. troops were not part of the UN operation and were only there at the request of the UN High Commissioner for Refugees. To the extent that the U.S. presence was formally authorized by the UN, this was done through Security Council Resolution 929, which welcomed the assistance of member states, operating under national command and control, until the UN peacekeeping force, United Nations Assistance Mission for Rwanda (UNAMIR), could be brought to full strength (UN Security Council 1994). The lackluster support for the mission in the executive branch was further evidenced by press reports, which started to appear in July and August, stating that the Department of Defense was unhappy with the operation and concerned about its effect on overall readiness (see, for example, Graham 1994; Lippman 1994b; Smith

1994). Indeed, from the very beginning of the crisis, the Pentagon had tried to stymie any move toward intervention (Power 2001).

The administration's weak commitment to Operation Support Hope created an easy opening for a skeptical Congress to limit its duration. On July 29, the Senate Appropriations Committee voted to cut $100 million from the $270 million Clinton had requested to fund the operation and stipulated that no funds could be used for operation after October 7 unless the president received congressional approval to extend the deadline. In addition, the Senate passed a measure barring any change in the nature of the mission from humanitarian assistance to peacemaking or nation building. Both provisions were agreed to by House conferees and became part of the 1995 Defense Appropriations Act (PL 103-335).

Congressional action seems to have had the desired effect in this case. The Senate Appropriations Committee action reportedly played a role in discussions within the administration and gave ammunition to Pentagon officials who wanted to see the mission curtailed (Smith 1994). While Defense Secretary William Perry originally suggested that U.S. troops could be deployed for "a year or longer" (Drogin 1994), they were in fact all removed by the October 7 deadline. The withdrawal took place even though the operation had not achieved all of the goals that had originally been set for it (see, especially, Smith 1994).

This case shows that Congress is not institutionally incapable of legislating limitations on military deployments—even those that have sustained no casualties. When the administration is weakly committed to an action, due to public skepticism and/or resistance from the Pentagon, then congressional resistance can increase the leverage of those in the executive branch who are opposed to the operation. It is possible that Clinton could have found a way to press ahead in the face of Congress's action, but clearly the costs of doing so had become larger than the benefits. At the same time, the outcome is consistent with the model's prediction that Congress is most likely to successfully block operations to which the president has few or weak public and international commitments. The administration's unwillingness to orchestrate and join a fully fledged UN operation in Rwanda was indicative of the lack of resolve that would ultimately make congressional resistance effective in this case. In addition, because the U.S. operation was separate from UNAMIR, by pulling the plug on the former, Congress was not undermining an international effort—it was simply passing responsibility to a more appropriate authority. With the United States outside of the UN mission rather than within it, opponents of the mission, such as Senator Byrd, could argue that "burden-sharing" mandated an end to the unilateral U.S. role (see, for example, 140 *Cong. Rec.*, S10995).

Conclusion: Will They Ever Learn?

A natural question raised by this analysis is whether members of Congress have learned something over time from their repeated failure to make their opposition effective. Presumably, if members understand their dilemma, they might take steps to do something about it. And, indeed, there is some prima facie evidence of learning in the timing of congressional action in post–Cold War cases of armed humanitarian intervention. From Somalia to Kosovo, there is a trend toward earlier moves by Congress in an effort to act before the president has engaged in the kind of costly commitments that would render congressional resistance futile. With Somalia, authorization votes took place after troops had already been deployed—four months after in the case of the House. With Haiti, the authorization vote came the day after troops landed. With Bosnia, the House voted to deny funds for the operation about a week before the first troops were sent. As we saw, evidence from that case clearly suggests that members opposed to the mission saw virtue in having the vote before it started. Still, both House and Senate votes on authorization occurred shortly after the first troops arrived in Bosnia. In the case of Kosovo, there was congressional action even earlier. With peace talks still under way, the House ignored pleas from the administration and held a vote on March 11, 1999, on whether to authorize U.S. participation in the peacekeeping operation that would have ensued had the talks been successful. The comments of congressional leaders make it clear that they wanted to vote early to avoid having their hands tied. In defending the action, Speaker of the House J. Dennis Hastert (R-IL) explicitly referred to the lessons of the recent past: "What we have continually done over the past six or seven years is, when the president has moved troops some place, we have acquiesced, just nodded our heads and done it." (Pomper 1999b, 621).[11] In the end, the House voted to authorize the peacekeeping force—a vote that became moot when Yugoslavia refused to sign a deal. The Senate never acted on the peacekeeping question, but it did vote to authorize the air strikes the night before they began.

While this pattern suggests some learning and response by members of Congress, we should be careful not to imbue it with too much meaning. After all, two other things also changed across time. First, the 1994 elections brought about a shift from unified to divided government and a general increase in conflict between the two branches. Moreover, because Republicans tend to be more skeptical of humanitarian intervention, this meant that opponents had not only greater numbers but also better control over the agenda. Whereas Democratic leaders deferred to the president's wishes to delay any vote on the Haiti operation, Republican leaders felt no such responsibility in the later cases. The second factor that changed over time was beliefs about the desirability of humanitarian operations. While the Somalia intervention was greeted with enormous optimism, all subsequent ones have taken place in the shadow of that mission's failure.

Still, there is some additional evidence of learning in failed Republican efforts to restructure the relationship between Congress, the president, and the UN. Shortly after they came into power, House Republicans brought forward the National Security Revitalization Act (HR 7) and Senator Dole proposed the Peace Powers Act (S 5). While these bills had many provisions that do not touch on the dilemmas considered here, two in particular are worth noting. First, both bills would have reaffirmed the intent of the 1945 UN Participation Act by requiring any agreement between the UN Security Council and the president on matters of international peace and security to be approved by Congress (Hendrickson 1998, 243–45). Second, both included a requirement that Congress receive prior notification before any actions are taken in the UN Security Council. The Peace Powers Act, for example, requires that

> at least 15 days before any vote in the Security Council to authorize any United Nations peacekeeping activity or any other action under the Charter of the United Nations . . . which would involve the use of United States armed forces or the expenditure of United States funds, the President shall submit to the designated congressional committees a notification with respect to the proposed action.

Dole, touting the measure in a *New York Times* editorial on January 24, 1994, argued that this provision was necessary to "put Congress in the loop," making it a "full partner in financing and deployment decisions, not an afterthought." Clearly, Republicans sought to reverse the pattern by which the president and the UN moved first and then dared the Congress to overturn it. HR 7 passed in the House 241-181, with virtually all Republicans voting in favor of it; neither the House bill nor the Peace Powers Act made any progress in the Senate, however. Hendrickson (1998, 246) suggests that Republicans were reluctant to go forward without a veto-proof majority and were concerned that the failure of Dole's initiative would only embarrass him in the lead-up to his presidential run. Thus, while congressional opponents of humanitarian intervention clearly understand the dilemma they have faced, the domestic institutional structure—in this case, the presidential veto—has worked against implementing an effective response.

One final conclusion emerges from this analysis. The manner in which domestic institutions react to challenges from international institutions depends upon preexisting arrangements within the country and, at a deeper level, the interests that undergird those arrangements. This can be seen by noting one area in which Congress was more successful in obstructing the UN: the issue of dues. By 1999, the United States had accumulated roughly $1 billion in unpaid debts to the international body, due primarily to congressional obstacles. Conservative critics of the UN sought to withhold funds in order to force reforms, and antiabortion legislators used the funding issue as a way to block U.S. assistance to oversees family planning organizations. Thanks to a compromise struck in November 1999, the United States agreed to start repaying these debts, but the payments were made contingent on the UN's accepting a number of reforms. These included reducing the United States' share of the regular UN budget from 25 to 20 percent and cutting its share of the peacekeeping budget from 31 to 25 percent (Pomper 1999c). Thus, Congress has challenged the UN through one policy instrument—power over the purse—that clearly falls within its domain, that it has all the incentive in the world to retain, and whose negative effects on policy outcomes are less direct and dramatic. Meanwhile, Congress has been unwilling to fight with a policy instrument over which jurisdictional issues are blurred (at least de facto) and that is seen as too risky to employ—war powers. It thus appears that, when faced with challenges from international institutions, actors within domestic institutions pick their battles carefully.

Appendix

This appendix presents the formal solution to the model discussed in the text. First consider the president's move at his final node. If Congress blocked the president, then he goes forward if $v > c - \delta a$, where δ equals one if the president made a commitment and zero otherwise. If Congress did not block the president, then he goes forward if $v > -\delta a$. We now conjecture that the president's equilibrium strategy takes the following form: The president makes a commitment and goes forward regardless of what Congress does if $v > c - a$; the president makes a commitment and goes forward only when not resisted if $c - a > v > v^* \geq 0$, where the cutpoint v^* remains to be derived; the president does not make a commitment if $v < v^*$ and then goes forward only if Congress does not resist him and $v > 0$. Notice that no president for which $v < 0$ would ever want to make a commitment, because the best payoff from doing so is less than the payoff of zero that can always be assured by not making a commitment.

Let q^C denote the legislator's posterior belief that the president will go forward in the face of resistance, given that he has made a commitment, and let q^N be the corresponding beliefs, given that the president has not made a commitment. If, as posited, $v^* < c$, then the legislator knows that resistance will work when the president has not made a commitment. Thus, $q^N = 0$, and by equation (2), the legislator always prefers to resist as long as $x > 0$. If the president does make a commitment, then q^C is derived as in equation (1), with $v^{**} = c - a$, and the legislator resists only if equation (2) holds.

Given these strategies, the president knows that Congress will resist him if he makes no commitment. Because all types that do not make the commitment in equilibrium also prefer not to go forward if resisted, the payoff from not making the commitment is zero. If he does make a commitment, then he expects to be blocked with probability

$$\Pr(x > q^C b) = 1 - G(q^C b) \equiv s. \tag{3}$$

For the cutpoint at v^* to be in equilibrium, it must be the case that a president of that type is indifferent between making the commitment and not making it. Because a president of this type will not go forward if resisted, this condition is met when

$$s(-a) + (1 - s)v^* = 0, \quad \text{or} \quad s = \frac{v^*}{v^* + a}. \tag{4}$$

In equilibrium, then, the value of s from (4) must equal the value defined in (3). Thus,

$$G\left[\frac{1 - F(c - a)}{1 - F(v^*)} b\right] = \frac{a}{v^* + a}. \tag{5}$$

While this expression does not permit a closed-form solution for v^*, we can guarantee that a unique solution does exist and that it satisfies $0 \leq v^* \leq c - a$ as long as $G(b) > (a/c)$.

If this last condition is not met, then the equilibrium takes a slightly different form. Let v^{**} denote a cutpoint in the range $[c - a, c]$ such that the president makes a commitment and goes forward if $v > v^{**}$ and does not make a commitment and does not go forward in the face of resistance otherwise. Thus, in this equilibrium, all types that make a commitment will go forward regardless of what Congress does. Given this, $q^C = 1$, and the legislator only resists in the face of a presidential commitment only if $x > b$, which happens with probability $1 - G(b)$. A president of type v^{**} must be indifferent between making a commitment and not making a commitment, which has a certain payoff of zero. Thus,

$$(v^{**} - c)[1 - G(b)] + v^{**}G(b) = 0, \quad \text{or} \quad v^{**} = c[1 - G(b)]. \tag{6}$$

Notice that $0 \le v^{**} \le c$, as posited. Moreover, $v^{**} \ge c - a$ as long as $G(b) \le (a/c)$.

The two comparative-static predictions discussed in the text are easily derived. First, notice that the probability of resistance given to a commitment is always lower in the second equilibrium, $1 - G(b)$, than in the first, $1 - G(q^C b)$. Thus, increasing the audience costs from a to a' leads to a decrease in the probability of resistance as long as $a' > G(b)c > a$. Notice, however, that the probability of resistance need not be decreasing in a in the first equilibrium because the derivative of v^* with respect to a, implied by (5), is indeterminate. Next, consider what happens if the president's value for the operation increases from v to $v + z$, holding the distribution of v constant. Applying the implicit function theorem to (5) shows that v^* is decreasing in z as long as

$$\frac{f(c - a - z)}{1 - F(c - a - z)} > \frac{f(v^* - z)}{1 - F(v^* - z)}, \tag{7}$$

which is ensured by the fact that $v^* < c - a$ and the assumption that F has a monotone hazard rate. Since v^* is decreasing in z, the probability of resistance, given in (4), is as well. In the second equilibrium, the probability of resistance does not depend on z.

Notes

1. Some individual events from the CRS list have been consolidated into the broader missions of which they were a part. Missions limited to the evacuation of U.S. citizens, embassy security, or drug suppression are omitted, as are several incidents in which military forces on routine missions responded to attacks.

2. I am grateful to an anonymous reviewer for pointing out this very important distinction.

3. For evaluations of the effect of the War Powers Act, see Fisher and Adler 1998 and Auerswald and Cowhey 1997.

4. Such a strategy is appropriate if one can think of legislators as being arrayed on a single dimension, in which case it is the preferences of the median that determine the action of the whole. To determine whether such an assumption is warranted in this context, I used Poole-Rosenthal NOMINATE scores, which locate all members of Congress on a left-right dimension using all of their roll call votes (Poole and Rosenthal 1997). The algorithm also estimates a cutpoint for each vote — that is, the point in the left-right dimension that best separates those who voted for the measure from those who voted against it. If a vote on a given measure is primarily driven by a single dimension, then the cutpoint in this dimension should do a good job of predicting which way any given legislator voted. If, on the other hand, the cleavages on a measure cut across the left-right dimension, then a cutpoint in this dimension will do a poor job of predicting actual votes. An analysis of all the votes taken on the Haiti and Bosnia mission confirms that a legislator's left-right position is an excellent predictor of her or his vote. For example, for the nine House roll calls on Haiti, the estimated cutpoints on the left-right dimension correctly predict an average of 90 percent of the votes; for the seven House roll calls on Bosnia, they correctly predict an average of 89 percent of the votes. The comparable figure for all House roll calls in the 103rd and 104th Congresses is 88 percent. Similar figures hold for the Senate. I am grateful to Keith Poole for sharing these data with me.

5. For the purposes of this analysis, it does not matter whether these costs derive primarily from domestic audiences (Fearon 1994) or international audiences (Sartori 2002).

6. The only restriction we impose on these distributions is that both have positive density over their whole support. Moreover, we assume that F has a monotone hazard rate, a characteristic of many common distributions (see, e.g., Fudenberg and Tirole 1991, 267).

7. The source for these data is Public Opinion Online. Except for the matter of other countries' participation, the wording of the questions in these polls was broadly similar. All ask about support for U.S. military action to restore the democratically elected government of Haiti.

8. Specifically, these questions included the phrases "no military assistance from other countries" and "regardless of whether other countries participate."

9. Specifically, these questions included the phrases "as part of a United Nations-sponsored multinational invasion force," "along with troops from other countries," "part of a United Nations multinational force," "if other countries participate," "along with other countries," or "the United States and its allies." In cases in which the question was asked so that respondents could either support unilateral or multilateral action, two data points are shown, one reporting the percentage supporting the former and one reporting the sum of support across both options. This reflects the assumption that,

if the poll had forced respondents to choose between multilateral action and nothing, those who supported unilateral action in the actual poll would have favored the former.

10. The order in which the questions were asked was randomized.

11. See also Pomper 1999b; Eilperin and Dewar 1999; and Mitchell 1999.

Part 3. Persuasion

The Social Effects of International Institutions on Domestic (Foreign Policy) Actors

Alastair Iain Johnston

There has been a growing interest in recent years in so-called sociological approaches in international relations (IR) theory. Typically these are juxtaposed with so-called economic approaches. In the study of international institutions and cooperation, this usually means juxtaposing arguments that stress socially constructed "ideas" versus material "interests" as the primary sources of motivation for actors inside institutions.[1] More specifically, the fairly common claim is that sociological approaches stress normative motivations (social obligation, for instance), while economic approaches stress material motivations.

The reality is a little more complex than the stereotyping (on both sides of this divide, I might add). Sociological approaches include many kinds of arguments, some of which are clearly not consistent with economic approaches but some of which are. The inconsistent ones are by now well known. Typically the difference is characterized as being between the logic of appropriateness and the logic of consequences. Economic approaches reflect the latter. The dominant economic approach in IR theory—contractual institutionalism—generally sees institutions as collections of rules and norms that constrain state actors primarily through material sanctions[2] but do not fundamentally alter actor preferences. At best, new information provided by, or inside, institutions will alter "beliefs" about all facets of strategic interaction but will not alter the underlying goals and desires of the actors. There are reasons for this argument—some methodological, some aesthetic[3]—but it is fair to say that for contractual institutionalism there is no theoretical reason to expect that strategic interaction among optimizing actors changes their underlying preferences. The functionalist features of this approach mean that there are objectively certain types of institutional designs and features that are optimal for certain kinds of cooperation problems. The problem becomes ensuring that actors have the information and resources to harmonize cooperation problems and institutional design (Martin 1993b; Wallander 1999). By extension, designs that are not suited for the cooperation problem at hand are inefficient. Outcomes will be suboptimal (for states and for solving the cooperation problem).

Sociological approaches, on the other hand, generally treat institutions as environments of social interaction rather than as "boxes" of material constraints. This means the research focus shifts to the nonmaterial (for example, psychological, affective, ideological) effects on progroup behavior that interaction with other human agents can generate. Concretely, it means that social interaction can change actor desires, wants, and preferences. Indeed, one would be surprised if social interaction didn't have these effects, given the tenuousness with which preferences over ends are held by most people. Specifically, the ways in which preferences and/or indifference curves among preferences change will be structured by three variables or moving parts: (1) socialization of actor 1 prior to entry into a social interaction; (b) socialization of actors $2 \ldots n$ prior to entry into a social interaction; (c) and the design of the institution within which this interaction takes place. (This latter variable refers to the features of the institution that either encourage or retard the changes in the desires, wants, and preferences established prior to interaction.) Once new preferences are internalized (or old ones reinforced) actor behavior is explained by role theoretic arguments. That is, actions that are consistent with the roles associated with a particular identity are enacted on normative grounds. Conversely, actions that are inconsistent with these roles are ruled out on normative grounds or are simply left unconsidered.

But the logics-of-consequences approach does not summarize the range of sociological arguments that one could make about institutions and cooperation. One can easily construct an optimization model of human behavior where the desire being maximized is nonmaterial and social, requiring interaction with other agents who, essentially, bestow or withdraw what is valued by the actor. As is evident, this is not much different in principle from economic arguments, though in practice the latter tend not to focus on nonmaterial optimization. Even so, as I will argue, social optimizing arguments do provide alternative explanations for cooperation that economic arguments tend to miss.

Thus, to clear up a misconception, sociological approaches do not exclude optimizing behavior. They can add a range of different things to be optimized, things that by definition only exist when two or more human agents interact socially — prestige, self-esteem, honor, status (all rooted in identity), for instance. They also suggest that when these goals are in conflict with material goals, the latter do not always win out. Or, even when material goals are the primary consideration, there are social processes that can lock in ways of doing things such that the long-term equilibrium behavior is not materially optimal.[4] But they also suggest that there may be motivations that are far less focused on obvious, individually beneficial consequences and that are so taken for granted that the calculus of the consequences becomes perfunctory at best. Options and outcomes may simply not be conceivable for one set of actors compared to another set, because of variation in the range of socially produced categories of analysis and evidence. Sociological approaches make the study of international institutions, therefore, much messier but more realistic—less precise but more accurate. But this messiness may be compensated by the possibility, as I will suggest at the end of this chapter, that there may be implications for the conditions under which cooperation emerges that heretofore have been missed.

Thus sociological approaches do not entirely replace economic motivations at the heart of methodological individualist predelictions of contractual institutionalism. Nor do they undermine "parsimonious" theory building about the impact of institutions on the behavior of states. Indeed, they validate such theory building by allowing genuinely alternative models of actor motivation. A parsimonious explanation may in the end be quite complicated and may require the incorporation of a range of values, including sociological ones. But we won't know this until the impact of these other variables is explored.

The aim of this chapter is to examine in preliminary fashion two social processes that may mediate the impact of international institutions on state foreign policy processes. One is persuasion and the other has been termed "social influence." This is not a rigorous test of these processes against alternative explanations, though I will address some of the possible alternatives during the discussion. Rather, it is merely a plausability probe that extends arguments in the literature on persuasion and social influence to cooperation in international institutions.

The chapter's mandate—the impact of international institutions on domestic (in this case foreign policy–related) agencies and actors—does mean, however, that we need to be explicit about what causes and what effects a sociological approach would look for. The dependent variable, strictly speaking, is not foreign policy outputs. Rather, it focuses on whether there are changes in the structure, identity, and interests of these agencies that are attributable to interaction with the international institution. This is a less demanding task than showing whether these changes have, ultimately, any impact on foreign policy. The effect of any of these changes in the foreign policy agency, or agencies, on state foreign policy will, of course, depend on the structure of the foreign policy process. But the first step in exploring the impact on outputs obviously is to determine whether social interaction has any impact on the identity and interests of the agencies and actors themselves. The independent variable, at base, is the degree of involvement in international institutions. Practically speaking, this means, How do two key variables, namely institutional design and prior identities or interests of an agent or actor, interact to produce changes in the identity, interests, and arguments of actors inside domestic institutions? The microprocesses that may govern this interaction are, as I noted previously, persuasion and social influence. Implicit in the arguments examined here is that noninvolvement will mean these effects don't appear. The "null" hypothesis, then, is that involvement should have none of the effects that socialization microprocesses suggest ought to appear. Since socialization, however, entails change over time in any particular agent (the effects of exposure to the socializing environment is, presumably, in some sense cumulative), it is hard to run a sophisticated quasi-experimental design where one can expose identical domestic agencies and actors to different starting conditions (involvement or noninvolvement in an international institution). So the best one can do at this stage is to ask, How do these features of a domestic institution change over time after exposure to an international institution (and its social environment), and do they change in ways that are consistent with persuasion and social influence? If the null hypothesis is rejected, we can then move on to a careful comparison with cases of noninvolvement. If the null hypothesis cannot be rejected, then there is no point in going on to such comparisons.

The unit of analysis here is the individual or small group (for example, the diplomats, analysts, strategists, and political leaders who are exposed to or participate in the social environments inside international institutions). This differs from many of the sociologically oriented studies to date. For the most part, when IR specialists or sociological institutionalists have looked for the effects of social interaction at the international level the unit of analysis has tended to be the state (or state elites in a fairly aggregated way). And the predominant method has been largely correlational, looking for the presence of new local practices that are consistent with new global norms (Eyre and Suchman 1996; Meyer et al. 1997; Finnemore 1996b, 1996c; Price 1998). This presents obvious problems when examining particular institutions as social environments since states as unitary actors don't participate in institutions; rather, state agents do—for example, diplomats, decision makers, analysts, policy specialists, and nongovernmental agents of state principals. Moreover, treating the state as a unitary actor presents problems when applying the most well-developed literature on socialization found typically in social psychology, sociology, communications theory, and even political socialization theory. Most of the literature examines the effects of socialization on individuals or small groups. And most of this literature acknowledges that there should be a fair degree of variation in the degree of progroup conformity due to local patterns of resistance and contestation. This variation tends to get lost in the extant sociological literature in IR. This neglect of microprocesses and local variation is surprising, given constructivists' focus on reflective action by multiple agents: If this kind of agency exists in the diffusion of norms, what happens when it runs into reflective action by multiple agents at the receiving end of these "teaching" efforts? This question is left unexplored.[5] The result is, however, that causal processes by which systemic normative structures (constitutive, regulatory and prescriptive) affect behavior are mostly assumed rather than shown.[6]

Thus a sociological approach allows (even demands) that the unit of analysis be the individual or small group. As Cederman (1997) points out in reference specifically to constructivism, its ontology can best be captured by the notion of complex adaptive systems whereby social structures and agent characteristics are mutually constitutive, or locked in tight feedback loops, where small perturbations in the characteristics of agents interacting with each other can have large, nonlinear effects on social structures (see also Axelrod 1997; Hamman 1998). Thus it matters how individual agents or small groups are socialized because their impacts on larger emergent properties of the social environment can be quite dramatic.[7] This focus on individuals and small groups also enables sociologically oriented analysts to deal with the legitimate critique from proponents of choice theoretic approaches that what is observed as the normatively motivated behavior of a group at one level may be the aggregation of the strategic behavior of many subactors at a lower level (Lake and Powell 1997, 33). There are good reasons, then, for sociological studies of international institutions to "go micro."[8]

The empirical data come mostly from China's behavior in international security institutions in the 1990s. From a research design perspective, this is not a bad place to go to look for the effects of sociological processes. Sociological perspectives suggest that the impact of social environments will be greatest on new members, inductees, and novices. That is, interaction between a novice or an inductee and a social group leads to changes in the actor's preferences over ends and actions, or both. Socialization is a process of creating members, inducting them into the preferred ways of thinking and acting. In Stryker and Statham's words, "Socialization is the generic term used to refer to the processes by which the newcomer—the infant, rookie, trainee, for example—becomes incorporated into organized patterns of interaction" (1985, 325). Berger and Luckman define the term as "the comprehensive and consistent induction of an individual into the objective world of a society or sector of it" (1996, 130). Ichilov refers to political socialization as "the universal processes of induction into any type of regime" (1990, 1).

Noviceness is, unfortunately, undertheorized in IR. Different states face similar exogenous choices with different "life" experiences. If the two major microprocesses of social interaction are to have a profound impact on state or substate actors, it should be most obvious in novices. Who are novices in IR? The obvious candidates are the agents of newly liberated or created states or of recently integrated states, such as the newly decolonized states starting in the 1950s and the newly independent states that emerged in the wake of the Soviet Union's collapse, for instance. These are states that are most likely to experience the IR equivalence of "primacy effects," where early experience and information will have out-of-proportion effects on inferences drawn from later experiences and information.[9] New states literally have had to set up foreign policy institutions, to determine what their foreign policy interests are on a range of novel issue areas, and to decide in which of a myriad social environments in IR they should participate (for example, which institutions, which communities of states—middle power, major power, developed, or developing—and which competitive and cooperative relations to foster).[10] It is precisely in the foreign policy communities of these kinds of states where one should expect social effects of involvement in international institutions to be greatest.

China is not exactly a novice in the same way as are, say, the newly independent states of the former Soviet Union. But in terms of its involvement in international institutional life, it clearly went

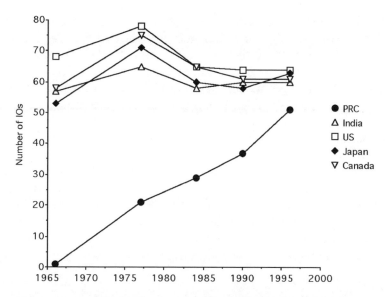

Fig. 1. Comparative involvement in IGOs. (Data from *Yearbook of International Organizations* 1985–86, 1989–90, 1996–99.)

through a period of noviceness in the 1980s and into the 1990s, as it moved from virtual aloofness from international institutions to participation rates that are not all that different from those of the United States and other developed states (see fig. 1).

But China is also a hard realpolitik state where novice foreign policy actors will nonetheless approach institutions with fairly skeptical arguments about the value of multilateral cooperation for achieving state security.[11] On top of this, Chinese leaders have had to calculate the costs and benefits of commitments to multilateral security institutions first in a bipolar era and then, after 1991, in a virtual unipolar era. These are material structural conditions under which involvement in, let alone agreement with, institutions that might constrain relative power should be viewed with a great deal of skepticism. In other words, whether one stresses domestic ideational constraints or systemic material constraints, one should not expect a whole lot of cooperation inside security institutions. Moreover, as I will discuss in more detail later, the cases from which I draw the evidence for these socialization microprocesses do not entail material sidepayments or sanctions as exogenous incentives to cooperate.

Thus China is an interesting place to start a plausibility probe, since its status as both a hard realpolitik state and a novice means that the effects of socialization microprocesses (if there are any) should be unlikely, but if they occur it should be relatively easy to observe the potential contrast between a pre- and postsocialized China.[12] This means, interestingly, that China is at one and the same time a most likely and a least likely case for socialization.

The evidence I use comes from acquired documents, interviews, and opportunities for participant observation while researching the development of China's arms control community and policy over the past fifteen years.[13] Certain ethnographic methods are unavoidable because of the opaqueness of China's policy process, especially as it relates to security issues. But the methodological value of the China case, combined with the real-world implications of China's participation in global and regional security institutions, justifies, I believe, this kind of evidence-challenged research.

Persuasion

As a microprocess of socialization, persuasion involves changing minds, opinions, and attitudes about causality and affect (identity) in the absence of overtly material or mental coercion.[14] It can lead to common knowledge (which may or may not be cooperative), or it can lead to a homogenization of interests. That is, actors can be persuaded that they are indeed in competition with each other or that they share many cooperative interests. The point is, however, that the distance between actors' basic causal understandings closes as a result of successful persuasion.

Persuasion is a prevalent tool of social influence. Social psychologists have shown, for instance, that in interpersonal relationships people tend to rank the changing of others' opinions very high in a list of influence strategies, regardless of whether the other is considered a friend or an enemy (Rule and Bisanz 1987, 192). Some political scientists have called persuasion the "core" of politics, the "central aim of political interaction" (Mutz, Sniderman, and Brody 1996, 1). In Gibson's view, politics is all about persuasion: "Real politics involves arguments; it involves people drawing a conclusion, being exposed to countervailing ideas, changing views, drawing new conclusions" (1998, 821; see also Berger 1995, 1).

The sociology-influenced literature in IR has tended to neglect how precisely persuasion works, despite its centrality to the constructivist argument. By usage persuasion usually means something akin to the noncoercive communication of new normative understandings that are internalized by actors such that new courses of action are viewed as entirely reasonable and appropriate. Here much of the literature tends to refer in some form or another to Habermas's theory of communicative action. The argument is that social interaction is not all strategic bargaining. Rather, it also involves arriving at shared basic assumptions about the deep structure of the actors' interaction: Who are legitimate players, what are the legitimate interests to be pursued, and what is a legitimate value to be bargained over? Even more important, this agreement needs to be narrow enough so that a vast range of potential equilibria that could arise in their strategic interaction becomes off-limits.[15] Thus bargaining is not simply a process of manipulating exogenous incentives to elicit desired behavior from the other side. Rather, it requires argument and deliberation in an effort to change the minds of others.[16] As Hasenclever, Mayer, and Rittberger put it, "the parties to a conflict enter a discourse where they first try to bring about agreement concerning the relevant features of a social situation and then advance reasons why a certain behavior has to be avoided. These reasons—as far as they are *convincing*—internally motivate the parties to behave in accordance with the previously elaborated interpretation and the justified expectations of others" (1997, 176–77, emphasis mine; see also Knoke 1994, 3; James 1998, 7).

The problem here is that it is not obvious that communications theory provides any insights into reasons for the success or failure of persuasion. That communicative action has to be convincing is a huge requirement, and thus far constructivists have not really shown how debates over common knowledge, for example, convince actors to agree to a "mutually arrived at interpretation" of social facts. Under what social or material conditions is communicative action more likely to be successful? How would one know? The conditions seem to be quite demanding, involving a high degree of prior trust, empathy, honesty, and power equality.[17]

There is a great deal of research in communications theory, social psychology, and sociology that focuses on these questions. Unfortunately, there is no obvious way of summarizing what is a disparate and complex literature (see Zimbardo and Leippe 1991, 127–67).[18] But let me try.

Essentially, for the purposes of this chapter, there are two main ways in which an actor is persuaded. First, the actor can engage in a high-intensity process of cognition, reflection, and argument about the content of new information—what Bar-Tal and Saxe call "cognitive capacity" (1990, 122). The actor weighs evidence, puzzles through counterattitudinal arguments, and comes to conclusions different from those with which he or she began. That is, the merits of the argument are persuasive, given internalized standards for evaluating truth claims. Arguments are more persuasive and more likely to affect behavior when they are considered systematically and, thus, when they are linked to other attitudes and schema in a complex network of causal connections and cognitive cues (Wu and Shaffer 1987, 687; Petty, Wegener, and Fabrigar 1997, 616; Zimbardo and Leippe 1991, 192–97). This process of cognition, linking one set of attitudes to another, is more likely to occur when the environment cues and allows for the actor to consider these connections. In other words, it is not likely to be spontaneous. As Gibson has shown with political intolerance among Russian voters, levels of intolerance and tolerance toward political opponents, and the overall balance between these two extremes, will change if counterattitudinal arguments are presented to respondents in ways that compel them to think harder about the implications of their initial attitudes. Thinking harder simply means people are cued, and have the time, to connect the implications of their initial attitude to outcomes that might affect their interests based on different sets of attitudes (1998, 826–31). Thus the probability of some change in attitudes through cognition increases in an iterated, cognition-rich environment (where there is plenty of new information that cues linkages to other attitudes and interests) (Sniderman, Brody, and Tetlock 1991, 210; Gibson 1998, 844).

Second, the actor can be persuaded because of her or his affect relationship to the persuader: Here the persuadee looks for cues about the nature of this relationship to judge the legitimacy of counterattitudinal arguments.[19] Thus information from in-groups is more convincing than that from out-groups. Information from culturally recognized authorities (for example, scientists, doctors, religious leaders) is more convincing than that from less authoritative sources. This will be especially true for novices who have little information about an issue on which to rely for guidance (Zimbardo and Leippe 1991, 70; Wetherell 1987, 154).[20] Information from sources that are liked is more convincing than that from sources that are disliked. Liking will increase with more exposure, contact, and familiarity. The desire for social proofing means that information accepted through consensus or supermajority in a valued group will be more convincing than if the group is divided about how to interpret the message (Petty, Wegener, and Fabrigar 1997, 612, 617, 623, 627, 629; Kuklinski and

Hurley 1996, 129–31; Napier and Gershenfeld 1987, 159; Isen 1987, 206–10, 211; Axsom, Yates, and Chaiken 1987, 30–31).[21]

Obviously persuasion in the end is a combination of all of these processes, and it is hard to run controls that might isolate the effects of any one.[22] People are more likely to think hard and favorably about a proposition, for instance, when it comes from a high-affect source, in part because affect helps trigger resistances to information from other sources (Mohr 1996, 81–82). But one can still identify ideal combinations that could, in principle, be tested. Given, then, an effort by a persuader to provide information with a view to changing basic principled, causal, or factual understandings, there are certain kinds of social environments that ought to be especially conducive to persuasion. These conditions occur under the following circumstances:

- when the actor is highly cognitively motivated to analyze counterattitudinal information (for example, a very novel social environment);
- when the persuader is a highly authoritative member of a small, intimate, high-affect in-group to which the persuaded also belongs or wants to belong;
- when the actor has few prior, ingrained attitudes that are inconsistent with the counterattitudinal message, say, when the actor is a novice or an inductee in a new social environment or when the perceived threat from counterattitudinal groups is low;
- when the agent is relatively autonomous from the principal (for example, when the issue is technical or is ignored by the principal);
- when the actor is exposed to counterattitudinal information repeatedly over time.

In practice, as I will discuss in a moment, these conditions are more likely to hold in some kinds of institutions than in other kinds.

These conditions suggest some more specific hypotheses about the relationship between international institutional design and persuasion effects among actors at the level of national foreign policy agencies. These hypotheses depend on some systematic conceptualization of variation in institutional design, that is, a typology of institutional forms or institutional social environments. Unfortunately, none exists in IR at the moment. But one could imagine at least several dimensions for coding institutions as social environments. Here I borrow and expand on the typology of domestic institutions developed by Rogowski (1999):

1. membership: for example, small and exclusive or large and inclusive
2. franchise: for example, where the authoritativeness of members is equally allocated or unevenly (though legitimately) allocated
3. decision rules: for example, unanimity, consensus, majority, supermajority
4. mandate: for example, to provide information, to deliberate and resolve, to negotiate and legislate
5. autonomy of agents from principals: low through high

Different institutional designs (combinations of measures of these five dimensions) would thus create different kinds of social environments, leading to differences in the likelihood and degree of persuasion and social influence. To take one extreme ideal, persuasion is likely to be the most prevalent and powerful socialization process when membership is small (social liking and in-group identity effects on the persuasiveness of the counterattitudinal message are strongest); when the franchise recognizes the special authoritativeness of a small number of actors (authoritativeness of the messenger is likely to be high); when decision rules are based on consensus (requires deliberation, with concomitant cognition effects); when the institution's mandate is deliberative (requires active cognition, and agents may be more autonomous since there is no obvious distribution of benefits at stake, thus there is less pressure to represent the principal); and when the autonomy of agents is high, for example, when the issue is narrowly technical or when the principal just doesn't care much (when the principal is less attentive or relevant).[23] All these design-dependent effects will be enhanced for novices who are exposed to the environment over long periods of time (Zimbardo and Leippe 1991, chap. 5).

Assuming that an actor enters the institution and its particular social environment with preferences and causal and principled beliefs that are at odds with those of the group, if persuasion is at work one should expect to see the actor's convergence with these preferences and beliefs after exposure to this environment. One would also expect to see conformist behavior later in the interaction with the group that would not have been expected earlier on.

Persuasion inside the ASEAN Regional Forum?

Broadly speaking, the empirical expectations from the literature on persuasion seem borne out by China's participation in the ASEAN Regional Forum (ARF). The ARF was set up in 1994 as a forum for high-level discussion among states in the region on security issues. It is the only intergovernmental security institution as such in the Asia-Pacific. It is relatively small (around twenty states) and is very weakly institutionalized, operating without its own secretariat, for instance. The language of the ARF underscores this informality: Members are called "participants" because "members" sounds too permanent. Around two years into its operation it finally set up intersessional meetings to allow more ongoing detailed discussions between the annual meetings of foreign ministers. The decision rule is flexible consensus, whereby the chair of all ARF meetings (who must be from an ASEAN country) has a fair amount of leeway and legitimacy to call a consensus even when some states might not be completely supportive. This norm allows the ARF to gradually move issues onto its agenda even when some actors are not entirely on board. Thus, unlike many other consensus institutions (Lindell 1988), there is, in practice, no veto or unanimity rule in the ARF.[24]

There are also no negotiations over the distribution of "goods." The ARF is not treaty institutions. The working philosophy of the institution—its ideology, if you will—is counterrealpolitik, drawing on notions of cooperative security, for example, the nonlegitimacy of military force for resolving disputes, security through reassurance rather than unilateral military superiority, nonprovocative defense, and transparency. Behavior that is reassuring rather than threatening should be the rule, such that the ARF can "develop a more predictable and constructive pattern of relations for the Asia-Pacific region."[25] This security philosophy implicitly assumes that states are essentially status quo (or can be socialized to accept the status quo), and as such ARF ideology takes it as both normatively and empirically true that reassurance behavior is a better route to security than traditional realpolitik strategies. Security is positive sum.[26] To this end, the normatively appropriate and empirically effective means for achieving security involve the building of trust through confidence-building measures and the defusing of security problems through preventive diplomacy and conflict management. This theory of security is supposed to be the basis for developing habits of cooperation among ARF participants.

In short, the ARF is almost explicitly designed to accentuate persuasion through social interaction. What effect has this environment had on Chinese diplomats and analysts who have participated in the ARF or its related Track II activities, such as the Council for Security Cooperation in the Asia Pacific (CSCAP) and ARF-sponsored working groups on confidence-building measures (CBMs)?[27]

It is quite clear that the public and internal discourse in China on multilateral security dialogues in the Asia-Pacific prior to China's entry into the ARF in 1994 was highly skeptical of their value. Such institutions, Chinese leaders worried, could be dominated by the United States or Japan. Or China would be outnumbered, and sensitive bilateral disputes where China might have an advantage in bargaining power might be multilateralized (Garrett and Glaser 1994; Yuan 1996; Johnston 1990; Interview 1996d). The skepticism of multilateralism was rooted in even deeper realpolitik assumptions about international relations where structurally (and sometimes ideologically) induced zero-sum competition among sovereign states necessitated unilateral security strategies.

Since China has entered the ARF, however, there have been some noticeable changes in the discourse. Initial statements made to the ARF (for example, Foreign Minister Qian Qichen's comments at the first ARF in 1994) stressed what can only be seen as traditional rules of the road for the management of relations among sovereign, autonomous states. These included the five principles of peaceful coexistence, economic ties on the basis of equality and mutual benefit, and the peaceful settlement of disputes (Yuan 1996, 11). Terms, concepts, and phrases associated with common or cooperative security were absent.

By late 1996 and early 1997, however, Chinese working-level officials directly involved in ARF-related affairs began to articulate concepts that were, to a degree, in tension with traditional realpolitik arguments.[28] Most significant in this regard was that by early 1997 ARF-involved analysts and officials had unofficially floated a concept of "mutual security."[29] The term meant, according to one Chinese participant, that "for you to be secure, your neighbor had to be secure," a common security concept based on the notion of "win-win" (see Chu 1997). It is possible the Chinese may have felt under pressure to develop an original Chinese contribution to the multilateral security discourse. So "mutual security" was preferred to "common or cooperative security," as these were terms too closely identified with the Organization for Security and Cooperation in

Europe (OSCE) process and thus were too provocative inside the Chinese policy process.

Around this time, another analyst involved in ARF-related work in a think tank attached to the State Council wrote a paper on confidence building in the Asia-Pacific. The paper provided a sophisticated explanation of Western theories of CBMs, noting for example the military reassurance purposes of CBMs. The author also elaborated on mutual security, noting that the concept was embodied in the April 1996 Five Power (China, Russia, Kazakhstan, Kyrgyzstan, Tajikistan) Treaty on CBMs (Liu 1997).

The invocation of the Five Power Treaty is important. The treaty comes as close to a OSCE-type CBM agreement as anything in the Asia-Pacific region, with provision for limits on the size and type of military maneuvers allowed within certain distances of borders, provisions for military observers and military exercises, and so forth.[30] In internal Chinese debates over multilateralism, whether one believed that the principles of the treaty had broader applicability to the region was an indicator of one's skepticism toward multilateralism in general.[31] That those articulating the concept of mutual security would also invoke the Five Power Treaty as an example, precedent, or exemplar suggests that the term signified an acceptance of more intrusive and formal security institutions. Publicly during most of 1997, however, the term "mutual security" was not fully integrated into policy discourse.

This situation changed by November 1997. The Chinese paper presented to the ARF Intersessional Support Group on CBMs in Brunei explicitly noted that the Five Power Treaty embodied the notion of mutual security and could be used as a source of ideas for the rest of the Asia-Pacific. Mutual security was defined as an environment where the "security interests of one side should not undermine those of the other side. . . . This kind of security is a win-win rather than zero-sum game" (China 1997, 3).

The concept of mutual security received the highest-level endorsement when it was included in remarks by Foreign Minister Qian Qichen of China at the Private Sector's Salute to ASEAN's Thirtieth Anniversary in December 1997. Since then the thinking on multilateralism has continued to evolve.

As expected, the thinking is closest to ARF ideology in the agency most directly involved in regional security dialogues, namely, the Ministry of Foreign Affairs' (MOFA) Asia Department. In 1998 the Asia Department, realizing that it required more sophisticated theoretical arguments to bolster and justify the mutual security discourse and policy inside the policy process, commissioned a study by a respected specialist in regional multilateralism from the Chinese Academy of Social Sciences (Interview 1999c).[32] The report explicitly argued that military power and traditional territorial-based concepts of national security were no longer the most important issues in China's future security in the region. Rather, the report argued, China faced an increasing array of nontraditional security problems that could not be solved through the augmentation of national military power alone and thus should focus more energy on developing multilateral cooperative solutions to security problems, including greater activism in the ARF. The report noted—in recognition of security dilemma dynamics—that China's behavior on the ground was one reason for states' worrying about China's rising power. To deal with this, the report argued, China had to signal that it basically accepted extant rules of international and regional order while trying to moderate these rules and norms through existing international institutions and procedures. In other words, China's rise was a potentially destabilizing element in international relations because of perceptions of Chinese power in the past, but China had to credibly signal that it was in essence a status quo power. The report explicitly borrowed arguments and concepts from Western, including Canadian, multilateralists and included an appendix that introduced some of the multilateralist lexicon to its audience (for example, integration theory, interdependence theory, and democratic peace theory) (Zhang 1998).

The Chinese discourse on multilateralism, then, has moved quite some distance—from public skepticism to informal articulations of mutual security and common security to public affirmation of the concepts. Moreover, the concepts have been explicitly linked to a real-world institutional exemplar of these principles, the Five Power Treaty, a document that is consistent with, indeed modeled in some ways after, OSCE-style concepts. This discourse is most prominently identified with people and organizations actively involved in ARF and ARF-related Track II activities.

My argument here rests, obviously, on the critical question of whether the multilateralism discourse has, in some sense, been internalized among those working most closely in the ARF environment. The evidence that this may be the case is indirect at the moment.[33] But China's involvement in the ARF and related processes seems to have led to the emergence of a small group of policymakers with an emerging, if tension-ridden, normative commitment to multilateralism because it is "good" for Chinese and regional security. ARF policy in China was put in the hands of the Comprehensive Division of the Asia Department of the MOFA. This division did the preparatory work for ARF meetings and Track II activities. Initially, in ARF activities the Chinese representatives were unaccustomed to the give-and-take of corridor debate and negotiation. They also came to the discussions with a watchful eye for developments that might impinge on sensitive security or domestic political issues. Over time, however, with experience in informal discussion and familiarity with the ARF norms of interaction, these officers have become more engaged, relaxed, and flexible.

Most interesting has been their apparent endorsement, within limits, of multilateralism as being compatible with Chinese security interests. More than one foreign diplomat in Beijing, interacting extensively with these MOFA officers, has suggested that their agenda is to tie China gradually into regional security institutions so that some day China's leaders will be bound by the institutions. They see ARF involvement as a process of educating their own government. Some have even remarked that involvement in the ARF has reduced the likelihood of China's resort to force over disputes in the South China Sea because there are now more diplomatic (read, multilateral) tools at China's disposal (Interview 1996b, 1998d; Acharya 1998). The main conduit for the infusion of these sorts of ideas, into this group at least, has tended to be experience in Track I and II activities, not so much the absorption of academic literature on multilateralism (Interview 1996b, 1996d).[34] It seems that this group's influence over Chinese ARF policy may have been helped by further institutional change in China. In January 1998, the Asia Department set up a separate division just to handle ARF and Track II diplomacy. It has been the Asia Department, and in particular the ARF division, that has most actively promoted internal research on how to flesh out concepts such as mutual security, cooperative security, and common security. The goal is to use these arguments internally to justify more activism in regional multilateral institutions (Interview 1998, 1999).

There is some intriguing concrete evidence of the commitment these individuals have in protecting China's multilateral activities from domestic political critics—hence an indication of their growing normative stake in the ARF. A senior Canadian official involved in ARF diplomacy reported that the Chinese delegates to ARF discussions apparently did not report back to Beijing any references by other delegations to the CSCE as a possible model for the ARF. The

Council on Security Cooperation in Europe (CSCE) is not just a symbol of a more intrusive, constraining regime; it is also a regime that deals with human rights (Smith 1996, 22). Downplaying this information was probably deemed important to preserve support or acquiescence for further institutionalization of the ARF. Other Canadian diplomats have reported that sometimes the multilateralists in the MOFA will help other states frame proposals for ARF-related activities in ways that will make these more acceptable in Beijing (Interview 1998d). While only anecdotal, this evidence suggests that over time the character of Chinese obstruction or resistance in its ARF diplomacy on the ground has shifted from protecting given Chinese interests to protecting Chinese multilateral diplomacy from potential domestic opposition. Tentatively speaking, one could plausibly see this as diplomacy more empathetic with the institution and less empathetic with other People's Republic of China (PRC) constituencies that may have different views of the value of multilateralism. In other words, it may reflect an emergent solidarity with the institution, its ideology, and its participants.[35]

Obviously, one would like to do a more systematic comparison of the attitudes toward multilateralism of those exposed to the ARF process and of those not exposed. Also, one would like to ascertain the routes through which persuasion has or hasn't worked inside the ARF. Why might Australian or Canadian ideas about common security be more persuasive than U.S. skepticism inside the ARF, for instance? One would expect to see a hierarchy of persuasion whereby diplomats in the MOFA directly exposed to the ARF environment would rank higher on some index of multilateralism followed by PLA officers who have also been exposed, followed by MOFA officials and PLA officers without any direct experience in the ARF. I have no way of conducting such systematic research, but based on observation and conversations with regional security specialists in China, I think this ranking generally holds. The truest believers are in the regional security division of the Asia Department in MOFA. And PLA officers who handle regional security in the Comprehensive Office of the Foreign Affairs Bureau of the Ministry of Defense are probably more sympathetic to multilateralism than are other PLA officers.

There are, of course, other possible explanations for the emergence of a multilateralist discourse within this ARF policy community. First, it could all reflect a deceptive effort to exploit cooperation from other states. A realpolitik actor would have incentives to use such a discourse deceptively: If one believed one were in a Prisoner's Dilemma (PD) environment, cooperative discourses might be designed to encourage others to cooperate, creating opportunities to acquire the "temptation" payoff. This would, in principle, be especially attractive to an actor in an institution like the ARF, with little or no monitoring capacity and no ability to punish defection. Many in the U. S. government view the mutual security discourse precisely as just that: a deceptive effort to redirect attention from inconsistencies between Chinese security behavior (sharp increases in military expenditures, provocative military exercises, and so forth) and the ideology of the institution, while trying to underscore the inconsistencies between U. S. bilateral alliance strategies in the region and the ideology of the institution.[36]

I am not convinced of the pure deceptiveness of this discourse, however, for at least two reasons. First, there is a relatively easy test of this hypothesis. If it is right, then the strongest proponents of the mutual security discourse, and the Five Power Treaty as an exemplar agreement for the region, should be the strongest opponents of U.S. bilateral alliances in the region, for example. A careful tracking of the discourse, as I tried to do earlier suggests that the strongest proponents are precisely those who in private interactions with diplomats and scholars indicate a deeper commitment to multilateralism—functional specialists in the MOFA are somewhat more pro-American voices in the strategic analysis community. While these people are generally opposed to the expansion of U.S.-Japanese security cooperation and would like to use multilateral diplomacy to pressure the United States to limit the scope of its military cooperation with Japan, they also recognize that the alliance is a reality and may indeed constrain Japanese remilitarization.[37] Those who are less enamored with the mutual security discourse are found mostly in the military, and it is in the PLA where some of the strongest skeptics of the U.S.-Japan alliance are found. Moreover, the Chinese CBM proposals that were clearly biased against U.S. military power in the region (for example, observers at jointly military exercises, reductions in military reconnaissance activities aimed at ARF members, and so forth) appeared first in 1995–96, well before the "mutual security" concept emerged, and were promoted by the PLA, not the Asia Department of the MOFA.

Second, if protomultilateralist arguments in China were all only deception, we would expect that, as the ARF handles increasingly intrusive and sensitive issues that may impinge on core interests or relative power issues, the PRC would balk at further change in the institution and agenda. That the ARF is already discussing the South China Sea in multilateral terms, intrusive CBMs, and preventive diplomacy mechanisms is evidence to the contrary. Moreover, that there are Chinese (proto)multilateralists who are now holding up the Five Power Treaty as a potential model for East Asia suggests that PD preferences are no longer uniform across the actors in the Chinese policy process. Finally, if the multilateral discourse were deceptive one would not find it promoted in internal studies and documents that are not supposed to reach the light of day.

Another possible explanation is that the acceptability of multilateralist discourses was due to new information about the benign nature of the ARF. As contractualists might put it, beliefs about, and hence strategies toward, multilateralism have changed, but preferences and interests have not. At most, more favorable attitudes toward multilateralism might serve instrumental reputational purposes. The problem I have is with the concept of "new information." IR theory has tended to underestimate the uncertain status of new information. Information is interpreted and the same information can be interpreted differently in the context of similar institutional rules and structures. Empirically, we know that the same information will be interpreted differently depending on whether it comes from "people like us" (the information is more authoritative and persuasive) or comes from a devalued "other" (Kuklinski and Hurley 1996, 127). Social context is an important variable in how well information reduces uncertainty in a transaction and in which direction this uncertainty is reduced (for example, clarifying the other as a friend or adversary).

Thus, if all of China's ARF decision makers were realpolitik opportunists (that is, if they believed they were playing a PD game in some form in East Asia) and if this basic worldview were fixed, then new information would be interpreted through these lenses. It is probably true that the initial signals provided by an underinstitutionalized and nonintrusive ARF in 1994 could have been interpreted as nonthreatening by realpoliticians.[38] But as the ARF agenda and institution evolved, the signals should have been interpreted with increasing alarm by realpoliticians, since the trend lines were toward issues and procedures that could place some limits on relative military power. Yet, for a small group of China's ARF policymakers these signals were reinterpreted in less, not more, threatening ways.[39] That this group of policymakers eventually believed this information *was* reassuring, while still expressing concern that others in the policy process (with more realpolitik views of multilateralism) might see this information as less reassuring, suggests that the information provided by the ARF is often not unproblematically reassuring. Protomultilateralists did not enter the ARF with this more sanguine interpretation of this new information. Rather, this interpretation of the information came with exposure to the ARF and related Track II processes.

Social Influence

Social influence refers to a class of microprocesses that elicit pronormative behavior through the distribution of social rewards and punishments. Rewards might include status, a sense of belonging, a sense of well-being derived from conformity with role expectations, and so forth. Punishments might include shaming, shunning, exclusion and demeaning, or dissonance derived from actions inconsistent with role and identity. The effect of (successful) social influence is an actor's conformity with the position advocated by a group as a result of "real or imagined group pressure" (Nemeth 1987, 237). The difference between social influence processes and persuasion is neatly summarized by the phrase Festinger used to describe compliance due to social pressure: "public conformity without private acceptance" (cited in Booster 1995, 96). Persuasion would entail public conformity with private acceptance (see also Betz, Skowronski, and Ostrom 1996, 116). The rewards and punishments are social because only groups can provide them, and only groups whose approval an actor values will have this influence. Thus social influence rests on the influenced actor's having at least some degree of prior identification with a relevant reference group. Social influence involves connecting extant interests, attitudes, and beliefs in one attitude system to those in some other attitude system; for example, attitudes toward cooperation get connected to seemingly separate attitudes toward social standing, status, and self-esteem in ways that had not previously occurred to the actor (Zimbardo and Leippe 1991, 34). Put differently, social influence involves creating or exploiting new indifference curves between previously unconnected preferences.

Like persuasion, the microprocesses of social influence are multiple, complex, and still the subject of much debate. Generally, however, the literature has isolated a number of possibilities. The first cluster of arguments comes from social identity theory but is rooted in hypotheses about the cognitive discomfort associated with perceived divergence from group norms. Social identity theory is founded on powerful evidence that mere self-categorization as a member of a particular group generates strong internal pressures to conform to the group's norms and practices. Group members hang their self-esteem on appearing to be progroup. If a real or imagined disjuncture between group norms and those of any individual member appears (or is exposed and pointed out), the trauma to self-esteem can motivate an actor to reduce this discrepancy through greater conformity.[40]

A second possibility has to do with social liking. Liking typically means that an individual experiences a sense of comfort interacting with others with whom she or he is perceived to share traits. Thus people will be more likely to comply with requests from friends than from strangers (Cialdini 1984, 1987).

A third possibility comes from consistency theory. There is considerable experimental and field research that suggests people are loathe to appear inconsistent with prior behavior or publicly affirmed beliefs. Cialdini found, for instance, that people were more likely to continue to conform to certain norms and behaviors after taking an on-the-record action that reflects these particular norms than if they were simply asked to conform (Cialdini 1984; 1987, 169; Petty, Wegener, and Fabrigar 1997, 620). This is, generally speaking, a positive evolutionary trait, since it means people will act more predictably, which can increase trust, the credibility of commitments, and the robustness of reciprocity (Cialdini 1984, 69). This does not mean that fear of losing a reputation for trust is the only motivation to behave consistently. Cognitive discomfort appears to be an important driver as well.

The desire to be consistent generates a powerful effect on individual conformity to the group. Membership in a group usually entails on-the-record statements or behaviors of commitment (for example, pledges of loyalty, participation in group activities, commitments to fulfill a membership requirement). These behaviors, even if relatively minor, establish a baseline or threshold identity such that behavior that diverges from these identity markers give rise to discomforting inconsistencies. That is, a behavioral commitment can generate a reevaluation of identity, such that a cluster of behaviors related to the new identity becomes appropriate and is reinforced by the desire to avoid defecting against this new identity (Jones 1985, 76; Petty, Wegener, and Fabrigar 1997, 612).

Finally, the desire to maximize status, honor, and prestige—diffuse reputation or image—can be another driver behind group-conforming behavior, as can their opposites, the desire to avoid a loss of status, shaming, or humiliation and other social sanctions. Status refers to "an individual's standing in the hierarchy of a group based on criteria such as prestige, honor and deference." Typically, status is closely related to others' "expectations of ability or competent performance" (Lovaglia 1995, 402; see also Choi 1993, 113). Competency or proficiency need not mean a mechanical ability to do some task but can mean a high ability to represent some normative ideal. A competent or proficient nonproliferator is, in the eyes of an antiproliferation community, a responsible actor, a consistent, effective proponent of nonproliferation norms. Image is the public manifestation of status. Image refers to the package of perceptions and impressions that one believes one creates through status-consistent behavior.

There are numerous motivations behind maximizing status. Often status brings with it power, wealth, and deference and vice versa (Gilpin 1981, 30–33). Often, however, status markers and immediate material gains are not correlated. For example, status markers such as citations, medals, or public recognition may have no obvious material reward. Moreover, the desire to maximize status need not entail efforts to defeat others to seize status: It can entail group-conforming behavior designed to "buy" status. The reward is psychological well-being from back-patting; the punishment is psychological anxiety from opprobrium.

A second possible motivation is to maximize reputational effects attributed to particular status markers. Here status is an instrument: A good image can encourage actors to deal with you in other arenas and can help build trust leading to reciprocity and decentralized (uninstitutionalized) cooperation (Kreps 1992). There are two problems with this conceptualization, however. The first is, as Frank (1988) points out, that if people know about this instrumentality then an actor's image or reputation as a cooperator has no advantage. So it is in the actor's interest to make cooperation automatic and deeply socialized to make the reputation for cooperation credible. But then no advantages can be accrued, since deception is abandoned. The second problem is that instrumentality assumes the actor is seeking some concrete, calculable benefit from having a good image, an image that can be translated into leverage in some explicit, linked, immediate issue area. Yet often there are no obvious concrete benefits, or they are quite diffuse and vague. Indeed, there are sometimes concrete material costs.

This is the third reason for a concern about status. A particular high-status image may be considered a good in and of itself. Frank, for one, argues that the desire to maximize prestige and status has psychological (even physiological) benefits (1985, 32). Harre attributes the drive to people's "deep sense of their own dignity, and a craving for recognition as beings of worth in the opinions of other of their kind," a craving that depends on public affirmation of one's worth, success, and status (1979, 3, 22). Hatch notes that "the underlying motivation is to achieve a sense of personal accomplishment or fulfillment, and the individual does so by engaging in activities exhibiting qualities that are defined by the society as meritorious" (1989, 349). Franck argues, in reference to the fact that most states abide by most institutional legal commitments most of the time in IR, that conformist behavior is due mainly to a desire to be a member of a club and to benefit from the status of membership (1990, 38; on the opposite effect, shaming, see Young 1992, 176–77; DiMaggio and Powell 1991, 4).

An individual will be sensitive to arguments that his or her behavior is consistent or inconsistent with his or her self-identity as a high-status actor. This sensitivity ought to depend as well on who is making these arguments. The more the audience or reference group is legitimate—that is, the more it consists of actors whose opinions matter—the greater the effect of back-patting and opprobrium (Dittmer and Kim 1993, 9, 14–15). The legitimacy of the audience is a function of self-identification. Actors more easily discount criticisms from enemies and adversaries than from friends and allies. Thus the strength of back-patting and opprobrium depends on two related factors: the nature of the actor's self-categorization and which other actors, by virtue of this self-identification, become important, legitimate observers of behavior.

For there to be observers, of course, one needs some "technology" or mechanism for observation. Thus social influence processes require a forum or institution that makes conformity or nonconformity a public, observable act. The forum could be something as loose as a process by which voluntary reporting on some agreed commitment is scrutinized, where defectors would stand out by either not submitting a report or by submitting shoddy and incomplete ones. Or it could be something as strict as a multilateral negotiation process by which actors are required to state bargaining positions, justify them, and then vote in some form on the outcome. Thus constructivists and contractual institutionalists are both right. Constructivists are right that normatively induced cooperation requires shared understandings of what appropriate behavior looks like. But this may not be enough without an institutional structure that provides information about the degree to which actors are behaving in ways consistent with this shared understanding.[41] This information publicizes the distance between an actor's behavior and the socially approved standard. It is this distance that generates back-patting and shaming effects. In principle, the larger the legitimate audience of cooperators, the more powerful are these effects. Legitimacy here refers to the degree to which it is the social norms of this particular audience that matter and that have an effect on a potential free rider. If, say, an actor completely rejected, or were unaware of, the social norms of a particular group, then no matter what the size of that group, it could not generate back-patting or shaming effects.

To summarize, the desire to maximize status and image—diffuse reputation—say, through the accumulation of back-patting benefits (symbolic status markers, praise, and so forth) can generate a number of incentives for prosocial behavior. Prosocial behavior motivated by status maximization is not directly altruisic (though the behavior required to acquire status might be). Rather, it reflects an actor's egoistic pursuit of social rewards and avoidance of social sanctions. But it cannot exist without the prior existence of a group and without a common understanding of the value or meaning that the group places on putative status markers. This much, at least, must be shared by the actor and the group. Identification with a group, role, or category creates sensitivity to particular kinds of status markers. The accumulation of these becomes a motivation for cooperative behavior. A particular identity is a necessary but not sufficient condition—it established who the reference group will be, the kind of status markers to be accumulated, and the kinds of behavior that elicit these markers. But action is not purely appropriate in a normative sense, nor is it purely optimizing in a materialist instrumental sense.[42]

If these are the reasons why actors might be sensitive to back-patting or opprobrium markers, how might this sensitivity affect the decision calculus of an actor who would prefer an outcome where she or he defects while others cooperate? Here we need to look at the effects of these social rewards and punishments on this actor's calculation of the costs and benefits of cooperation.

Assume, for the moment, that the actor in question has internalized a hard realpolitik concern about shielding relative power (military and economic) from potentially constraining commitments to international regimes. As a first cut, one can model this type of actor's diplomacy using a simple N-person's PD model (fig. 2).[43] The C line represents the payoffs to the actor who cooperates when exactly k other players cooperate, in the sense of limiting their military activities. The

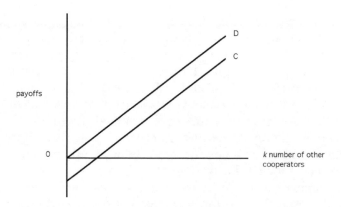

Fig. 2.   Free riding

D line represents the payoffs to the actor from defection when exactly *k* other players cooperate, in the sense of limiting their military activities. If the realpolitik actor were the only cooperator (for example, if it were the only one trying to reduce some global security "bad" while others continued to maximize their relative power) its payoff would be negative, since it would be constraining its relative power while having little effect on stabilizing the security environment. If it did not cooperate while others also defected, although it could not derive any benefits from the cooperation of others, it would be better off than had it unilaterally cooperated. Thus it would pay not to cooperate even if there were no other cooperators. This payoff from defection would hold even as the number of cooperators increased. As these players contributed to a public good the actor would benefit from the provision of this good, but by free riding it would not incur the cost of providing its share of the good. Thus the payoff line from defection will always be greater than the payoff line from cooperation. In an *N*-person PD game, this actor should never have an incentive to cooperate.

Suppose, however, that this actor is also sensitive to its diffuse image, to the desire to maximize status markers as well as relative power. Suppose, too, that all players have a capacity to praise and shame. Under these conditions, social interaction can induce caution in the pursuit of pure defection strategies that might have an adverse effect on status. Within international organizations and institutions the participating or cooperating audience is relatively large. While the opportunities to free ride are potentially greater—given the number of potential cooperators—the scrutiny of each player is more in-

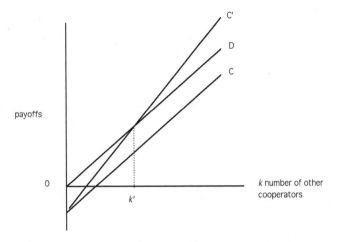

Fig. 3.   Back-patting

tense and state behavior is often more transparent than in bilateral
relations, due to the rules of these institutions. In this context, a concern about image has two very different effects on a realpolitik
actor's payoff structure, corresponding to the effects of back-patting
and opprobrium.

Back-patting is a benefit incurred from being seen as a cooperator or an active prosocial member of a group. An actor receives
recognition, praise, and normative support for its involvement in the
process. Back-patting can reaffirm an actor's self-valuation, its self-
categorization as a high-status actor, with concomitant payoffs for
self- and public legitimation. Ceteris paribus, as the size of the cooperating audience grows, the actor accrues more back-patting benefits.
Thus for every additional member of the institution, a potential defector receives a certain added payoff from back-patting as long as it
cooperates. The benefits are cumulative. As figure 3 indicates this increases the slope of the payoffs from cooperation (from *C* to *C'*).

Opprobrium, of course, carries social costs—a denial of the prior
status and prestige of the actor—as well as psychological ones—a denial of the actor's identity as one deserving of back-patting. Opprobrium can also be modeled as an accumulation of shaming markers
that diminishes the value of free riding as the number of participants
or cooperators in a regime increases. A certain social cost is incurred
with each additional participant or observer in the reference group.
As the group increases, the criticisms accumulate, which increases the

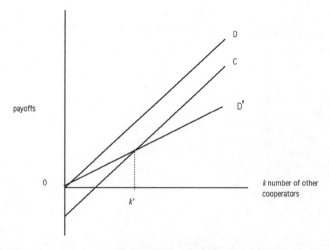

Fig. 4.   Opprobrium

costs of defection. The effect, as shown in figure 4, is to depress the slope of the payoffs from defection (from D to D'). At a certain point, an increase in the slope of the payoffs from cooperation and/or a decrease in the slope of the payoffs from defection may create a crossover point in the two lines. This is the point where the size of the audience (k') is such that the back-patting benefits and opprobrium costs change the cost-benefit analysis. It is at this point that it begins to pay to cooperate, as the size of the audience increases.

When back-patting benefits and (implicit or threatened) opprobrium costs are combined, this can dramatically reduce the size of the audience needed to make it pay to cooperate (this is shown by k'' in figure 5). The policy objective for other players, at its simplest, is to make this n as low as possible such that it does not take a large audience of cooperators to induce a defector's cooperation.

Note that the net effects of social influence on the cost-benefit calculus of cooperation in a institution are similar to the provision of material sidepayments and sanctions. It is important to point out, however, that back-patting and shaming change this cost-benefit calculus in a very different way than do sidepayments or sanctions. Sidepayments or sanctions, whether provided by the institution or by a key player or players in the institution, typically have a constant effect on an actor's utility regardless of how many others cooperate, participate, backpat, or shame. Put graphically (fig. 6), the effect of

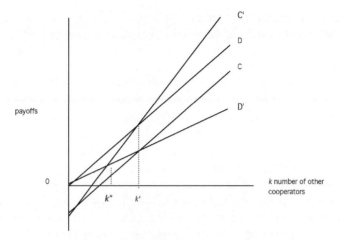

Fig. 5.   Opprobrium and back-patting

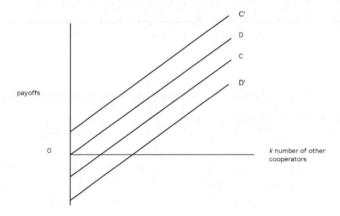

Fig. 6.   The effects of material sidepayments and sanctions

the sidepayments and sanctions is to raise the entire C payoff line and/or depress the entire D payoff line respectively, while not changing their slopes, such that the C' payoff line ends up above the D payoff line or that the D' payoff line ends up below the C payoff line. A sanction for defection (imposed by an enforcer or hegemon, for instance) is equally costly regardless of the size of the group cooperating. Cooperation brings higher utility than defection regardless of what other members of the group do. Put another way, the institution, the forum in which the audience is active, is irrelevant for the initial decision to cooperate. Back-patting or shaming, on the other hand, have cumulative effects that depend precisely on how many others cooperate, participate, backpat, or shame. That is, cooperation as a result of material sidepayments or sanctions is not a social effect of the institution. Cooperation due to social influence, however, is a social effect only and would not exist without the existence of, and interaction with, the group. Back-patting and opprobrium lose their impact outside of a social group. These alternative forms of social influence would not carry this weight if unilaterally directed by one actor toward another in a bilateral, institutionless relationship.

The conditions under which one might expect social influence to be greatest will depend in part on the type of environment to which the national actors are exposed. Returning to the typology of institutional designs I suggested earlier, given the microprocesses of social influence, back-patting and opprobrium are more likely to be at work than is persuasion when membership is large (maximizes the accumulation of back-patting or shaming markers): when the franchise is equally allocated (no obvious authoritative source of information); when decision rules are majoritarian (behavior is on record and consistency effects may be stronger); when the mandate involves negotiations over the distribution of benefits; and when the autonomy of agents is low (agents have to represent principals, thus reducing the effects of persuasion on agents).

But how would one know if social influence had led to prosocial or pronormative behavior in international institutions? Controlling for effects on relative power and the presence or absence of material sidepayments and punishments (discussed later), if social influence is at work, one should expect to see the following effects:

- commitments to participate and join power-constraining institutions should take place in the absence of material sidepayments or threats of sanctions;
- arguments for joining or participating should stress back-patting and image benefits, diffuse reputation benefits, and opprobrium costs;
- initial bargaining positions, if stuck to, will put the state in a distinct minority, isolating it from the cooperating audience or reference group. Thus, commitments to prosocial behavior will only be made when it is clear that noncommitment will be highly isolating.

The Aggregation Problem

Before I get to the evidence for social influence, I need to be clear about the level of analysis here. The focus on sociological and social psychological microprocesses in IR compels one to look at individuals or small groups, to examine the effects of social influence on them, and then to trace the effects of these individuals on the policy process. This is a legitimate research process when one starts from a constructivist, complex adaptive systems ontology, as I do here. States as unitary actors are not persuaded, are not influenced by back-patting and opprobrium, and do not mimic.

The problem comes with observing social influence effects, in particular, on top-level decision makers. Who in the decision-making system is sensitive to back-patting or opprobrium? How do agents in institutions transmit international social influence signals back to political leaders? In the China case, why and how would people on the Foreign Affairs Leading Small Group—the institution in which the final decisions to sign onto regional security and arms control commitments were probably made—be sensitive to back-patting and opprobrium directed at the Chinese delegation in arms control negotiations? I don't think there is an especially good theoretical or empirical answer to these sorts of questions. There is evidence that leaders tend to anthropomorphize the state themselves (indeed, the language of the state and its diplomacy is always highly anthropomorphic, for example, fatherlands, motherlands, prestige, dignity, unitary national interests, and so forth). They, and their attentive publics, tend to isomorphize criticism or praise of the state with criticisms and praise of the national in-group and of each individual in the in-group.[44] In interviews with governmental and nongovernmental intellectuals and analysts in China, many of whom are critics of the regime's repressiveness, a common argument was that leaders and the state are isomorphized when Chinese leaders interact with the external world. How Jiang Zemin is personally treated, for instance, is seen as a direct indicator of how China the collective is treated. There is no reason to believe that decision makers themselves don't engage in this type of isomorphization and anthropomorphization. The process might go in the other direction as well: Criticism of the collective is personalized by decision makers. As one example from environmental diplomacy, Qu Geping, at the time the head of China's National Environment Protection Agency, expressed personal frustration with the "pressure" he felt whenever he attended international conferences because of the stories told about Chinese eating wild and endangered animals (Qu 1990, 195).

There is a growing sense among Chinese specialists of Chinese foreign policy that the current, post-Deng leadership in particular is much more sensitive both to China's international image and, with lines between the two blurred, to their own. Jiang Zemin, in particular, is viewed as being especially sensitive to how China is portrayed and to the implications of this both for his own personal image and for his domestic legitimacy. That Jiang allowed himself to enter a very public debate with Clinton over human rights during both the U.S. and the China summits in 1997 and 1998 was seen as a sign of his strength, confidence, and stature internationally: He could debate the president of the United States on equal terms and, in Chinese views, hold his own.[45] Jiang has emphasized that one of the key themes of Chinese foreign policy should be precisely the promotion of China's image as a responsible major power.[46]

China and the CTBT: A Case of Social Influence?

The Comprehensive Test Ban Treaty (CTBT) negotiations, conducted inside the UN Conference on Disarmament (CD), ran from January 1994 to August 1996.[47] The goal of the negotiations was, essentially, to ban the testing of nuclear weapons in underground explosions. Proposals for a CTBT had floated around for decades but had run into opposition from one or more of the permanent members of the UN Security Council (P5) at different times. The original goal was to prevent states without nuclear weapons from acquiring them and to limit the modernization of weapons in the hands of states with extant weapons programs. Without an ability to test, states could not be confident in the reliability of their weapons designs, reducing the value of nuclear weapons in their arsenals. Over time the constraining effect of test bans on new and extant programs declined with advanced in computer simulation, nuclear power technology, and manufacturing skills. Nonetheless, there are certain kinds of advanced weapons designs that could still be severely limited by an inability to test through underground explosions (for example, the nuclear explosion–pumped X ray laser, enhanced electromagnetic pulse [EMP] weapons, microwave weapons, and superenhanced radiation weapons). The CTBT had also long been considered by developing states as an important pillar in the global nonproliferation regime because, in principle, it would restrain the P-5's ability to proliferate vertically.

Right from the start, China signaled its discomfort with a CTBT. When the CTBT moved onto the CD agenda in 1993, Chinese arms control specialists and government officials let it be known that they considered the value of a treaty for reducing the demand for nuclear weapons to be quite secondary to things such as no-first use declarations and security assurances (Wu 1994, 11–12; Liu 1993; Chen 1993). Their worry was that a treaty might freeze China's nuclear capabilities in perpetual inferiority vis-à-vis the two major nuclear states. In particular it might inhibit the development of a survivable second-generation nuclear missile capability.[48] Many in the nuclear weapons technical community and within the PLA have serious doubts about the credibility of China's second strike capability. And there are some in the PLA who support the development of a limited nuclear war-fighting capability to control escalation in the event of a conventional and/or nuclear crisis. This would require a more flexible operational capacity that might include, among other requirements, multiple independently targetable reentry vehicles (MIRVs), theater and tactical nuclear weapons, a capacity to penetrate space-, air-, and ground-based ballistic missile defenses, and an ability to hit smaller, hardened military targets. Most of these systems involve smaller weight-to-yield ratios and hence new warhead designs.[49]

Once negotiations got under way Chinese negotiators began to present bargaining positions that most observers believed were designed to slow down negotiations, at least until China had completed a test series on its second-generation warhead. Initially, negotiations proceeded under the assumption that a treaty would be ready for submission to the General Assembly (as is required before a CD-negotiated treaty becomes open for signature) by September 1996. The Chinese indicated too that they hoped a treaty would be complete by the end of 1996. It is likely that, given a spring and fall testing schedule, approximately, with two tests per year (generally four to six tests are needed for a new design), China's decision makers would have needed at least until the fall of 1996 before they knew whether a new design was possible.[50] Thus when negotiations began in 1994, it is safe to assume that China's weapons testing community argued that delaying tactics might be needed for at least two years. This was a high-risk strategy, since there was no guarantee that the testing series would be successful, or successful enough, for a robust design.

Thus China's delegation led off in 1994 with three positions that were likely to delay the treaty in some way. The first was a demand that the CTBT include a statement that committed states to unconditional no-first use and security assurances (NFU/SA). The second was essentially a demand that the treaty allow for peaceful nuclear explosions (PNE) (Conference on Disarmament, plenary session statement CD/PV.676, March 24, 1994, 20–21). The third was a proposal for an extensive international satellite monitoring system for verification purposes.

The first two positions were nonstarters (or "treaty killers") for some or all of the other P-5. U.S. nuclear doctrine was adamantly opposed to NFU and SAs. And PNEs were opposed by almost all other states, including most of the G-21 (the developing states group in the CD), mainly because it was too difficult to differentiate between a PNE and a test explosion for military purposes, making verification of a CTBT impossible. Nonetheless, the Chinese apparently pushed for PNEs to delay the negotiation process if necessary. The third position was considered by many delegations to be frivolous, redundant, and excessively expensive.

These three positions were the core of China's bargaining in the CTBT from 1994 to mid-1995. By the late summer of 1995, however, two additional positions emerged, both having to do with verification. One stated China's opposition to the use of national technical means (NTM—information gathered from spy satellite and other technical means of espionage) as a source of information for triggering on-site inspection (OSI) of a suspected CTBT violator. China's negotiators insisted that under no circumstances could NTM be used, given the asymmetries in NTM capabilities around the world.[51] The other position concerned the decision rules leading to OSI. Essentially the Chinese supported a green light system; that is, OSI would not start automatically when a state requested OSI of a suspected violator. Rather, it would start after a decision by the treaty's Executive Council to do so. The Chinese proposed a voting rule of two-thirds. Western states wanted a red light system where OSI started automatically unless stopped by a decision of the Executive Council.

As negotiations entered the first period in January 1996, China continued to stick with its treaty-killing positions on NFU and PNEs, as well as its positions on NTM and OSI. Observers and members of other delegations were unsure whether, with these stances, China would even sign a treaty.[52] A major break in the Chinese bargaining occurred with the introduction in late May 1996 of a "clean" chair's draft treaty.[53] The draft left out language proposed by China on NFU/SAs and PNEs. This was, in a sense, a face-saving way of dropping these two positions: It required only that China agree to use the clean draft as the basis of negotiations instead of having to publicly retreat from its NFU and PNE positions.[54] Sha Zukang, the head of the delegation and the chief decision maker on arms control in the MOFA, had announced China's flexibility on PNEs after he returned from Beijing in early May. This suggests that it was during the break between the first and second negotiating periods (April) that the Chinese interagency process made a final decision to abandon the PNE position. The reason, apparently, was that China did not want to be seen as the major obstacle to the treaty.[55]

The Chinese position on OSI and NTM did not change, however, with the introduction of the clean draft. The draft treaty accepted a green light system for OSI but proposed a simple majority rule for triggering inspections rather than China's preferred two-thirds rule. It also allowed for some use of NTM as a source of evidence for requesting OSI. Both of these were resolved after intensive bilateral negotiations with the United States in late July, around the time of China's last nuclear test. The United States, intent on getting a treaty before the United Nations General Assembly (UNGA) opened in September 1996, was willing to compromise with China on OSI: Both sides agreed to a three-fifths voting rule for triggering OSI, a compromise between the U.S. preference for simple majority and the Chinese preference for two-thirds.[56] The Chinese essentially caved on NTM, however, as most states were supportive of some role for NTM. With these compromises made, China signed the treaty and declared a unilateral moratorium on testing, abandoning at the last moment its longstanding position that it would stop testing with entry into force.

How precisely did China get to this point when it had initially considered the treaty to be potentially detrimental to China's relative power capabilities? Let me address the alternatives to a back-patting/opprobrium explanation first. The simplest explanation—drawing from certain realist premises—is that the treaty was, in the end, costless. This argument could come in two forms. The first is that China had, by July 1996, finished its testing series for a second-generation warhead design; the testing and weapons communities were essentially satisfied with the information gathered from the tests.

There are at least two problems with this argument, however. First, many in the testing and weapons communities have since expressed dissatisfaction with the treaty. Many consider the treaty to be a sacrifice for China.[57] While it is possible that sufficient information came from the last series of tests to design a newer, lighter, and smaller warhead and to increase confidence in the safety of warheads, it is not clear that the weapons designers believe this does much to reduce the technical asymmetries (for example, relative power capabilities gaps) between China's nuclear weapons and those of the superpowers. Nor can China test for the reliability and safety of the 1996 design. Even U.S. government specialists in Chinese nuclear weapons believe that the moratorium on testing will create difficulties for the Chinese, with stockpile aging after 2000. There are continuing complaints that U.S. possession of simulation technology and China's lack of such technology mean that the United States can develop new generations of weapons designs while China is essentially frozen with its second-generation warheads.[58] In other words, the CTBT may worsen China's relative capabilities (Zou 1998, 43–44).

Second, there is some evidence that China's leaders essentially decided to sign the treaty in the fall of 1995, prior to the negotiation session in January 1996. A comparison of the composition of China's CTBT delegation over time is revealing on this score.[59] It wasn't until the January session that China sent the most senior official in charge of the nuclear weapons and nuclear arms control research in the military-industrial complex, General Qian Shaojun. Qian's presence probably indicated that the Chinese believed negotiations had entered the endgame, that a treaty was inevitable, and that now the task was to ensure that the provisions that really mattered to China were in the treaty. Given the quickened pace of negotiations in an endgame, Qian's presence also reduced the amount of time it would take for China's nuclear weapons community to respond to changes in the treaty. Qian was also, roughly speaking, the military's equivalent to Sha Zukang. This meant that decisions on how to respond to negotiations could be made more quickly and between relative equals, both probably with a mandate to decide on China's final bargaining positions. To have this mandate, however, they would have needed instructions basically approving China's signature in the first place, thus the likelihood that the basic decision to sign was made by China's top political leaders in late 1995.[60]

The timing of China's positions on OSI and NTM would roughly fit a decision to sign in 1995. From the third negotiation session in the late summer of 1995 through the first negotiation session of 1996 China focused its bargaining on verification and dropped the treat-killing provisions on PNEs and NFU. That China introduced two key positions related to verification in late 1995 suggests that its leaders had deduced that a treaty was inevitable, that China's treaty-killing positions would run into tremendous flack in the CD, and that China should start to focus on those parts of the treaty that it could really change to its advantage.

Thus the decision to join almost certainly came prior to at least the last two nuclear tests, both conducted in 1996. This would suggest that the decision came before there was conclusive information about the success of the second-generation warhead design.

A second general realist explanation for why the treaty was probably costless relates to India's refusal to sign unless the CTBT explicitly included a time-bound commitment from the P-5 for nuclear disarmament. India's refusal meant that the treaty would not enter into force and thus China would not be legally restricted from testing as long as India was outside the treaty. There are some problems with this argument too. While the timing is unclear, if China did indeed decide to sign in 1995, this came *before* India began to link its signature to a timetable for disarmament, that is, before China could have known that India's position would prevent entry into force. The Indians had been hinting at such linkages starting in January 1996, especially leading up to, and after, the elections in May, when the Hindu nationalist BJP formed a coalition government. But it wasn't until June that India stated firmly it would not sign unless there was a time-bound commitment to disarmament. China had insisted on India's inclusion in the treaty as a condition for entry into force, but this insistence had come well before India came out in opposition to the treaty (Zou 1998, 36).

In a sense, the more interesting Chinese decision was the one to enter the negotiations in the first place in 1994. At that time India was a strong supporter of the CTBT (the Hindu nationalist influence on foreign policy didn't affect India's bargaining until late 1995 and into 1996). Thus India's later opposition could not have factored into China's calculations. At the time, though, the British and the French appeared unhappy with the idea of a treaty.[61] China could have probably blocked the treaty before its negotiations had started, linking with the other two medium-sized nuclear powers to prevent a P-5 agreement to negotiate a treaty in the CD. It could have done this behind the scenes, with little fear of superpower retribution. Indeed, before the CTBT or any of its major provisions could be brought before the CD, the P-5 in general had to reach a consensus on doing so (Zou 1998, 37). Yet China chose to accept the CD's mandate to negotiate a treaty, even though in 1994 Chinese decision makers were even more uncertain than in 1996 about the technical benefits a test series might produce.

In short, there is little evidence that China's decision makers believed the treaty process was relatively inconsequential for its relative military power capabilities. China's decisions to join the negotiations and accept a treaty are still puzzles from mainstream realist perspectives.

In contrast to neorealist explanations, contractual institutionalism would look for positive or negative incentives that mediated the military costs of the treaty, for example, sidepayments and sanctions or reputational benefits for immediate exchange relationships. Interestingly, the United States concluded early on that sidepayments might be necessary to ensure Chinese signature. In November 1994 it apparently offered China help in developing computer simulation technology that would allow the Chinese to maintain confidence in the safety and reliability of their weapons. According to one highly placed Department of Defense official the offer came to nothing because the Chinese didn't have sufficient data from their tests to use the software effectively. Apparently another approach was made in 1996, but nothing came of it either. The Chinese military has continued to float suggestions that the United States provide this kind of technology, implying that China alone among the P-5 still doesn't have it.[62] Some nuclear warhead designers in the United States also doubt that China could develop sophisticated new warhead designs using simulation technology alone.[63] So, on balance, the Chinese do not appear to have received any useful technological sidepayments to join.

There were also no threats of sanctions—at no point was there any implicit or explicit threat of economic or technological sanctions should China not join CTBT negotiations, should it delay, or should it not sign. Indeed, since the election of a large number of conservative republicans in the 1994 congressional elections, the U.S. Congress has been very leery of the treaty.

What about short-term reputational incentives? In a sense this is the hardest to deal with precisely because the behavioral effects one would expect to see are essentially identical to diffuse image or status concerns. But I have two problems with the immediate reputational argument. The first is that institutionalists typically haven't developed scope conditions that might differentiate between immediate reputational concerns and very diffuse ones. This makes the claim that a decision maker was worried in an instrumental fashion about his or her reputation as a cooperator almost unfalsifiable. In this specific instance, there was no particular exchange in the Sino-U.S. relations to which one can point where Chinese leaders believed that signing onto the CTBT would lead to a better deal for Beijing. Sino-U.S. relations had deteriorated in the wake of the March 1996 Taiwan Strait crisis, but both sides moved quickly at the highest political levels to improve relations, independent of the CTBT. Moreover, since the CTBT was opposed by the U.S. Senate, it is unclear what political leverage China could acquire with the making of U.S.-China policy by signing onto the treaty. It certainly bought no credit with Congress. Second, in none of my interviews did my Chinese interlocutors mention this short-term instrumental consideration. Indeed, one could plausibly expect that such an admission would be easier to make than an admission of diffuse image concerns. The former implies that any Chinese concessions are at least justifiable, given the need to maintain good relations with the most powerful state in the system. This is easier to sell publicly than to admit that concessions were made because of a diffuse sense of pressure from a large number of states. This is something, presumably, decision makers would prefer others not to know. Thus, admitting that diffuse image concerns were a critical motivation would seem to be a more credible statement than admitting that instrumental reputational calculations were key.

But what, then, is the positive evidence for social influence effects? The consistent refrain in interviews I conducted with people involved in the interagency process and with observers of Chinese bargaining from other countries was that China could not stay out of, or in the end sabotage, the CTBT because of the costs to China's international image and because of the status benefits from participating in one of the pillar treaties of the nonproliferation regime, a regime supported by an overwhelming majority of states in the system. The language used by Chinese interlocutors to discuss joining and then signing was status oriented. The CTBT was a "great international trend"; there was a nebulous "psychological pressure" to join once the United States, Russia, United Kingdom, and France had committed and there was clear strong support in G-21; China's signing was consistent with it being a responsible world power, and joining the treaty was part of a "global atmosphere," such that China would have been isolated had it ignored this atmosphere.[64] One of the members of the Chinese CTBT delegation argued publicly (the first statement of this kind as far as I am aware) that one of the key reasons why China ended up supporting the CTBT was opinion among developing states: "Taking into account its historical friendly relations with them, China had to maintain its image in third world countries. China's image as a responsible major power is reportedly moving to the fore. *The necessity of maintaining its international image* was a reason for China's decision to adjust its position on the CTBT negotiations" (Zou 1998, 15, emphasis mine).[65] These are unusually direct admissions of the impact of this form of international pressure from a regime that has traditionally publicly claimed that diplomatic pressure on China is counterproductive.[66] That the Chinese bargained hard over verification issues—in particular OSI—even in the face of considerable dismay among delegations, does not undermine the argument about social influence. Bargaining to dilute the verification and punishment elements of the treaty in the last months of negotiations was premised on the existence of a basic acceptance of the core distributional features of the treaty.

There is, as one might expect, given the nature of the institutional environment in which China was operating, little evidence that normative persuasion affected the decision making behind CTBT accession. In this case one would look for two arguments in particular that would reflect an internalization of the theory behind the CTBT's value as a treaty. The first would be arguments in the policy process to the effect that the CTBT would have a critical stabilizing effect on vertical and horizontal proliferation. This was after all the primary argument made in favor of test bans well back in the 1950s. Even though technological change through to the 1990s meant that non-testing would not have as dramatic a constraint on the development of some new weapons designs (particularly for the United States with its advanced simulation technologies), the general argument behind the CTBT still held—a ban on testing would reduce the reliability of, and hence the value of, nuclear weapons, putting some constraints on vertical and horizontal proliferation. One did not find this argument in the Chinese policy process. Indeed, Chinese arms controllers involved in the process continued to express doubts about the value of the CTBT in this regard.

A second argument, somewhat less obvious and more controversial among the proponents of a CTBT, would be that the CTBT does not undermine the deterrents of the nuclear states because, above a certain threshold of capabilities, more is redundant and does not buy security. In other words, for many advocates the CTBT has been implicitly premised on the notion of minimum deterrence: Once a nuclear power has enough to inflict unacceptable damage, there should be no need for continued testing. Minimum deterrence would be a transitional strategy toward a nonnuclear world. The question of whether Chinese strategists accept the notion of minimum deterrence is controversial. There is substantial evidence that many believe minimum deterrence makes a virtue out of necessity and that China needs a somewhat larger, more flexible limited war-fighting capability to control escalation from conventional to nuclear conflicts and to control nuclear escalation itself. While the evidence as to the impact of these ideas on force posture and operations is unclear, there is no evidence that the concept of minimum deterrence was used in the Chinese policy process to support signing the CTBT. Thus persuasion—in this case the internalization of new cause-and-effect arguments about how to achieve security embodied in the philosophy of a CTBT as an institution—appears not to have been at work in this case.

In sum, it appears that Chinese decision makers' sensitivity to China's image and status as a responsible major power was a critical driver in their decision to sign onto the CTBT. This sensitivity—a function, I would argue, of an emerging identity in which its key status markers come from participation in international institutions that regulate interstate affairs—was especially acute because of the high profile and legitimacy of the nonproliferation regime, of which the CTBT was one important pillar. This identity created new trade-offs between status and relative power that had not existed in the Maoist (or early Dengist) period in Chinese foreign policy. The pressure to choose status over relative power was, as one would expect, especially great in such an institution. Can one develop a metric for determining a distribution of states (and state identities) in terms of sensitivity to status and security? Possibly. Indeed, it would be essential for comparing across identity types and for further testing social influence hypotheses about the relationship between institutional design and back-patting or opprobrium effects. I think that the CTBT case shows, at least, the plausibility of these hypotheses.

Conclusion

This chapter has examined some broadly sociological arguments about the effect of participation in international institutions on domestic foreign policy processes. To summarize the arguments and evidence, let me simply outline some of the implications for understanding how cooperation between domestic actors (in this case, foreign policy actors) and international institutions might work.

The first set of implications has to do with persuasion and institutional design. Typically, contractual institutionalists argue that efficient institutional design depends on the type of cooperation problem; for example, a PD-type problem requires information (monitoring) and sanctions, and an assurance problem primarily requires reassurance information (Martin 1993b). The flip side is that one can identify inefficient institutional designs for a particular cooperation problem as well (for example, an institution that is designed only to provide assurance information but has no monitoring or sanctioning capacity would be inefficient for resolving PD-type problems). In addition, Downs, Rocke, and Barsoom (1997) argue that so-called transformational institutions (inclusive institutions that bring genuine cooperators and potential defectors together in an effort to instill norms and obligations in the latter) are less likely to provide efficient solutions than a strategic construction approach. This latter approach to institutional design stresses exclusive memberships of true believers where decisions are made on the basis of supermajority rules. The gradual inclusion of potential defectors under these conditions ensures that the preferences of the true believers predominate as the institution evolves. Downs, Rocke, and Barsoom's critique of the transformational approach rests explicitly on skepticism that the preferences of potential defectors can change through social interaction. The problem is that they do not develop any operational indicators for determining whether interests, desires, and goals undergo endogenous change as state actors move into and become more involved in institutions.

In any event, if one considers the possibility of preference change among individuals and small groups of actors inside institutions, then one is forced to revisit these common notions of efficient institutional design. An institution that appears inefficient to contractual institutionalists (for example, an assurance institution for a PD problem), may actually be efficient for the cooperation problem at hand. If, say, a player (or subactors in a policy process) with PD preferences can be socialized (persuaded) to internalize stag hunt preferences through interaction in a social environment with no material sanctioning or sidepayments, then assurance institutions may work in PD-like cooperation problems. An efficient institution might then be reconceived as the design and process most likely to produce the most efficient environments for socializing actors in alternative definitions of interest. As I have argued, the ARF case, and the sociological literature on which it rests, suggests that such an institution may have to be informal, weakly institutionalized, and consensus based—the opposite of an institutional design appropriate for dealing with PD problems.

A second broadly theoretical implication of social influence is for collective action. Social influence effects may provide insights into how groups resolve the collective action problem that hinders resolving collective action problems. That is, traditionally scholars have argued that a critical solution to free riding is to offer material sidepayments (and sanctions) to make collective action pay for the individual. The conundrum has been, however, that the offering of sidepayments is itself a collective action problem. Who will take up the burden of offering sidepayments, given the resources required to do so? Hegemons and activists are usually part of the answer to this puzzle (though why activists should exist in the first place is hard for collective action theorists to specify a priori). Social rewards and punishments, however, are a particularly interesting kind of incentive for overcoming collective inaction. They are relatively cheap to create but are often infused with a great deal of value. This means that new status markers can be manufactured and distributed without necessarily diminishing their value. In principle any member of a group therefore can provide social sidepayments at relatively low cost, indeed at zero cost if the member can also receive these kinds of sidepayments for providing them to others. This is, after all, what back-patting entails—a mutual, virtuous circle of bestowing and receiving social rewards. Cheap, but social, talk, then, can indeed be cheap to produce but nonetheless can still be considered credible precisely because of its social value.[67] Thus, because status markers are so highly valued, it doesn't take much of a costly commitment by providers of these markers to establish the credibility of promises to bestow, or of threats to retract, these markers. All this suggests that one reason why collective action problems are often less frequent and debilitating than theorists expect (Green and Shapiro 1994, 72–97) may have to do with the fact that actors are also motivated by the desire to maximize social rewards and that these are relatively easy for groups to produce and distribute.

Following from this argument about collective action, social influence arguments also suggest that the conventional wisdom about optimal size of institutions and groups may need rethinking. Drawing from Mancur Olson's work, the contractual institutionalist argument is that ceteris paribus more actors make cooperation more difficult (collective action problems, problems of monitoring and punishing defection, and so forth). Transaction costs increase with more actors. Decentralized institutions are therefore handicapped in dealing with "problems of transaction costs and opportunism" (Abbott and Snidal 1998, 15). From a social influence perspective, however, more may be better. Status back-patting and opprobrium effects are likely to be stronger when the audience or reference group is larger.

In sum, sociological approaches introduce at least two new and different processes by which actors come to cooperate inside institutions—persuasion and social influence. These, added to the more traditional focus on material sidepayments and sanctions and on instrumental reputational concerns, present a more complete range of possible causal processes at work inside international institutions. Indeed, they bring to IR theory a set of motivations for behavior that have long been recognized as central to the study of politics.[68] They suggest broad scope conditions for examining the relationship between international institutional design and state action—in large, high-profile, formal negotiation institutions one should expect that social influence, material sidepayments or sanctions, and reputational concerns will be the most likely candidates for explaining cooperation. In smaller, informal, consensus-based deliberation institutions, the key processes will likely be those, or some combination, of persuasion, instrumental reputation, and sidepayments or sanctions. In bilateral relationships material sidepayments or sanctions, instrumental reputation, and possibly persuasion would be processes for which to look.

These plausibility probes suggest, therefore, that with further refinement some important and genuinely competitive empirical arguments could be set up to test the variable effects of institutional designs on state behavior, tests that could examine the relative importance of social processes and motivations and economic processes and motivations. This is the first step to truly understanding the scope conditions under which these kinds of motivations are or are not at work. Surely this will make for a more accurate and precise understanding of the effects of international institutions than if one were to start from the assumption that only one or the other is relevant.

Notes

I would like to thank Jean-Marc Blanchard, Dan Drezner, Kathryn Hochstetler, Steve Krasner, Helen Milner, participants at the conference "The Interaction of Domestic and International Institutions," and the anonymous reviewers for their comments and criticisms.

1. This juxtaposition is increasingly under attack from two very different sources. Critical constructivists have pointed out the illogic of assuming that there is an arena of human activities where "ideas" are not present in the in-

terpretation of interests (Laffey and Weldes 1997). Some of those coming out of the contractual institutionalist community have also argued that there is no inherent contradiction between a thin rational choice epistemology and an interest in explaining where preferences come from. See Katzenstein, Keohane, and Krasner 1998.

2. Contractualists will admit that sanctions could be social or that non-material considerations such as reputation could provide incentives to accept the constraints of the institution. As I will note this points to an area of convergence with sociological approaches. As a practical matter, however, almost always the empirical work focuses on material incentives. Moreover, the goal of improving one's reputation from one set of interactions is usually to apply this reputation to acquire, most commonly, material benefits from another set of interactions.

3. See Frieden 1999 for a sophisticated statement of the reasons for assuming fixed preferences.

4. I am referring here to mimicking. I have not discussed mimicking—copying the descriptive norms of a group as opposed to internalizing its prescriptive norms—and its path-dependent effects on organizations because one could debate whether it clearly falls within a sociological perspective.

5. For similar critiques see Checkel 1998, 332; Moravcsik 1997, 539.

6. This may change as scholars pick up on Finnemore and Sikkink's summary of some plausible causal processes (1998).

7. This is, after all, the point of much of the work on how transnational networks affect state behavior (Keck and Sikkink 1998; Evangelista 1999), "teaching" and the diffusion of norms, and the creation of national interests (Finnemore 1996b).

8. Ruggie calls this a focus on "innovative micro-practices," a hallmark of constructivist research (1998, 27).

9. See Choi 1993, 52–53.

10. See for instance the argument in Chafetz, Abramson, and Grillot 1996. The authors argue that the debate in the Ukraine in the 1990s over whether to sign the Non-Proliferation Treaty (NPT) was in large measure a debate over whether Ukraine's identity was that of a great power (hence it could legitimately keep and develop nuclear weapons) or a middle European power (in which case it should denuclearize and join the NPT).

11. On China's realpolitik see Christensen 1996; Johnston 1999a.

12. I do not use socialization here in a normative sense. Nor do I believe that Chinese actors prior to entry into these institutions were in some sense unsocialized. They were merely differently socialized.

13. The documents come from the Conference on Disarmament record, a collection of over one hundred conference papers presented by Chinese arms controllers at international conferences over the last ten years, and articles from major internal and open sources journals. In addition I have conducted around ninety interviews with Chinese, American, Canadian, Japanese, and

Singaporean arms control officials over the past approximately six years on the topic of China's involvement in international security institutions. Finally, I have been a participant observer in a number of Track II conferences on security, where I could interact intensively with Chinese arms control experts and officials, including two sessions of the Summer Study in Science and World Affairs, organized by the Union of Concerned Scientists (1993, 1996), the ISODARCO Beijing Arms Control Seminar (1994), meetings between the Ford Foundation and several arms control research institutions in China (1998), meetings between the MIT arms control group and Chinese nuclear weapons and missile design institutions (1996), and the Monterey Institute of International Studies Second U.S.-China Arms Control Seminar (1999).

14. This section draws heavily from Johnston 1999b.

15. See Johnson 1993, 81, on this point.

16. For an excellent exegesis of Habernas's theory of communicative action, see Risse 1997.

17. See the conditions explicated by James (1998, 7–11, 15–17).

18. Despite the volume of this literature, "To date there is precious little evidence specifying who can be talked out of what beliefs, and under what conditions" (Berger 1995, 8).

19. Sometimes scholars identify a third condition for persuasion, namely, the characteristics of the persuadee herself or himself, for example, innate cognitive processing abilities (the greater, the strength of existing attitudes, the greater the degree to which an individual is sensitive to appearing consistent).

20. Or as Gibson puts it, "Especially when people do not have much experience with political institutions and processes, it is easy to imagine that their initial viewpoints are poorly anchored in a highly articulated and constrained belief system, and that considerable potential for effective persuasion exists" (1998, 821).

21. There is a signaling literature that is beginning to address the scope conditions for persuasion as well. Lupia and McCubbins (1998) argue that there are two basic conditions, namely, that the persuadee believes the persuader to be knowledgeable about an issue and that the persuadee believes that the persuader's intentions are trustworthy. Any other factors, such as ideology, identity, culture, and so forth, are only predictors of persuasion to the extent that they reveal information to the persuadee about the persuader's knowledge and trustworthiness. The problem here is that the argument, in my view, avoids the more interesting question about the empirical frequency with which *social* variables such as perceived ideology, identity, and/or cultural values are in fact the primary cues that people use to determine the degree of knowledge and trustworthiness of a persuader and thus come prior to beliefs about knowledge and trustworthiness. The answer has important implications for how social interactions lead to socialization and how different institutional designs might lead to different socialization paths. Lupia and McCubbins tend to focus on the role of external forces in clarify-

ing beliefs about knowledge and trustworthiness of persuaders. Since, they argue, social and political environments are rarely ones in which persuader and persuadee interact face to face over long periods of time, the familiarity or personal interaction route to beliefs about the persuader's knowledge and trustworthiness tends to be less common. This may be true at the national level of persuasion (for example, political messages from politicians aimed at masses of voters), but it is not necessarily true at the level of social interaction in international institutions among diplomats, specialists, and analysts. Here the first route—familiarity, iterated face-to-face social interaction— may be more common, hence affect based on identity, culture, and ideology may be more critical for persuasion than external forces and costly signals.

22. Jorgensen, Kock, and Rorbech (1998) found in a study of televised political debates in Denmark, for example, that the most persuasive debaters were those who used a small number of extended, weighty discussions of specific qualitative examples. The use of these specific, straightforward, and logical examples seemed to accentuate the authoritativeness of the debater, and they were easier for viewers to assess and adjudicate.

23. Risse argues, for instance, that nonhierarchical and networklike international institutions "characterized by a high density of mostly informal interactions should allow for discursive and argumentative processes" (1997, 18). Martin and Simmons, coming at the question from a contractual institutionalist perspective, also imply that institutions where participants are reliant on "expert" sources of information should be "most influential in promoting cooperation" (1998, 742). See also MacLaren 1980, 67–68, for similar hypotheses.

24. Efforts to buck or shirk flexible consensus decisions will generate more negative peer pressure than if clear opposition is registered through a vote (Chigas, McClintock, and Kamp 1996, 42–43). Obstinance in a consensus system threatens to undermine the effectiveness of the entire institution because this is premised on consensus. Obstinance is judged to be fundamentally at odds with the purposes of the institution. "Principled stands" against efforts to declare consensus are viewed as less principled than had they been expressed in a losing vote (Steiner 1974, 269–71).

25. ARF (1995). See also the comments by Defense Minister Hajib Tun Rajak of Malaysia, cited in Dewitt 1994, 12–13, and Lee Kwan-yew's comments about the ARF as a channel for China's reassuring Southeast Asia about its status quo intentions in Makabenta 1994.

26. These are the security principles of the OSCE as well. The primary difference between OSCE and ARF definitions of common and cooperative security is that the former includes human rights and liberal domestic governance as a component of interstate security. The ARF, sensitive to the postcolonial sovereign-centric ideologies in ASEAN and China, excludes this element.

27. Track I refers to official meetings and institutions: Track II refers to non-official meetings that involve officials, academics, and other nongovernmental

personnel. CSCAP has emerged as the primary Track II institution for the ARF, where ideas and arguments that might be too controversial at the official level can be floated and discussed less formally, without requiring national policy commitments.

28. See the paper presented by Shi Chunlai (a former ambassador to India and a key figure in China's CSCAP committee) and Xu Jian at the ARF-sponsored Paris workshop on preventive diplomacy (November 1996). Shi appears to have been China's first authoritative participant in ARF-related activities to have used the term "common security." The paper argues that common security was central to the post–Cold War need for a "renewal" of old security concepts based on the "dangerous game of balance of power" (see Shi and Xu 1997).

29. They did this at the first Canada-China Multilateral Training Seminar in January 1997. The seminar brought together a small number of key officials handling the ARF in the MOFA Asia Department and a couple of analysts from China's civilian intelligence institution—China Institute of Contemporary International Relations (CICIR)—who were also in the ARF interagency process.

30. For a systematic comparison of the Five Power Treaty on CBM and the CSCE Vienna Document of 1994, see Acharya 1997a, 16–23.

31. This was the distinct impression I received when interviewing military and civilian specialists on the ARF in 1996. Interviews in 1998 and 1999 with analysts involved in discussions of multilateralism also suggested that officials in the MOFA Asia Department were more likely to see the potential applications than, say, PLA officers and traditional security analysts.

32. While an internal study, the document itself is not classified or stamped with the words "internal circulation only." Technically the report was commissioned by the MOFA Policy Research Office, but the primary consumer was the Asia Department.

33. The following information comes from Interview 1996b, 1996c, 1996d, 1997a, 1998d; Smith 1996.

34. The MOFA-commissioned study on comprehensive security, however, clearly lists sources and notes from Canadian and American academic specialists in multilateralism.

35. One key issue is how this change in attitudes toward multilateralism has affected China's diplomacy inside the ARF. Since this doesn't fall within the mandate of this chapter, strictly speaking, I will not address it here. The short answer is that this growing acceptance of multilateralism has enabled China to accept changes in the institutionalization and agenda of the ARF that it would not have accepted at the start in 1994—namely, a greater level of institutionalization (for example, the creation of functionally specialized intersessional meetings) and more intrusive agendas (for example, certain CBMs, discussions of preventive diplomacy, and so forth). I expand on these changes in the ARF in Johnston 1999b.

36. The argument is outlined in Garrett and Glaser 1997. My own conversations with Pentagon officials involved in Asia policy confirms this particular interpretation.

37. This argument was made by some of the civilian analysts and military officials involved in ARF policy-making I interviewed in 1998 and 1999. Indeed, the MOFA-commissioned report on comprehensive security is explicit in stating that China should not and need not replace U.S. military superiority in the region and that China needs to balance militarily against U.S. power, especially if effective, practical multilateral security institutions can be set up in the region (see Zhang 1998, 20–21, 26–27).

38. Even this is problematic from an institutionalist perspective. As realpoliticians, the Chinese should have been especially suspicious of an institution that activist states such as Canada, Australia, and to some extent the United States supported. The information that their involvement should have supplied, for realpolitician skeptics, was precisely that the ARF was a potentially constraining institution.

39. These interpretations were consistent across public and private internal discussions.

40. On social identity theory (SIT) and the psychological discomforts of nonconformity, see Turner 1987; Gerard and Orive 1987; Stryker and Statham 1985; Barnum 1997; Axelrod 1997.

41. Keohane notes, for instance, that one of the things international institutions do is provide a forum in which an actor's conformity with group standards can be evaluated. He links this to a more instrumental notion of reputation than I do here, however (1984, 94).

42. This distinguishes status concerns from obligation and from material interest as a source of cooperative behavior. It blends the economic language of optimizing with the sociological language of group processes or social interactions and thus helps to underscore why (small r) rationalist and sociological or constructivist approaches are not necessarily mutually exclusive. (I use small r rationalism to refer to the assumption that agents are optimizers or maximizers in the expected utility sense. Big r Rationalism refers to the ontological and epistemological assumptions of positivism and modernity [that there is an observable and knowledge external world independent of the normative preferences of the observers]).

43. The reasons behind using this type of game for illustrative purposes are twofold: First, while security dilemmas can be modeled using PD or stag hunt assumptions, the former is a tougher cooperation problem because of its assumption about opportunism. So, in a sense, using an N-person PD presents a hard case for the promotion of cooperation through social influence mechanisms. Second, empirically, it is my view a valid simplification to assume that the realpolitik of Chinese decision makers leads them to view their own security environment more in PD terms than in stag hunt terms.

44. On the question of aggregation see Finnemore and Sikkink 1998, 904.

45. Conversation with Chinese foreign policy specialist, Foreign Affairs College, October 1998.

46. This is based on conversations with scholars from the Foreign Affairs College and the Institute of World Economics and Politics at the Chinese Academy of Social Sciences, October 1998.

47. Many of the details of the negotiations come from Rebecca Johnson's excellent reportage on behalf of the NGO community. See her "Geneva Updates" and "Acronym Reports" on the DFAX web page at <http://csf .colorado.edu/dfax/index.htm>.

48. See the summary in "Guowai dui women he shiyan de fanying" [Foreign Reaction to Our Tests], in *Guowai hewuqi dongtai* [Trends in Foreign Nuclear Weapons], 12, no. 6 (1994.12.2): 1. See similar concerns expressed in other internal circulation materials such as Fu 1994, 7; Wu Zheng 1996, 10; and Zou 1998, 12.

49. See Johnston 1995–96 for details on the concept of limited deterrence. Adding to the uncertainty of the effects of a test ban on China's deterrence is that apparently there has been little discussion inside China over how many penetrated warheads against what targets is enough to constitute a deterrent. This dearth of discussion has also hindered China's ability to think through the pros and cons of a fissile material production cutoff. The weapons community was also worried that a ban on testing would bring economic hardship to its large testing infrastructure, including the city of Malan, which serviced the Xinjiang test sites.

50. China had lobbied behind the scenes at the UNGA First Committee (disarmament) in the fall of 1995 to prevent a vote calling for a treaty by the fall of 1996. The committee in fact voted overwhelmingly for the date, and in the end China abstained rather than having to stand publicly in opposition to the vote.

51. See comments by Sha Zukang in CD/PV.717, September 5, 1995, 6.

52. I interviewed a member of the U.S. delegation in the fall of 1995, and he was not at all certain that China would sign.

53. Up until this point delegates were negotiating a rolling text with as many as 1,200 brackets, indicating disagreements over wording, grammar, and punctuation. A clean text was introduced by the ad hoc nuclear test ban (NTB) committee chair, Rammaker of the Netherlands, presented as a flexible fait accompli for more focused negotiation. The presentation of the clean text, and its acceptance as a basis for bargaining, signaled the endgame of negotiations.

54. The cover for China's concession on PNEs was "an assurance that such explosions could be reviewed at periodic review conferences, although Chinese officials acknowledged that such reviews were unlikely to lead to revisions of the prohibitions" (Zou 1998, 38).

55. This is implied by Zou's summary that "When people gradually came to the conclusion that PNE was one of the obstacles to signing the treaty, China finally made a major move on this issue in early June 1996" (1998, 23).

56. The United States wanted the triggering of OSI to be as easy as possible, hence its preference for a simple majority. China, determined to minimize the intrusiveness of the verification system, initially wanted OSI to be as difficult as possible. For a fascinating description of negotiations on this question, see Zou 1998, 31–35.

57. Recent allegations that the Chinese had "stolen" information about U.S. nuclear weapons designs have been remarkably ambiguous about what information was acquired, how, and when. The intelligence community consensus, in contrast to the more hyperbolic Cox Report, is that it is unclear what information was acquired, when, how, and with what significance for the flexibility of China's nuclear options. Actually, the Cox Report implies in places that the CTBT, if enforced, does negatively affect the reliability of China's second-generation warheads. Until these issues are clarified, I believe that the concerns that had been relayed in public and private by China's testing community about the constraints a CTBT will place on warhead modernization are still credible ones. For a discussion of these issues see May 1999.

58. Interviews with analysts in the Institute of Applied Physics and Computational Mathematics (IAPCM), China Academy of Engineering Physics (CAEP), PLA, and U.S. Department of Defense. See also Li and Zhou 1997, 241. For a critique of the CTBT for its irrelevance in reducing incentives to proliferate, see Chen and Wang 1996.

59. See CD/INF.37 (1995) and CD/INF.38 (1996).

60. One of the Department of Defense members of the U.S. CTBT delegation also speculated that this timeline is probably correct (Interview, January 1998). The January 1996 Chinese delegation also included a deputy director and arms control expert from the IAPCM. This too would suggest that the issue for China by January 1996 was not whether to sign but which specific provisions at the margins in the treaty that might affect the nuclear weapons community were acceptable.

61. One Chinese informant, a well-respected arms control specialist outside of the formal CTBT interagency process, claimed that the French had approached him early on about possible cooperation to prevent a CTBT. I have no way of verifying this claim independently, however.

62. The issue came up in my discussions with specialists connected to the Chinese military in January 1998.

63. Conversation with U.S. government specialist, August 1998.

64. These arguments come from interviews with arms control officials and experts in MOFA, the Chinese military, the Chinese nuclear weapons research community, and the U.S. Department of Defense. The interviews were conducted in 1996 and 1998.

65. The Chinese were made very aware of the specific pressure from developing states after its May 1995 nuclear test, which took place forty-eight hours after the end of the NPT extension conference. In Zou's words, "The May 15, 1995 test inflicted the most political damage to China. . . . This test

made the Non-Aligned Movement very angry" (1998, 13). This is an interesting and exceedingly rare public admission of sharp differences between China and other developing states on nuclear disarmament issues.

66. In some cases, when I followed up with questions specifically on the role of image concerns, my interlocutors would quickly downplay what they had just said, since this implied that China was indeed susceptible to external pressure.

67. This is not dissimilar to Johnson's (1993) argument that cheap talk, in the context of persuasion whereby interests and identities converge inside a social relationship, establishes focal points that are necessary to reduce the strategic indeterminacy of bargaining games.

68. These motivations parallel the three that James Q. Wilson (1973) identifies: material incentives, purposive incentives (persuasion), and solidarity incentives (social influence).

International Commitments and Domestic Politics: Institutions and Actors at Two Levels

Duncan Snidal and Alexander Thompson

In the last two decades, international relations (IR) scholars have responded to the parsimony of systemic theory, with its exclusive focus on interactions among states, by looking both above and below the level of states. Thus international cooperation and institutions, on the one hand, and domestic politics and institutions, on the other, have assumed important positions as both independent and dependent variables. However, surprisingly little attention has been paid to the interaction of international and domestic institutions, although there is no theoretical reason to presume that the two should be analytically separated. The primary exception is the two-level games literature (Putnam 1988; Evans, Jacobson, and Putnam 1993) and related work on how domestic political constraints shape international cooperation (Milner 1997) and the ability of states to make credible international commitments (Cowhey 1993; Martin 2000). Much less effort has been devoted to the reverse channel of influence—how international institutions constrain domestic politics.[1]

This volume investigates how actors use international institutions to overcome domestic political obstacles. It addresses two principal impediments that may confound the pursuit of political goals. On the one hand, highly centralized states are plagued by commitment problems: When government power is not checked, then other actors, both within the state and internationally, cannot be sure that the policy will be maintained over time and so may be unwilling to take actions desired by the policy initiators. Decentralized states, on the other hand, face domestic veto problems because the consent or participation of key actors ("domestic veto points") is required for policies to succeed. The involvement of international institutions can potentially solve both of these political dilemmas.

In his introductory chapter, Daniel W. Drezner provides a framework for exploring the conditions under which actors use supranational institutions to pursue policies, as well as when they will be successful and what the long-term implications might be. He eschews state centrism by dividing the relevant actors into policy initiators (who have the power to propose change and may be internal or external to the nation-state in question) and policy ratifiers (who have the ability to veto policy initiatives). The number of necessary ratifiers defines the degree of centralization in the relevant polity. Drezner's framework then helps us understand how international institutions shape the interaction of initiators and ratifiers through a variety of influence mechanisms—including contracting, coercion, and persuasion.

The empirical chapters explore how international institutions influence these interactions. They are diverse in terms of both subject matter and methodological approach. The authors address a broad array of substantive issue areas, including humanitarian intervention (Schultz), trade dispute settlement (Reinhardt), economic development (Blanchard), democratic transition (Pevehouse) and security cooperation (Johnston). This broad case selection has the virtue of incorporating developing countries, which are too often ignored in IR, as well as less prominent international organzations (IOs). This helps correct a potential bias in the literature, namely that repeated studies of the usual suspects—in terms of states and IOs—will lead to conclusions that are not representative of the universe of countries and institutions. The potential for generalizability is thus great.

The authors specify and assess their arguments using game theory, quantitative analysis, and qualitative case studies, often in combination. Although the empirical chapters lie generally in the rationalistic tradition of treating actors as purposive and instrumental, they show how international institutions also shape the interaction of domestic and international politics through other influence mechanisms more commonly identified with constructivist approaches.[2] Thus IOs allow policy initiators to establish credible commitments and to contract more effectively; they provide information, resources, and expertise; and they help to persuade, legitimize, and transmit norms to domestic actors. This causal eclecticism, encouraged by Drezner's analytic exploration of contracting, coercion, and persuasion, is virtuous in its inclusiveness: There is no a priori reason to expect any one paradigm to dominate in this domain.

The volume adds considerably to our understanding of interactions between international and domestic institutions while retaining nuance at both levels. The state is broken down in terms of structure (centralized versus decentralized) and through the identification of individual actors (initiators versus ratifiers). International institutions are problematized in terms of their design and their multiple sources of influence. Indeed, one reasonable criticism is that the volume attempts too much in embracing such complexity. This critique is misplaced insofar as the project sets the stage for an expanding research program; its greatest contribution lies in generating new hypotheses and probing their plausibility.

Drezner's introductory chapter provides a rich set of theoretical propositions to guide the empirical analysis. We have distilled these propositions into five general hypotheses (see table 1). These have been selected because they capture the essential elements of Drezner's argument and are addressed by the empirical case studies. In this concluding chapter, we will synthesize the volume's results with an eye to deepening their theoretical implications and identifying further paths of inquiry.

The first section of this chapter advances Drezner's theoretical agenda beginning at the domestic level. We expand on the concept of centralization and then develop a simple game theory model to clarify the different relations between state structure and the demand for international institutional involvement. The second

TABLE 1.   The Volume's Hypotheses

State Structure

H1   Initiators from decentralized states use international institutions to overcome domestic veto points in order to implement and lock in policies.

H2   Initiators from centralized states use international institutions to establish credible commitments.

Long-Term Implications

H3   Repeated interactions enhance the power of policy initiators at the expense of ratifying institutions.

International Institutional Structure

H4   Institutional design matters. Whether and how initiators use international institutions is partly a function of their design features.

Initiator Location

H5   External initiators have less success in their interactions with domestic institutions than domestic policy initiators.

section surveys the evidence from the volume with regard to hypotheses H1, H2, and H3. The cases strongly support H1—that initiators from decentralized states use international institutions to overcome domestic veto points. Some support is found for H2—that centralized states use international institutions to make credible commitments—but the more important conclusion concerns the need to refine our understanding of centralization and to identify more precisely the underlying commitment mechanisms. Finally, H3—that repeated interactions favor initiators over ratifiers—has some validity but needs to be refined in terms of the identities of the initiator and ratifier and to incorporate learning and persuasion into the analysis.

The third section turns to the international level and discusses the findings with regard to H4 and H5.[3] The empirical evidence on H4—that international institutional design matters—indicates a need to develop more fine-grained propositions and to distinguish more carefully between the qualitatively different roles of formal versus informal institutions. Furthermore, the Drezner framework portrays IOs as excessively passive and thereby overlooks their important role as agents of interaction and change. Finally, the volume offers insufficient evidence to reach a definitive conclusion regarding H5—that external initiators will be less successful than domestic initiators—but the limited evidence presented suggests that it is incorrect as stated. A speculative but plausible revision is that external initiators need domestic allies to succeed.

An important implication of the theory and evidence is that international institutions work both through the manipulation of rational incentives (by withholding benefits or sanctioning, by facilitating signaling and commitment, and by providing information and resources) and through sociological and normative mechanisms (such as persuasion and collective legitimation). Indeed, the same institution may perform these functions at different times or even simultaneously. This illustrates that rationalist and constructivist approaches often are complementary and provide different lenses through which to view the same phenomena and outcomes. We proceed in this spirit.

The concluding section refines several of the hypotheses and discusses how the framework might be extended along several theoretical and empirical avenues. We consider how the state structure and international institutional design variables might be modified to produce novel insights and how an expanded analysis might treat the roles of initiator and ratifier as endogenous. In particular, ratifiers may adopt some of the same strategies as initiators to capture first-mover and agenda-setting advantages. We end by asking several questions, inspired by the volume, about the broader role of international institutions — and especially formal organizations — in world politics.

State Structure and International Commitments

The central explanatory theme of this volume is that states use international institutions to solve commitment problems and to overcome domestic veto points. But they do so in different ways, depending on their state structure. State structure determines the type of commitment or veto problem a state faces and how it uses international institutions to solve it.

Drezner defines "state structure" in terms of the centralization of decision making. A centralized state can be viewed as a single, cohesive decision-making body unencumbered by the need to achieve agreement from other decision-making bodies. This corresponds to the classical IR conception of the state as a unitary actor, although here it is taken as a reasonable approximation of domestic politics rather than as a "black box." However, whereas traditional IR takes the unitary actor assumption as a license to ignore domestic politics, Drezner argues that even centralized states need to worry about the response of domestic actors to their policies. By contrast, a decentralized state structure has multiple independent decision points, and there is no central actor that can act on its own. Here state action requires overcoming potential domestic veto points directly. The veto points are not limited to formalized institutional arrangements (for example, voting); ratifiers may include actors such as firms or unions whose active support is essential to policy success.

Of course, there is considerable variation along a continuum from decentralization to centralization — some states are only somewhat decentralized because they have a few veto points, whereas others are highly decentralized because they include many veto points. Moreover, the degree of centralization often varies across issue areas even within the same state. For example, states are typically highly centralized on security issues but more decentralized on issues such as trade or the environment, where different actors play key roles and political motivations are distinct. This more nuanced centralized-decentralized distinction captures refinements in the traditional "strong" versus "weak" state categories and recognizes variation both across states and within the same state.[4] Drezner's framework allows us to cast these considerations in terms of the strategic interrelation between initiators and ratifiers and an analysis of the commitment problem, as we show later.

This very general theoretical conception of (de)centralized state structure has the virtue of bringing together the wide range of substantive cases analyzed in the volume. Two chapters—Eric Reinhardt's analysis of WTO trade disputes and Kenneth A. Schultz's examination of U.S. humanitarian intervention—use centralization to refer to the relationship between the executive and legislative branches. Here centralization is defined in terms of formal institutional rules such as ratification. These analyses show how international institutions strengthen the advantage that the president enjoys over Congress in obtaining trade liberalization and in deciding on the use of force abroad, respectively.

Jon C. Pevehouse's focus on newly democratizing states offers a quite different view of centralization. These regimes are decentralized not so much because of their formal structure but because of their dependence on other actors.[5] Domestic business and international investors are each in a position to scuttle the government's plans if they do not find them suitable. More ominously, opposition groups and the military may veto government policies, or even the government, when they oppose policies. This dependence on other actors is exacerbated by the fluid nature of the posttransition setting: The government may not be sure which actors will pose a threat and under what institutional rules or power relationships they will interact. The result, Pevehouse argues, is that democratizing regimes turn to international institutions to credibly commit to policy reform.

Finally, a comparison of the two chapters involving China shows how different cuts at the "same" case may lead to different conceptualizations of centralization. Jean-Marc F. Blanchard investigates efforts by subnational and supranational actors to promote a multinational development project along the Tumen River involving the bordering states of China, Russia, and North Korea. In doing so, he defines centralization in terms of relations between the central government and its provinces, where the provinces are the key initiators in his analysis. Alastair Iain Johnston's study of how other states use persuasion and social influence to convince Chinese policymakers to join regional security regimes does not focus on centralization as a key variable, but it still provides an interesting contrast. Military policy formulation is generally a centralized state activity, as it is in

China. But a more microscopic view of interagency relations within the security bureaucracy begins to reveal these processes as somewhat decentralized—even though defense policy is highly centralized from a more macroscopic perspective. Thus in both cases—and even in an authoritarian system—some degree of decentralization becomes apparent according to how we define the problem and units of analysis. This flexibility of the centralization concept suggests both its potential power and the dangers of stretching it too far.

Such fine-grained differences are important in the empirical studies, but for theoretical purposes it is often more insightful to begin with comparisons between the endpoints of the continuum—as we do in the remainder of this section. The importance of centralization is reflected by its fundamental role in Drezner's theoretical arguments. Drezner develops what could be labeled a paradox of centralization: Highly decentralized states are so weak domestically that they cannot implement coherent policies, whereas highly centralized states are so strong domestically that they cannot credibly commit to policies. International institutions help both types of states solve these problems by increasing the costs of changing policies. But they do so in different ways that are worth clarifying.[6]

A decentralized state confronts a domestic veto point when a domestic ratifier can block its policies. The game tree in figure 1a represents this situation by showing the state initiator I with a choice to propose a policy (P) or not, followed by a choice for the domestic ratifier R to accept or veto the policy (V). The ordered pairs at each terminal node refer to the payoffs to the initiator and ratifier, respectively, as indicated by the subscripts. (The b_R and c_R terms reflect the impact of an international institution and are in brackets to indicate that they are initially equal to zero and should be ignored for now.) The domestic veto problem arises because, while the initiator benefits from the policy ($P_I > 0$), the ratifier prefers to veto the policy ($V_R > P_R$) after it is proposed. The result is that the initiator's policy goals will be frustrated. They may only be partially frustrated if I finds it useful to propose the policy and accept the veto (which it will do if $V_I > 0$, perhaps because some compromise results), or they may be completely frustrated if I declines to even propose the policy because of the political damage it suffers by being defeated (if $0 > V_I$).[7]

Drezner argues that the initiator state can resolve the problem by working through an international institution to change the incentives of domestic ratifiers, as indicated by the bracketed payoffs in figure 1a. International institutions can reward domestic ratifiers for accepting

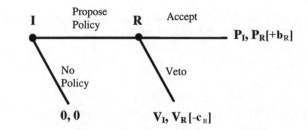

(a) Decentralized state facing a veto problem

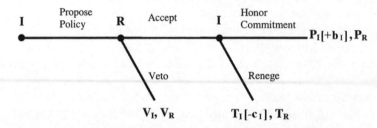

(b) Centralized state facing a commitment problem

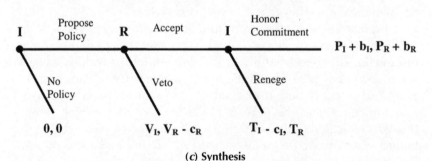

(c) Synthesis

Fig. 1.   The dilemmas of state structure

government policies $(+b_R)$—perhaps by providing outside resources to offset any losses caused by the policy. They can also impose costs on the exercise of domestic vetoes $(-c_R)$—perhaps because states that do not fulfill commitments made through international institutions will be ineligible for subsequent programs that benefit the ratifiers.[8] If this combination of carrots and sticks is strong enough (that is, $c_R + b_R > V_R - P_R$, where $V_R - P_R$ is the gain that domestic ratifiers make from vetoing rather than accepting the policy), the initiator's policy can be made effective. We postpone a fuller elaboration of how international institutions create costs and benefits—the substance behind the terms used here—until a later discussion.

Intervention by the international institution is most compelling—on normative grounds that may also provide a positive basis for international intervention—if the initiator policy represents a broader social good that some narrow constituency or special interest is seeking to block. If the initiator instead represents a narrow interest (for example, a self-serving or predatory elite), whereas the ratifier incorporates a broader social interest (for example, interests of economic development in general), intervention is less compelling.[9] In either case, however, international intervention will be contested when domestic interests are opposed.

An important variation of the veto problem occurs when the interests of the initiator and state are not strictly opposed. Even if the ratifier is a beneficiary of the initiator's policy ($P_R > 0$) so that both are better off at $\{P_I, P_R\}$ than at the $\{0,0\}$ status quo, R may still have an incentive to act opportunistically by vetoing the proposed policy ($V_R > P_R$). This might be the case if significant political gains accrue from opposing the policy and outweigh the gains from the policy itself. But if this leads the initiator not to propose the policy (because $0 > V_I$), both sides are worse off than if the domestic ratifier did not have a veto. In these highly contested political situations—where the veto is costly to the initiator and therefore a self-defeating threat for the ratifier—both sides may welcome the role of the international institution in resolving the veto problem. Finally, note that this situation can now be thought of as a commitment problem from the perspective of the domestic ratifier. If the ratifier could commit to working with the government's policy—for example, by forswearing its veto alternative before the government announces the policy—the government could propose the policy, the ratifier would accept it, and both sides would be better off.

Figure 1b presents the alternative case, where the ratifier supports the policy ($P_R > V_R$) but the centralized state is so strong that it cannot credibly commit to its policy. The game tree begins with initiator I announcing a policy after which ratifier R must decide whether to trust the government by accepting the policy. If R trusts I by accepting the policy and I honors its commitment, they each benefit from the policy ($P_I > V_I$ and $P_R > V_R$). (Again, bracketed terms b_I and c_I refer to outcomes when the commitment is made through an international institution and so initially equal zero.) Unfortunately, I receives a higher payoff ($T_I > P_I$) by not honoring its commitment, while R receives less than if it had not trusted I ($T_R < V_R$).[10] Thus R

will not trust I, the policy will be ineffective, and the outcome will be $\{V_I, V_R\}$.[11] The dilemma is that both actors are worse off because I cannot make a credible commitment to its policy P (if it could, R would trust I and the payoff would be $\{P_I, P_R\}$).

This commitment problem can be resolved if an international institution either imposes costs on initiators who break commitments ($-c_I$ in fig. 1b) or provides benefits ($+b_I$) to initiators who honor their commitments. Provided the combination of punishments and rewards is sufficiently powerful (that is, $b_I + c_I > T_I - P_I$, where $T_I - P_I$ is the benefit the initiator gets from reneging), then the commitment to the policy is credible; R can trust I, who will honor the policy.

Note that in both figures 1a and 1b, it would be preferable from the institution's perspective to promote the policy by threatening punishments rather than by providing benefits. Benefits are costly (that is, an amount b has to be provided to one or both actors), whereas effective punishments never have to be administered since the threat is sufficient to induce appropriate behavior.[12] But if the ability to threaten punishment provides a cheaper way of solving commitment problems, it raises the question of whether international institutions can do so credibly. Are the "forum" effects of being condemned rhetorically in an international setting, the "compliance pull" of international agreements (Franck 1990), or the costs of being viewed as a rule violator sufficiently powerful incentives to change an actor's behavior? And even when IOs have the capacity to impose punishments (for example, IMF cutoffs), can they solve their own commitment problems to make credible threats? In the case of the IMF, for example, Randall Stone's (2002) research shows that the IMF can credibly threaten smaller countries such as Bulgaria and Poland but not large countries such as Russia and the Ukraine. This is especially true when, for geopolitical reasons, the latter receive support from the United States that further undermines IMF credibility. Some of these effects, and the ability of institutions to punish and provide benefits more generally, depend on the details of institutional design. We will return to these substantive issues subsequently.

Although the simple model does not include uncertainty—the actors, their choices, and their payoffs are completely known to all— it can be introduced informally by considering the impact of uncertainty regarding payoffs. In figure 1b, for example, the problem may be that, although the initiator prefers to honor its commitment, the ratifier is unsure whether this is the case (that is, T_I ? P_I). In this circumstance, the international institution may serve as a screening device if, for example, only states that prefer to honor their commitment would accept the requirements of the institution or be allowed into it. Alternatively, in a more dynamic setting, the institution might perform monitoring functions that reduce incentives to renege by providing early warning of any change in policy.

Figure 1c combines the two problems into one interaction, reflecting the possibility of domestic veto and commitment dilemmas occurring together. After I proposes the policy, it is subject first to a veto by R (if $V_R > P_R$) and then to reneging by I (if $T_I > P_I$). Either possibility is sufficient to cause the policy not to be offered in the first place. Working through an institution can resolve the problem only if the incentives of both initiators and ratifiers are altered (that is, so that $b_I + c_I > T_I - P_I$ for I and $b_R + c_R > V_R - P_R$ for R).

Pevehouse's discussion of newly democratizing states is an instructive example of such complicated interrelations. On the one hand, the opposition often wonders whether a new democratic regime is truly committed to reform or will renege on its policies at some opportune time. On the other hand, the new regime depends on other actors (such as domestic business and international investors) to accept its policies to succeed. Moreover, when the simple static model is placed in the context of a turbulent world of uncertainty and ongoing choices, Pevehouse points out how the problems feed on each other. Doubts regarding the credibility of the initiator's commitment to the policy make ratifiers increasingly hesitant to accept the policy, which leads the initiator to partially renege on the policy, which in turn reinforces the ratifier's doubts. A vicious cycle ensues.

Drezner makes a useful analytic simplification when he separates the two problems, as in figures 1a and 1b. He argues that decentralized states cannot abandon their commitments unilaterally because of the same domestic veto actors that make it hard for them to change policies in the first place.[13] Conversely, he argues that the strength of centralized states, which makes it hard for them to credibly commit, also means they do not face domestic veto players who can block their policies. However, many real-world problems lie in the middle such that both forms of commitment problems emerge. A speculative bright side is that the symmetry of the problem may ease its solution. Thus even if neither side understands why it cannot be trusted and why external intervention is needed, each may be willing to engage an international institution to deal with the problem "caused by the other."

Three further limitations of this stylized framework should be noted. First, these arguments make sense in terms of formal institutional rules but may be less compelling when we consider the implementation of policies. Decentralized states may be unable to change policies unilaterally, but they may well have a capacity to renege on their implementation. Similarly, even the strongest centralized states depend on other actors participating in their policies and so are subject to some type of domestic implementation "vetoes." Second, international institutions are not the only way to solve commitment and veto problems. We discuss the use of domestic institutions for these purposes below; reputation staking provides an alternative mechanism. Finally, veto and commitment problems are hard to distinguish empirically because both predict the same outcome—that states will use international institutions. Of course, states differ in their motivations for doing so, and the roles of the international institutions differ in terms of which actors' payoffs are affected. These issues are best resolved empirically in terms of specific case studies, as reflected in the design of the overall project.

As a final note, while this discussion has been developed in rationalist terms, Johnston's social influence argument can also be represented through the payoffs. Insofar as interaction within international institutions creates social rewards and pressures for the actors, these can be reflected in the benefits (that is, b_I, b_R) and costs (that is, c_I, c_R) imposed through the institution. Persuasion, on the other hand, changes private values, not just costs and benefits. Since persuasion results in new conceptions of interests, its impact will be reflected in the preferences of the actors and only thereby in the payoffs. This allows the substantive analysis to distinguish other ways that international institutions affect the choices of states beyond creating costs and benefits. Of course, these representations do not fully capture the actual social process involved any more than the payoffs fully capture the underlying rational decision processes. But the framework can still be useful provided the underlying "calculus" is interpreted broadly.

Variation in State Structure: Findings and Extensions

The cases provide empirical evidence on the two hypotheses (H1 and H2) captured in figure 1. The first hypothesis—that initiators from decentralized states use international institutions to overcome domestic veto points—fares very well. All four cases with internal initiators from decentralized states show them using international institutions this way.

Schultz provides very strong support for this hypothesis with respect to humanitarian intervention by the United States. He does it theoretically by elaborating the hypothesis in the important case of president-Congress relations and by connecting this argument to the well-known parallel commitment devices at the domestic level. Schultz confirms the hypothesis empirically in the cases of Haiti (1994) and Bosnia (1995), where presidential commitments through IOs "create a momentum that members of Congress are unwilling to stop." Conversely, he shows that when the president did not establish clear international commitments in Rwanda (1994), Congress was able to block any substantial humanitarian initiative. Indeed, among the strongest evidence Schultz provides about the validity of the "overcoming veto points" hypothesis concerns congressional efforts to act before the president is able to make a commitment. It may be bad for public policy if the executive and legislative branches must race to be precipitous, but this race does confirm the power of commitment through international forums.

Pevehouse provides strong quantitative support for the proposition by showing that recently democratized states, which are especially subject to veto points in the wake of transition, are much more likely to join IOs—presumably as part of a strategy of locking in democracy against domestic opposition. However, Pevehouse argues that this tendency "may have little to do with international outcomes." We disagree, since the power of an international institution to lock in democracy comes through its ability to provide benefits or costs to the ratifiers (as in fig. 1a). Also, while Pevehouse correctly points out the need to investigate the issue of enforcement by IOs, it is valuable to remember that one important form of enforcement comes through the (potential) withdrawal of the benefits of membership. This is especially relevant because states are often reluctant to join institutions that have a significant capacity to coerce and enforce. Thus, while Pevehouse is correct that the impetus to join the institution may come from domestic sources, the impact of IOs in the domestic realm implicitly rests on their ability to be consequential and effective in the international realm.

Blanchard's analysis of the Tumen River Area Development Programme (TRADP) shows the importance both of China's Province of Jilin as a subnational initiator and its reliance on the facilitating role of the United Nations Development Programme (UNDP). The UNDP provided research funding for the project both initially and at key junctures and set the agenda for the development of the project. Its role was not centrally one of overcoming domestic veto points, since Blanchard does not indicate any significant opposition to the project within China. However, the UNDP did play a valuable role in reassuring the Japanese and Americans and thus in avoiding *international* veto points. (This suggests a mild broadening of H1 to include external "ratifiers" of domestic policies.) Finally, the limitations of the role of the international institution are clearly demonstrated in the slowing progress once the TRADP became embroiled in broader PRC-Russia diplomacy.

Reinhardt's chapter offers an interesting extension of H1. Although he supports the basic argument that international institutions help overcome domestic veto points, he shows that these relations are not always as simple or straightforward as the hypothesis implies. In his analysis, the initiator (the president) uses its informational advantage regarding an international organization (the WTO) to tie the hands of the ratifier (Congress).[14] The possibility of an adverse ruling from the WTO and the resulting sanctions make protectionism too costly for Congress. Because the cost of vetoing $(-c_R)$ is too great, Congress prefers ratifying the liberalization policy over vetoing it $(P_R + b_R > V_R - c_R)$.

Although Reinhardt captures essential elements of how U.S. trade politics are shaped by the threat of WTO litigation, his "tying hands without a rope" logic is a specialized argument that applies when a ruling is pending, when certain assumptions about asymmetric information and transactions costs apply, and when there is the possibility of enforcement by the institution. This is a narrower and different version of the commitment problem than the one presented by Drezner.[15] The lesson is that specific cases need more detailed investigation and theoretical guidance than that offered by the hypothesis. On the other hand, as a way to summarize the central dynamic of the case, the argument of "using international institutions to overcome domestic veto points" does very well.

While the empirical support for H1 is strong, some caution is appropriate. First, this conclusion is based on a small number of cases even if it is strengthened to the extent that the details of the commitment mechanism are elaborated in each. Second, there is always the danger of an unintentional selection bias if cases were chosen because they were instances of commitments through international institutions. Finally, as we noted earlier and will discuss again later, the very definition of centralization versus decentralization is at play according to how analysts define their objects of study. For these reasons, the findings on H1 should not be taken as a test of the theory in any but the weakest sense. What they do provide, however, is a rich playing out of the hypothesis in different settings that suggests an important mechanism is at work.

By contrast, the cases offer limited evidence regarding H2—that initiators from centralized states use international institutions to establish credible commitments—because they contain little treatment of centralized states as initiators. The exception is Reinhardt's analysis of unified government, that is, a situation in which the president and Congress have identical (protectionist) preferences. He finds that as the transaction costs of working through the institution increase, the result is increased liberalization of trade policy proposals, despite the unified preference to the contrary. It is difficult to interpret this finding in light of H2, however, since Reinhardt does not discuss his results with respect to the centralized-decentralized variable. When initiators and ratifiers have the same preferences in a decentralized state (a unified government), should we expect the same commitment strategies and outcomes as with a centralized state? Nevertheless, Reinhardt adds another useful dimension to the state structure variable by looking at actor preferences in addition to formal structures.

In his introduction, Drezner suggests that Pevehouse's analysis of newly democratizing states also bears on H2. Although Pevehouse offers some relevant evidence, his more important contribution is to show how the hypothesis might be reworked in a broader way. The nascent democracies in Pevehouse's analysis face a credibility problem not because they can do as they want (as with the centralized states of H2) but because it is unclear what they want or what they can do. Since the government is new to power, other actors do not know yet if it is controlled by true reformers or by imposters. The government has no track record that either answers this question or creates a reputation that the government would have incentives to preserve. Finally, the difficulties of transition and the short time horizons of a fragile government may create severe time-inconsistency problems (that is, incentives to quickly renege on commitments) that make their policy pronouncements unbelievable. Thus they face a commitment problem of convincing other actors that they will stay whatever course they announce. In such circumstances, international institutions can help transitional governments establish the durability of their commitment to reform and thereby increase their capacity to achieve policy goals.

The other contributors deal almost exclusively with decentralized states and so provide little evidence for or against H2.[16] This may simply be a result of the failure to include initiators from centralized states among the empirical cases. It is not because centralized states never use institutional arrangements to limit their power—as the examples of central banks (Broz 1997; Maxfield 1997), independent judiciaries (North and Weingast 1989), federalism (Weingast 1995), separation of civil and military authority, and separation of powers illustrate. But these examples further suggest that centralized states can often find *domestic* institutional means to make self-limiting commitments if they are so inclined. We can speculate that, when domestic means are available, states will not grant such substantial authority to an external agent for "sovereignty cost" reasons (Abbott and Snidal 2000). An important exception is the growing emergence of currency board arrangements among less developed countries otherwise unable to manage their monetary affairs effectively.

An alternative explanation for such strong support for H1 and relative silence on H2 is the elasticity of the concept of centralization discussed earlier. If even highly authoritarian states begin to look quite fragmented under sufficiently close examination (as in Blanchard's and Johnston's chapters), then the "observed" level of centralization or decentralization may depend primarily on the power of our analytic microscope. The observed level of centralization may also depend on the types of decisions being examined. Top authority has to delegate some decision-making powers to lower authority in any regime, but that may vary as much by issue area as by regime type. Such measurement problems need not be problematic for longitudinal studies of one case or for comparisons across cases where the same operationalization of centralization is employed. But they confound comparisons across cases that employ different conceptions of centralization. For example, Blanchard sees both China and Russia as decentralized in the sense that provincial subunits have some autonomy in conducting international affairs. But is this degree of decentralization greater or lesser than the decentralization modeled by Reinhardt or Schultz, who divide a Western democratic regime into executive and legislative branches? And, following Reinhardt, what difference should we expect it to make if the legislature and executive are from the same party and/or have the same preferences? Does decentralization only matter contingent upon policy differences?

These difficult questions do not impair the project's central goal of examining how domestic politics lead states to use international organizations. What the measurement problem does impair is a clear identification of which of the two mechanisms—overcoming veto points or making commitments—should be operative in a given case. One way to resolve this empirically is by identifying the actual channels through which international institutions exert influence in a given case. We have begun to clarify those channels in figures 1a–c in terms of theoretical predictions as to when international institutions will have their primary impact on initiators or ratifiers.

However, there are several reasons why it will remain difficult to sort out commitment and veto problems. First, beyond the general difficulty of measuring benefits and costs in the model, problems of credible commitments and deterring vetoes necessarily depend on benefits and/or costs that are never observed if the institutional arrangement is effective (that is, they lie off the equilibrium path). For example, if a domestic opposition group is deterred from exercising a veto in figure 1a because of a (potential) cost that can be imposed through an international institution $(-c_R)$, we never observe the cost being imposed and so cannot (directly) measure it. Second, some institutional effects may simultaneously solve both the commitment and the veto problems. For example, in figure 1c, an effective institution will likely raise both b_I and b_R, and so the two effects will be difficult to sort out. Finally, as our theoretical integration of the model suggests, these mechanisms are not necessarily as mutually exclusive as the centralized-decentralized dichotomy suggests. In reality, states often face both types of problems, and therefore they turn to international institutions for both reasons (fig. 1c).

To consider these issues more carefully, we need to bring international institutions into the analysis directly. Before doing so, however, we assess the evidence in light of H3, which addresses the long-term implications of two-level interaction for initiators and ratifiers.

The Long-Term Effects of Interaction

Speculating on the long-term effects of interactions between domestic and international institutions, Drezner hypothesizes that longer time horizons "should inevitably enhance the power of policy initiators at the expense of ratifying institutions." His intuition for H3 is that any transfer of authority from the national to the international level should on average benefit policy initiators at the expense of ratifiers since initiators usually have closer relations with international institutions. This leads to greater influence—including superior access and formal voting power—and knowledge in the realm of IO affairs. A complementary logic is that, as a state's relationship with an IO deepens and becomes more valuable over time, the influence and constraining effect of working through the organization may be enhanced. In other words, the values of the b's and c's in figure 1 increase, making the IO strategy more effective for the initiator.[17] The empirical chapters provide some support for this proposition. However, the hypothesis ignores other processes that also take place over time—such as updating, learning, and socialization—that may support or challenge the power balance between initiator and ratifier.

Pevehouse's case provides the clearest support for H3. When the "winners" of democratization use IOs to consolidate their hold on power and create stability, they clearly gain at the expense of the "losers." However, the other two commitment stories—by Reinhardt and Schultz—leave open the possibility that the ratifier (Congress) might learn over time and counter moves by the initiator (the president). Schultz explicitly recognizes this possibility and finds evidence that Congress began opposing humanitarian missions at earlier stages to preempt the president before he was able to establish a costly commitment. Similarly, although Reinhardt does not discuss the possibility, Congress could respond to the executive's manipulation of the WTO dispute settlement process by using its oversight and lawmaking capacities to counter the power of the president. For example, Congress can pass protectionist trade laws that constrain the executive,[18] and it can threaten to cut the budgets of relevant agencies. Thus we should not always expect the initiator (the president) to gain power over time at the expense of the ratifier (Congress).

The Blanchard case is indeterminate with regard to H3. The initiators (the UNDP and Province of Jilin) succeeded in their policy effort at the expense of the ratifiers (the Russian state and especially the Primorskii region). However, beyond the outcome in this episode, there is no reason to assume any cumulative effect. The UNDP and Jilin will not necessarily be more powerful actors in future policy conflicts—at least there is no logic outlined for why this might be the case. On the other hand, a possible path-dependence argument is that an initiator's early gains from interactions with an international institution may generate self-reinforcing changes in state bureaucracies, in the interests of nonstate actors, or in asset-specific investments that promote the goals of the initiator. Alternatively, the path-dependence effect could operate through the inculcation of new or stronger normative commitments to the initiator's policies or policy-making processes—especially after their validation at the international level.

The effects of social influence and persuasion are particularly interesting in light of H3. In Johnston's case, the external initiators—other states that wish to bring China into the relevant regimes—clearly benefit from the outcome. At least in the case of persuasion within the ASEAN Regional Forum (ARF), however, this does not come at the *expense* of China since China's interests themselves change. Some officials in the Chinese policy process developed a normative commitment to multilateralism, and this internalization of norms entails a redefinition of interests such that membership in the ARF is viewed as desirable. When interests are endogenous to the analysis, as in the case of persuasion or socialization, H3 is either incorrect or irrelevant. But since Johnston argues that social pressure involves acquiescence without private acceptance, it is reasonable to conclude in the CTBT case that the external initiators have institutionalized their policy preference at the expense of China, offering support for H3.

A possible explanation for why the hypothesis does not consistently make accurate predictions is that it implicitly assumes that the initiator is the state and thus also the gatekeeper for IO-related activities inside it. However, Drezner clearly recognizes that initiators need not be executives or "centers of government" but could include other governmental actors or even (we would add) nonstate actors. The cases illustrate this possibility: Subnational actors such as the Province of Jilin and external actors, including other states and IOs, may also be policy initiators. This indicates a need to refine H3: If the initiator controls access to IOs, repeated interactions through international institutions will enhance the power of the policy initiator at the expense of the ratifiers. But if the initiator does not control access—perhaps because the initiator is not the state or because the IO is an independent actor—this conclusion should not hold. For example, domestic human rights initiators will not be strengthened by their government's interactions with international institutions that are strictly state based. But if nonstate initiators are able to invoke IO support (for example, a human rights group able to secure outside international legal support), H3 again applies. Similarly, external initiators—such as other states and IOs themselves—are typically more active at the international level than are subnational actors and so benefit at the expense of ratifiers when international institutions influence domestic politics over time. In short, the impact of repeated interaction is contingent on the relationship between the initiator and the international institution.

Therefore an important strategy for ratifying actors is to insert themselves as initiators to influence the agendas and behavior of states and IOs. Vigorous NGO participation in international environmental institutions is an example (Raustiala 1997b; Clark, Friedman, and Hochstetler 1998), as are the activities of norm-based entrepreneurs such as the International Campaign to Ban Landmines, which mobilized public concern on the road to establishing the 1997 Convention on the Prohibition of Anti-Personnel Mines. Activists, who typically relied on reacting to and blocking policies emanating from states and IOs in the past, now increasingly focus on actively pursuing their agendas (Keck and Sikkink 1998). For example, antiglobalization protesters sought direct access to the 1999 WTO meetings in Seattle to increase their influence on policy at the initiation stage rather than simply to react to WTO policies later. These are examples of learning by groups that attempt to capture the benefits of being an initiator when it comes to interactions between international and domestic institutions. H3 would need significant refinement to accommodate the shifting identities of initiators (and hence of ratifiers) over time.

Taking International Institutions Seriously

This volume makes an important contribution to a fledgling literature on the relationship between domestic politics and international institutions (Cortell and Davis 1996; Martin and Simmons 1998), thereby helping to correct a state-centric bias in regime theory and neoliberal institutionalism. Moreover, parallel with recent calls to incorporate formal IOs into the theoretical study of IR (Abbott and Snidal 1998), the authors shed light on the complex relationship between IOs and domestic political processes. We are presented with both an analytical framework for understanding the variety of roles IOs play in their interaction with internal politics and an important set of empirical illustrations. As the study of domestic-international interactions moves forward, students of IR and comparative politics should be equally sensitive to the role of international institutions as intervening variables that shape political strategies at the domestic and international levels.

Drezner and his collaborators go beyond merely showing that international institutions matter. As discussed in the previous section, they theorize and adduce evidence for a variety of causal mechanisms—from rationalist contracting and commitment to ideational processes such as persuasion and legitimation—by which policy initiators and ratifiers interact through IOs. In addition, several authors explicitly discuss variation in institutional design and its impact on behavior and outcomes. As Drezner states in the introduction, "IOs vary according to structural dimensions, making them useful in different situations." In other words, the framework explicitly argues that institutional design matters.

Despite this orientation, the volume does not sufficiently explore the complexity of institutional design. The impact of different international institutional features—including various levels of informational, operational, adjudicative, and enforcement capacities—is not adequately distinguished. More important, IOs are treated as largely passive; insufficient attention is given to their role as active actors that may even initiate policies. With these critiques in mind, we turn to the findings on H4 and H5.

Variation in Institutional Design:
Findings and Extensions

The volume contains a number of interesting conclusions with regard to the "institutional design matters" proposition (H4).[19] Since the hypothesis is cast at a very general level, it offers no testable implications. Instead it prompts an analysis of how certain design features shape the interaction of domestic and international institutions. These insights are worth clarifying and extending, and we address two questions in particular. How does institutional design matter for whether initiators can use international institutions to influence domestic politics? How does institutional design affect the influence mechanism through which the institution operates? Three of the empirical contributors—Pevehouse, Reinhardt, and Johnston—discuss international institutional design issues explicitly; Schultz and Blanchard provide evidence that is implicitly relevant.

Pevehouse argues that joining IOs provides a contracting mechanism for policy initiators in new democracies. It allows the winners of political transition to credibly commit to liberal reform, thereby assuring would-be domestic opponents who are naturally suspicious of the new regime. However, not all IOs are able to perform this function. The ability to credibly commit by joining IOs is enhanced when the organization has precise conditionality rules, when fulfilling this conditionality is costly, and when the IO can monitor and enforce reform. Pevehouse posits that "democratic" IOs—those whose members are democracies—perform this function best since they are most likely to impose democracy-related conditions on membership and because "more homogeneously democratic IOs are more likely to enforce the conditions imposed on membership." The special role played by "democratic" IOs is a potentially important elaboration of the general claim of H4 that institutional design matters.

The analysis raises questions about how exactly "democratic" IOs are different than others. Pevehouse is not clear why his three design features—precision of conditionality rules, costly fulfillment of conditionality, and capacity to monitor and enforce—are necessarily characteristics of IOs with democratic members. His empirical analysis does not resolve this issue since democratic membership, not the underlying features it is intended to capture, is used as the independent variable. Moreover, "democratic" IOs seem to matter not so much because of their membership but rather because of how they operate: They impose conditions and pressure members who do not fulfill them. The WTO, for example, is a nondemocratic IO but still serves as a device for committing to liberal reform since it operates in a similar manner. These points show that a fuller treatment of H4 requires a more fine-grained analysis to explore specific design features and thorough process tracing to establish the causal link between "democratic" IOs and the ability of newly democratized regimes to commit.

The chapter by Johnston lends strong support to the proposition that institutional design matters when IOs influence actors through sociological mechanisms. Using Rogowski's (1999) typology of domestic political institutions, he argues that the conditions that facilitate persuasion and/or social influence are more likely to hold in some institutions than in others.[20] For example, the ARF has relatively few members, is weakly institutionalized, and makes decisions by consensus, features that make it ideal for persuasion. As Johnston notes, "the ARF is almost explicitly designed to accentuate 'persuasion' through social interaction." By contrast, back-patting and opprobrium—the two mechanisms by which social influence operates—are more influential under a different set of design conditions. For example, Johnston argues that a large audience is conducive to social influence, as in the case of the CTBT negotiations. The result is a clear prediction regarding institutional design: Initiators should pursue persuasion strategies when IO membership is small and should prefer social influence when members are more numerous.[21]

Johnston's analysis suggests that notions of "efficient" institutional design employed in rationalist institutionalism must be complemented by analyses of the sociological processes by which institutions shape actor preferences. Consistent with his constructivist approach, he recognizes that institutions vary not only according to formal design features but also in terms of less tangible processes, internal cultures, and "working philosophies." In other words, they are social environments as well as incentive structures.[22] This leads Johnston to consider institutional dimensions such as whether the "authoritativeness" of members is equally or unequally allocated (what he calls the "franchise" dimension). Although his case studies can provide only suggestive evidence for his institutional design hypotheses (a limitation he recognizes), Johnston generates several useful and plausible propositions that are amenable to further testing.

Reinhardt shows that the impact of IOs on domestic politics is contingent on institutional design, arguing, for example, that IOs can serve as commitment devices for presidents only if the transaction costs of working through them are sufficiently high. In his case of trade dispute settlement, high costs of litigation are a necessary component of his "tying hands without a rope" equilibrium. In contrast to the neoliberal institutionalist literature, this implies that executives might want international institutions that generate rather than mitigate transaction costs. Moreover, even by modestly increasing the potential for enforcement, an IO can fundamentally change the dynamics of domestic political relations, especially when domestic actors hold information asymmetrically.

Schultz asks if the involvement of IOs helps the U.S. president overcome congressional opposition to humanitarian intervention. The mechanisms by which IOs aid the president combine constructivist and rationalist logics: IO approval increases public support by bestowing legitimacy on the operation while increasing the costs of turning back. This increases the president's obligation to proceed, as well as the expected value of proceeding, and thus decreases the likelihood of successful resistance. However, Schultz does not directly explore issues of institutional design. Since NATO is less independent of U.S. power and interests than is the UN Security Council (where four other members have veto power), we might expect the latter to be more effective in the legitimation and commitment roles (Thompson 2001). Yet these quite distinct institutions, the UN Security Council and NATO, play similar roles and are used by the same initiator, somewhat defying the "institutional design matters" hypothesis—or at least challenging us to refine it. One possibility, for example, is that Congress considers NATO a more like-minded source of information than the UN Security Council and so it constitutes a more effective institutional device for the president.[23]

Blanchard's chapter on the TRADP finds that the UNDP played a variety of roles consistent with both rationalism and constructivism. The UNDP provided resources and facilitated contracting between the policy initiators and ratifiers (rationalist mechanisms), but it also legitimized the initiative and provided a setting for persuasion (ideational mechanisms). Like Schultz, Blanchard does not explore the institutional design implications and draws no direct implications for H4. Since only one international institution is involved, and since it plays a wide variety of roles—as Blanchard writes, "the UNDP influenced the course of the TRADP through its involvement in interest and policy formulation, agenda setting, agreement development, negotiation, ratification, and project implementation"—it is difficult to map particular design features onto particular influence mechanisms. Nevertheless, the UNDP clearly derived authority and influence from its combination of expertise and political neutrality, neither of which the primary initiator (the Province of Jilin) possessed. One implication is that some IO characteristics simultaneously generate both material and sociological influence effects. Thus by convening meetings the UNDP both reduces the transaction costs of negotiation and creates a setting for persuasion. By backing the project and sharing knowledge about its potential benefits, the UNDP transmits information that changes actors' incentives and lends legitimacy to the project's goals.

Based on these findings, we can draw some preliminary conclusions about the conditions under which initiators will choose certain institutions. When initiators rely on rationalist mechanisms such as tying hands and contracting, we should expect them to turn to more formal and bureaucratic organizations such as the EU, the WTO, the UN, and NATO. Commitments to such organizations are more explicit and more difficult to reverse. Among the sociological or ideational mechanisms for influencing ratifiers, if an initiator simply wants to legitimize a policy with an external endorsement, a politically independent IO with a large and diverse membership represents the best avenue for channeling its actions. On the other hand, if the initiator's success depends on changing the interests or values of its opponents, then a more functionally focused institution with expertise and authority in a particular issue area might be more effective.[24] Moreover, direct contact and discussion are important in these cases, as in the ARF meetings that influenced Chinese thinking and the conferences sponsored by the UNDP during the Tumen River project. This finding is consistent with recent theorizing on the dynamics of public deliberation (Risse 2000; Lynch 1999).

In summary, the same or similar institutions may perform a variety of influence functions. This indicates some fungibility in the roles played by a given institution so that their causal impact depends on the needs of the initiator in a given case.

Formal versus Informal Institutions

Although institutions in IR "may take the form of bureaucratic organizations, regimes (rule-structures that do not necessarily have organizations attached), or conventions (informal practices)" (Keohane, Haas, and Levy 1993, 5),[25] the volume does not analytically distinguish among institutional forms. This conflation is explicit in the introduction—where IOs, regimes, institutions, and even epistemic communities are included in the same framework—and Drezner recognizes that it entails a loss of precision. Similarly, while Pevehouse, Blanchard, and Schultz expressly distinguish formal organizations from other institutional forms, the implications of this distinction are not addressed in depth in the empirical chapters.

All of the institutions addressed in the empirical chapters are formal IOs with independent resources and decision-making capacities. The evidence points repeatedly to IOs as the key intervening institutions, and in many cases the internal logics of the arguments seem to apply exclusively to IOs. This suggests that even if informal and more decentralized institutions can help overcome obstacles to policy-making, there may be added benefits to working through formal IOs. Thus an important extension of the volume would be to examine the validity of recent theoretical claims that formal or legalized institutions play a qualitatively different role in IR than do their less formal counterparts (Lipson 1991; Abbott and Snidal 1998; Goldstein et al. 2001).

In Pevehouse, for example, the conditionality of joining an international institution represents a costly signal of reform, since monitoring and some enforcement powers are delegated to a third party. Such forms of supranational authority are typically associated with formal IOs. Although Reinhardt's model could certainly apply beyond the GATT and WTO, it is driven by an impending ruling by a supranational court and thus assumes that a highly legalized institution is involved. Schultz makes the interesting and valid point that post–Cold War humanitarian missions conducted by the United States "had not just a multilateral cast but the explicit blessing of an international organization." This is an implicit recognition of important qualitative differences between multilateralism as a generic institutional form and formal multilateral IOs.[26]

Johnston's findings are more mixed. Formal IOs are clearly important in his cases, but he does not distinguish them analytically and sometimes conflates IOs with other institutional forms in his theoretical discussion. The ARF and CTBT negotiations addressed by Johnston were not themselves independent and formal bureaucratic organizations, yet they were held under the auspices of ASEAN and the UN Conference on Disarmament, respectively. His typology of international institutions includes some features that might well apply to less formal institutions, and he focuses on informal social processes to show the causal influence of persuasion and social influence. It is not clear to what extent formality is a necessary condition for his arguments to operate.

For the most part, the theoretical arguments and conclusions of the volume apply to formal IOs rather than to international institutions more generally. This is not a weakness of the volume; rather, it is a finding that should be highlighted. A closer examination of the cases might reveal that various informal institutions—such as epistemic communities, transnational activist networks, and legal norms—are playing equally important roles. Further analysis could then be aimed at determining whether these informal sources of governance influence international and domestic politics in qualitatively different ways.

Of course, formality itself is not what makes institutions more effective at performing functions such as contracting and persuasion—it is the underlying capacities and features of formal organizations that make them politically important. For example, formal IOs tend to be more centralized and independent from state influence than other institutions. Initiators need institutions that can affect the b and c terms as represented in figures 1a–c, and those that allow states to make clear and public commitments and to stake their reputations should be the most effective at this. Characteristics of formal IOs such as centralization and political neutrality—in establishing rules, monitoring behavior, and collecting information—facilitate the various influence mechanisms outlined in this volume, which helps explain why initiators choose formal organizations.

International Organizations as Agents

Despite the important role granted to formal IOs in the volume, international institutions are treated as almost entirely passive rather than active agents. The introduction portrays IOs as instruments that are "used" by initiators to influence politics. This characterization is contradicted by recent theorizing[27] and by the empirical chapters themselves, which provide considerable evidence that IOs can be active and even strategic. At the very least, IOs often supply valuable goods to states and cannot be easily manipulated at the whim of governments.

For example, IOs only serve as commitment devices (as in Pevehouse, Reinhardt, and Schultz) if they provide benefits to a state that can be forfeited or withdrawn if ratifiers veto or initiators renege (as in the c_R or c_I terms in fig. 1c).[28] Otherwise, violations of the commitment are not costly and the commitment would not be credible. In the Pevehouse chapter, democratizing regimes benefit from joining IOs that allow them to signal sincere preferences for reform. However, while signaling may reveal preferences, it does not solve the time-inconsistency problem, as Pevehouse recognizes when he raises the issue of policy reversals. Only a credible commitment can perform this distinct function.[29] Formal IOs that have the power to expel or punish a state in response to violations of conditionality are the most effective vehicles for commitment, since violating the commitment comes at a high cost.

Thus IOs must have either carrots (internationally provided benefits) or sticks (punishment for rule violation) in order for states to use them as commitment devices. Treating them as passive tools to be manipulated for domestic political gain ignores the fact that IOs often actively "supply" membership and benefits in order for the "demand" from states to be met (see Mattli 1999). The UN and NATO must endorse humanitarian intervention in the first place for the president to reap the legitimation benefits described by Schultz, yet congressional support is treated as problematic in his chapter, whereas the origins of IO support are not explored. Even Johnston's institutions, which perform the passive role of establishing "social contexts," interact with other actors in a sense, since "social structures and agent characteristics are mutually constitutive." In fact, the ARF was quite active, moving issues onto the agenda without all member states on board and thereby exercising considerable agenda-setting power.

The most striking example of an active and strategic IO is Blanchard's analysis of the UNDP. Blanchard recognizes that IOs are distinct from "regimes" in that the latter can only work passively and goes on to show that the UNDP was far more than a passive instrument of states during the formulation of the Tumen River project. The UNDP convened meetings, provided funding for studies and reports, and lobbied in capitals to stimulate support. UNDP officials even reached out to Japan and the United States—potential veto players—to head off any possible objections. The agency thus played a critical agenda-setting role. In fact, the UNDP was a policy initiator (along with the Province of Jilin), revealing that IOs can be important and active agents for change.

This finding has direct implications for H5—that external initiators will have less success in their interactions with domestic institutions than will internal initiators. We cannot draw robust conclusions since there are only two examples of external initiators in the volume, the UNDP in Blanchard's chapter and other member-states of the ARF and CTBT in Johnston's study. Nevertheless, in both cases outside initiators were successful in creating policy change. This casts some doubt on H5.[30] We also see, however, that external initiators were dependent on subnational actors for support: the Province of Jilin in Blanchard's cases and China's foreign affairs bureaucrats in Johnston's. This suggests that external initiators may only be successful when they have an ally at the domestic level.

Extending the Framework

The volume taken as a whole provides strong support for its central premise that policy initiators use international institutions to influence domestic politics. The most important message with regard to the individual hypotheses, however, is that they need substantial refinement to explain real-world situations, both in the case studies presented and beyond. Here we briefly consider some avenues along which the theory could be extended.

The framework uses the dimension of centralization as a simplifying yet widely encompassing concept to characterize domestic polities. This provides a powerful way to see the similarity between, for example, the decentralization of federal systems and the decentralization created through domestic checks and balances. As we outlined in the first section, however, identifying the relevant state structure—centralized versus decentralized—depends on the level of analysis: A state may appear centralized from a macroperspective but decentralized when decision making is scrutinized more closely. This is why authoritarian China may appear centralized from the outside but somewhat decentralized when we look at its internal politics or bureaucracy. States are also more or less centralized depending on the policy issue at stake. Military-security policy may be formulated in a fairly centralized manner while trade policy allows for decentralized input from various other governmental and private actors. These considerations require a more contingent conceptualization of the centralized-decentralized dimension and detailed qualitative work to specify the texture of state structure in a given case.

The relation between centralization and decentralization is interesting in other ways as well. Drezner argues that centralized states sometimes turn to IOs because they cannot make credible commitments on their own. However, an alternative is for the state to create this capacity to make credible commitments by establishing more decentralized institutions. Historically, tying hands has been accomplished domestically, through constitutional design such as internal checks and balances and independent judiciaries and through the establishment of autonomous agencies such as central banks. The availability of an international alternative raises an important question: Under what conditions do states seek domestic sources of commitment, and when do they seek international sources? Internal and external sources of commitment may be more or less effective for different substantive issues and for different types of states. They also impose different types of costs in terms of how they impinge on the domestic and international autonomy of decision makers. Further analysis could thus build on Drezner's framework to explore which sources of commitment are most common and effective for given properties of states and issue areas.

Although states typically have an advantage in dealing with IOs, ratifying domestic groups also need to consider the impact of IOs. This is especially the case with respect to interactions over time (H3), which add an additional strategic dimension regarding how ratifiers respond to the internationalization of issues by policy initiators. Do ratifiers learn to respond effectively to the strategic advantages gained by initiators who work through IOs? Schultz raises this possibility in the context of Congress's responding to the president's desire to conduct humanitarian intervention, and yet overall there is little evidence in the empirical chapters of ratifiers learning over time. This puzzle requires further analysis. Another strategic response by ratifiers is to change the game by becoming initiators themselves. NGOs are actively pursuing such strategies in areas such as human rights and the environment. In other cases, ratifiers relinquish much of their control over international agreements—a congressional grant of fast-track, or "trade promotion," authority to the president is an example—to solve their commitment problem (as discussed earlier with regard to H1). Here change within a domestic institution (that is, the rules for approving the agreement) is used to augment the role of the IO. Such considerations open up a range of questions as to how ratifiers learn, when they will seek to become initiators, and when they will agree to restrict their powers.

With regard to international institutional design issues (H4), more fine-grained hypotheses linking design features to influence mechanisms follow from the case studies. For example, we speculated that rationalist influence mechanisms are most effective when the most formal IOs are involved; that policy legitimation and social influence require a politically independent IO with a large and diverse membership; and that persuasion (involving the internalization of new preferences and interests) requires an IO with authority in a particular issue area to generate direct contact and discussion among members. The complementarity of these different roles also shows how IOs can operate through—and be understood in terms of—both rationalist and constructivist mechanisms.

The case studies further suggest that formal IOs have a special role in IR. But what features and capacities allow IOs to perform functions that less formal institutions cannot? Do IOs require an ability to monitor behavior, to provide access to domestic groups, or to sanction behavior to be effective? The need for specific design features might fruitfully be subjected to empirical testing both within the "interaction of international and domestic institutions" context and more generally. The analysis might be extended further to treat international institutions endogenously. Though it goes beyond the purview of this volume, the multiple roles for international institutions outlined in the various chapters have interesting implications for why they are created and how they are designed. In many cases, however, it is not so much a matter of designing an institution as of selecting one to handle a specific problem. Studies of "forum shopping," where actors choose among alternative institutional venues, should provide insight into the design features they seek when facing a given set of circumstances (Mattli 2001).

While this volume has focused on the initiation and ratification of policies, the framework could be extended to consider their subsequent implementation. This goes to the heart of the analysis since the credibility of commitments ultimately depends on the willingness and ability of actors to follow through on their agreements. By examining how IOs dampen incentives for states (or other initiators) to renege at the implementation stage, the research would directly engage the institutional details of how IOs affect state behavior. In some cases, it is not the initiator or ratifier who must implement but a third party (for example, firms, fishermen, soldiers), sometimes operating transnationally. This suggests that implementation may depend not only on the actions of the ratifier and the initiator but also on the role of the IO itself.

Finally, if states must operate through IOs to make their commitments credible or to lock in policies, IOs must acquire some capacity to constrain states. Credibility requires that this capacity be independent of the committing state, or else it will be meaningless. What then are the implications for IOs in their relations with states? Do IOs become independent sources of international authority? Or can states collectively constrain IOs even if they cannot do so individually? And does collective control become a means for some states to effectively constrain others? These questions are of great importance if the claim that actors use IOs to make commitments is credible.

Notes

We thank Dan Drezner, Jack Goldsmith, Jon Pevehouse, Eric Reinhardt, and Louise Steen-Sprang for their valuable comments on earlier drafts of this chapter.

1. Exceptions include Cortell and Davis 1996; Goldstein 1996; and Thompson 2000. Putnam's (1988, 446–47) discussion of "reverberation" recognizes that international bargaining could be used by leaders to influence domestic politics, but this possibility has gone largely unexplored.

2. Only the case study by Johnston is explicitly constructivist in orientation, but it is quite sympathetic to rationalist arguments. For example, many of his insights are similar to those discussed by Olson (1965) as "social incentives." While Johnston's "social influence" mechanism operates in a similar way, the interesting difference is that Olson sees social incentives as less

significant in large groups, whereas Johnston treats them as more important. The other chapters draw on rational choice but, as we show later, allow an important role for constructivist insights. We emphasize the value of combining perspectives throughout this chapter.

3. Ironically, we separate the domestic and international levels in our discussion, defying the spirit of this book and the two-level games literature. This is done only for convenience, and at each stage we are sensitive to the interaction of the two levels.

4. Stephen Krasner (1978, 60) defines one dimension of the domestic strength of a state as varying according to whether it "can formulate policy goals independent of particular groups within its own society" and recognizes that it will vary across issue areas. For further refinements and critiques of the "state strength" variable, especially the need to move beyond a single dimension of state strength, see the contributions to Evans, Rueschemeyer, and Skocpol 1985.

5. See Katzenstein 1978 for a conceptual and comparative discussion of the (de)centralization of major Western states.

6. In focusing on these extreme cases, we are not implying a Goldilocks theory that some intermediate level of centralization is neither "too hot" nor "too cold" but "just right." Although states often have a level of domestic centralization that is appropriate to particular problems they face, intermediate levels of centralization may sometimes leave a state vulnerable to both commitment and veto problems, as we discuss later.

7. Thus the consequences of a veto include not only the failure to obtain the policy—in which case the payoffs at $\{V_I, V_R\}$ would be the same as at the $\{0,0\}$ status quo point—but also any political and other consequences that accrue to the actors through their interaction.

8. These rewards or punishments may also affect the initiator government. For simplicity, we do not include those effects since they do not affect the analysis.

9. Of course, the utilitarian or other calculus implicit in this evaluation can be complicated. In practice, international institutions probably weight state initiator preferences more heavily than ratifier preferences—because they face their own veto problem in terms of needing state support to implement their policies, because states are the members of the IO, and because of geopolitical and other considerations.

10. Economists use the terms "dynamic" or "time inconsistency" to describe this problem, emphasizing the time sequence of play. The government "commits" to the policy at the outset of the game to encourage the compliance of the ratifiers, but once it obtains compliance it has an incentive to renege on its earlier policy. See Kydland and Prescott 1977 for an early exposition and Drazen 2000 for a recent overview.

11. Figure 1b does not include an option for the initiator not to propose the policy—thus implicitly assuming that $V_I > 0$. If $V_I < 0$ (with $T_I > P_I$), note that the initiator will not propose the policy because the ratifier will

veto it. This makes the situation appear to be a domestic veto problem even though the ratifier supports the policy; the "real" problem is one of commitment on the initiator's side. Figure 1c integrates the two problems.

12. It may be costly to set up and maintain some punishment mechanisms, although others—such as a threat of expulsion from a cooperating group—may be inexpensive to put in place. See Drezner 1999–2000 for a discussion of limits to using inducements, although he focuses heavily on transactions costs, which we set aside here.

13. This is not true in all cases—that is, the existence of veto points in making policy does not always imply their existence in breaking policy. The U.S. president, for example, must obtain Senate ratification to establish treaties but can often modify or terminate them unilaterally. We thank Jack Goldsmith for this point.

14. Reinhardt's "tying hands" language differs from standard usage in that the president is tying not his own hands but the hands of Congress. That is why we discuss his results under H1 even though "tying hands" would normally fall under the commitment logic of H2.

15. This difference is partly a function of empirical contexts: Whereas Drezner is concerned with how states use international institutions to commit, Reinhardt looks at compliance with commitments that are already made.

16. Johnston's chapter is difficult to categorize according to the centralized-decentralized dimension since he does not explicitly identify or discuss the state structure of the initiators (which are other states trying to influence Chinese policy from the outside). We thus discuss Johnston only peripherally as we address H1 and H2.

17. This assumes either that the initiator's and IO's goals correspond (i.e., b's correspond with initiator's preferences) or that the initiator can limit IO intervention to cases where they agree. This may not apply if IOs are relatively autonomous or are heavily influenced by third parties (e.g., the United States) to support policies contrary to the preferences of the initiator.

18. A classic example is the Omnibus Trade and Competitiveness Act of 1988, which required the president under certain circumstances to retaliate against foreign "unfair" trade practices (the so-called Super 301 and Special 301 amendments).

19. Complementary analyses of how institutional design matters include Mitchell 1994 and the articles in Koremenos, Lipson, and Snidal 2001.

20. Johnston defines persuasion as "the noncoercive communication of new normative understandings that are internalized by actors such that new courses of action are viewed as entirely reasonable and appropriate," whereas social influence refers to the application of social rewards and social costs without private acceptance of new norms by the state being influenced.

21. One of Johnston's assertions seems puzzling on its face. He argues that "[w]ithin international organizations and institutions the participating/cooperating audience is relatively large." However, deliberating within a

given institution often *limits* the size of the audience if membership is restricted, an institutional feature that Johnston explicitly recognizes elsewhere in his chapter.

22. Johnston is careful to recognize that material and social interests influence actors simultaneously and thus that rationalism and constructivism are not mutually exclusive.

23. We thank Dan Drezner for suggesting this possibility.

24. For an additional example beyond this volume, see the role played by UNESCO in Finnemore 1993.

25. For further conceptualization of this variation, see Thompson and Snidal 2000.

26. On multilateralism as an institutional form, see Ruggie 1993.

27. Constructivist scholars in particular have shown that IOs can act as agents for change. See Finnemore 1996b and McNeely 1995. Less formal institutions, such as epistemic communities (Haas 1992a) and transnational advocacy networks (Keck and Sikkink 1998), may also perform active governance functions.

28. To include active IOs in our model, they might be modeled as having autonomous choices to make and receiving payoffs of their own. Alternatively, IOs could be conceived of as strategic actors that represent the collective choices of member states.

29. For a discussion on signaling and commitment as analytically distinct problems, see Morrow 1999.

30. There may be a selection bias problem with drawing any inference from this evidence: Potential external initiators who believe they cannot influence domestic politics effectively will not initiate policies in the first place and are also less likely to become objects of scholarly study.

References

Abbott, Kenneth W., and Duncan Snidal. 1998. "Why States Act through Formal International Organizations." *Journal of Conflict Resolution* 42, no. 1 (February): 3–32.

Abbott, Kenneth, and Duncan Snidal. 2000. "Hard and Soft Law in International Governance." *International Organization* 54 (3): 421.

Acharya, Amitav. 1996. "The New Frontier of Multilateralism: Canada and the ASEAN Regional Forum." Paper prepared for the Canadian International Development Agency, November.

Acharya, Amitav. 1997a. "The ASEAN Regional Forum." Department of Foreign Affairs and International Trade, Ottawa, Canada, February.

Acharya, Amitav. 1997b. "Ideas, Identity, and Institution-Building: From the ASEAN Way to the Asia-Pacific Way." *Pacific Review* 10 (3): 319–46.

Acharya, Amitav. 1998. "The Impact of Multilateralism on Chinese Regional Security Thinking and Behavior: Snapshot of Beijing Views." Unpublished paper.

Adler, Emanuel. 1992. "The Emergence of Cooperation: National Epistemic Communities and the International Evolution of the Idea of Nuclear Control." *International Organization* 46 (1): 101–45.

Adler, Emanuel. 1998. "Seeds of Peaceful Change: The OSCE's Security Community-Building Model." In *Security Communities*, ed. Emanuel Adler and Michael Barnett. Cambridge: Cambridge University Press.

Adler, Emanuel, and Michael Barnett. 1998. "A Framework for the Study of Security Communities." In *Security Communities*, ed. Emanuel Adler and Michael Barnett. Cambridge: Cambridge University Press.

Adler, Emanuel, and Peter M. Haas. 1992. "Conclusion: Epistemic Communities, World Order, and the Creation of a Reflective Research Program." *International Organization* 46 (1): 367–87.

Agénor, Pierre-Richard. 1994. "Credibility and Exchange Rate Management in Developing Countries." *Journal of Development Economics* 45 (October): 1–16.

Aguero, Felipe. 1995. "Democratic Consolidation and the Military in Southern Europe and South America." In *The Politics of Democratic Consolidation*, ed. Richard Gunther, P. Nikiforos Diamandouros, and Hans-Jurgen Puhle. Baltimore: Johns Hopkins University Press.

Alexseev, Mikhail A., and Tamara Troyakova. 1999. "A Mirage of the 'Amur California': Regional Identity and Economic Incentives for Political

231

Separatism in Primorskiy Kray." In *Center-Periphery Conflict in Post-Soviet Russia: A Federation Imperiled,* ed. Mikhail A. Alexseev. New York: St. Martin's Press.

Anderson, Jennifer. 1997. *The Limits of the Sino-Russian Strategic Partnership.* Oxford: Oxford University Press.

Archer, Clive. 1992. *International Organizations.* 2d ed. London: Routledge.

ARF (ASEAN Regional Forum). 1995. "The ASEAN Regional Forum: A Concept Paper."

Arnold, R. Douglas. 1990. *The Logic of Congressional Action.* New Haven: Yale University Press.

Asiwaju, Anthony I. 1994. "Borders and Borderlands as Linchpins for Regional Integration in Africa." In *Global Boundaries,* ed. Clive H. Schofield. London: Routledge.

Auerswald, David P., and Peter F. Cowhey. 1997. "Ballot Box Diplomacy: The War Powers Resolution and the Use of Force." *International Studies Quarterly* 41 (September): 505–28.

Austen-Smith, David. 1993. "Information and Influence: Lobbying for Agendas and Votes." *American Journal of Political Science* 37:799–833.

Axelrod, Robert. 1997. *The Complexity of Cooperation.* Princeton: Princeton University Press.

Axelrod, Robert, and Robert O. Keohane. 1985. "Achieving Cooperation under Anarchy: Strategies and Institutions." *World Politics* 38 (October): 226–54.

Axsom, Danny, Suzanne Yates, and Shelley Chaiken. 1987. "Audience Response Cues as a Heuristic Cue in Persuasion." *Journal of Personality and Social Psychology* 53 (1).

Ball, R. 1999. "The Institutional Foundations of Monetary Commitment: A Comparative Analysis." *World Development* 27 (10): 1821–42.

Banks, Arthur S. Various years. *Political Handbook of the World.* Binghamton, NY: CSA Publications.

Banks, Arthur S., and Thomas C. Mueller. 1998. *Political Handbook of the World.* Binghamton, NY: CSA Publications.

Banks, Jeffrey. 1989. "Agency Budgets, Cost Information, and Auditing." *American Journal of Political Science* 33: 670–99.

Barnum, Christopher. 1997. "A Reformulated Social Identity Theory." *Advances in Group Processes* 14.

Barshefsky, Charlene. 1999. "Testimony of Ambassador Charlene Barshefsky, U.S. Trade Representative, Hearing on Preparations for the Upcoming World Trade Organization Ministerial Meeting, United States Senate, Committee on Finance." September 29. <http://www.senate.gov/~finance/9-29bars.htm>.

Bar-Tal, Daniel, and Leonard Saxe. 1990. "Acquisition of Political Knowledge: A Social-Psychological Analysis." In *Political Socialization, Citizenship Education, and Democracy,* ed. Orit Ichilov. New York: Teachers College Press.

Beck, Nathaniel, and Jonathan N. Katz. 1997. "The Analysis of Binary Time-Series-Cross-Sectional Data and/or the Democratic Peace." Paper presented at the annual meeting of the Political Methodology Group, Columbus, OH.

Beck, Nathaniel, and Richard Tucker, 1996. "Conflict in Space and Time: Time-Series-Cross-Section Analysis with Binary Dependent Variable." Paper presented at the annual meeting of the American Political Science Association, San Francisco.

Beck, Nathaniel, Jonathan N. Katz, and Richard Tucker. 1998. "Beyond Ordinary Logit: Taking Time Seriously in Binary Time-Series Cross-Section Models." *American Journal of Political Science* 42:1260–88.

Berger, Charles R. 1995. "Inscrutable Goals, Uncertain Plans, and the Production of Communicative Action." In *Communication and Social Influence Processes,* ed. Charles R. Berger and Michael Burgoon. East Lansing: Michigan State University Press.

Berger, Peter L., and Thomas Luckman. 1966. *The Construction of Reality: A Treatise in the Sociology of Knowledge.* New York: Anchor Books.

Betz, Andrew L., John K. Skowronski, and Thomas M. Ostrom. 1996. "Shared Realities: Social Influence and Stimulus Memory." *Social Cognition* 14 (2): 113–40.

Biddle, Bruce J. 1985. "Social Influence, Self-Reference Identity Labels, and Behavior." *Sociological Quarterly* 26 (2).

Bilveer, S. 1998. "East Asia in Russia's Foreign Policy: A New Russo-Chinese Axis?" *Pacific Review* 11 (4): 485–503.

Bird, Graham, and Dane Rowlands. 1997. "The Catalytic Effect of Lending by the International Financial Institutions." *World Economy* 20 (November): 967–91.

Blanchard, Jean-Marc F. 1996. "Chinese Nationalism and the Tumen River Area Development Programme." Paper presented at the annual meeting of the American Political Science Association, San Francisco.

Blanchard, Jean-Marc F. 1998a. "Borders and Borderlands: An Institutional Approach to Territorial Disputes." Ph.D. diss., University of Pennsylvania.

Blanchard, Jean-Marc F. 1998b. "The Political of Multilateral Economic Cooperation in Northeast Asia: China and the TRADP." Paper presented at the annual meeting of the Association for Asian Studies, Washington, DC.

Blanchard, Jean-Marc F. 2000. "The Heyday of Beijing's Participation in the Tumen River Area Development Programme, 1990–95: A Political Explanation." *Journal of Contemporary China* 9 (24): 271–90.

Blanchard, Jean-Marc F., and Norrin M. Ripsman. 1996. "Measuring Economic Interdependence: A Geopolitical Perspective." *Geopolitics and International Boundaries* 1 (3): 225–46.

Blanchard, Jean-Marc F., and Norrin M. Ripsman. 2001. "Rethinking Sensitivity Interdependence: Assessing the Trade, Financial, and Monetary

Links between States." *International Interactions* 27, no. 2 (June): 95–128.

Bleaney, Michael, and Paul Mizen. 1997. "Credibility and Disinflation in the European Monetary System." *Economic Journal* 107 (November): 1751–67.

Bollen, Kenneth. 1979. "Political Democracy and the Timing of Development." *American Sociological Review* 44:572–87.

Booster, Franklin J. 1995. "Commentary on Compliance-Gaining Message Behavior Research." In *Communication and Social Influence Processes*, ed. Charles R. Berger and Michael Burgoon. East Lansing: Michigan State University Press.

Bowens, Gregory J. 1993. "Somalia: House Backs Measure Allowing U.S. Role in UN Operation." *Congressional Quarterly Weekly Report*, May 29, 1373.

Boylan, Delia 2001. "Democratization and Institutional Change in Mexico: The Logic of Partial Insulation." *Comparative Political Studies* 34 (1): 3–30.

Braithwaite, John, and Peter Drahos. 2000. *Global Business Regulation*. Cambridge: Cambridge University Press.

Broz, J. Lawrence. 1997. *International Origins of the Federal Reserve System*. Ithaca, NY: Cornell University Press.

Burns, Katherine G. 1994. "Subnational Power and Regional Integration: The Case of Tumen River Development." Paper presented to the MIT Japan Program, MITJP 94-10.

Burns, Katherine G. 1995. "Battling for Foreign Capital in Primorsk Kray." *Transition* 1 (17): 18–23.

Burton, Michael, Richard Gunther, and John Higley. 1992. "Elites and Democratic Consolidation in Latin America and Southern Europe: An overview." In *Elites and Democratic Consolidation in Latin America and Southern Europe*, ed. John Higley and Richard Gunther. New York: Cambridge University Press.

Busch, Marc L., and Helen V. Milner. 1994. "The Future of the International Trading System: International Firms, Regionalism, and Domestic Politics." In *Political Economy and the Changing Global Order*, ed. Richard Stubbs and Geoffrey R. D. Underhill. New York: St. Martin's Press.

Calvo, Guillermo A. 1986. "Incredible Reforms." In *Debt, Stabilization, and Development*, ed. G. Calvo, R. Findlay, P. Kouri, and J. Braga de Macedo. London: Basil Blackwell.

Calvo, Guillermo A., and J. A. Frankel. 1991. "Credit Markets, Credibility, and Economic Transformation." *Journal of Economic Perspectives* 5 (4): 139–48.

Cameron, David R. 1995. "Transnational Relations and the Development of European Economic and Monetary Union." In *Bringing Transnational Relations Back In: Non-State Actors, Domestic Structures, and Interna-*

tional Institutions, ed. Thomas Risse-Kappen. Cambridge: Cambridge University Press.

Caporaso, James A. 1997. "Across the Great Divide: Integrating Comparative and International Politics." *International Studies Quarterly* 41:563–92.

CBS News/New York Times. 1994. CBS News/New York Times Monthly Poll 1, August (computer file). 2d ICPSR version. New York: CBS News (producer), 1994. Ann Arbor, MI: Inter-university Consortium for Political and Social Research (distributor), 2000.

Cederman, Lars-Eric. 1997. *Emergent Actors in World Politics: How States and Nations Develop and Dissolve.* Princeton: Princeton University Press.

Cerny, Philip. 1995. "Globalization and the Changing Logic of Collective Action." *International Organization* 49:595–625.

Chafetz, Glenn, Hillel Abramson, and Suzette Grillot. 1996. "Role Theory and Foreign Policy: Belarussian and Ukrainian Compliance with the Nuclear Nonproliferation Regime." *Political Psychology* 17 (4).

Chayes, Abram, and Antonia Handler Chayes. 1995. *The New Sovereignty: Compliance with International Regulatory Agreements.* Cambridge: Harvard University Press.

Checkel, Jeffrey T. 1997. *Ideas and International Political Change.* New Haven: Yale University Press.

Checkel, Jeffrey T. 1998. "The Constructivist Turn in International Relations Theory." *World Politics* 50 (January): 324–48.

Chen, Jian. 1997. "Challenges and Responses in East Asia." Speech to the First Council on Security Cooperation in the Asia Pacific General Meeting.

Chen Xueyin (IAPCM). 1993. "The Objectives, Definitions, and Related Issues of a Comprehensive Test Ban." (June 1993) JPRS-TND-93-026, August 10.

Chen Xueyin and Wang Deli. 1996. "The Top Priority of Current Nuclear Arms Control: Some Comments about the CTBT and the Production Cut-Off." Paper prepared for the Fifth ISODARCO-Beijing Seminar on Arms Control, Chengdu, November 11–16.

Cheung, Peter T. Y. 1998. "Introduction: Provincial Leadership and Economic Reform in Post-Mao China." In *Provincial Strategies of Economic Reform in Post-Mao China: Leadership, Politics, and Implementation,* ed. Peter T. Y. Cheung, Jae Ho Chung, and Zhimin Lin. Armonk, NY: M. E. Sharpe.

Chigas, Diana, Elizabeth McClintock, and Christophe Kamp. 1996. "Preventive Diplomacy and the Organization for Security Cooperation in Europe: Creating Incentives for Dialogue and Cooperation." In *Preventing Conflict in the Post-Communist World: Mobilizing International and Regional Organization,* ed. Abram Chayes and Antonia Handler Chayes. Washington, DC: Brookings Institution.

China. 1997. Paper presented to the ARF Intersessional Support Group on CBMs in Brunei. November 3–5.

Choi, Young Back. 1993. *Paradigms and Conventions: Uncertainty, Decision Making, and Entrepreneurship.* Ann Arbor: University of Michigan Press.

Christensen, Thomas J. 1996. "Chinese *Realpolitik.*" *Foreign Affairs* 75, no. 5 (September/October): 37–53.

Christoffersen, Gaye. 1994–95. "The Greater Vladivostok Project: Transnational Linkages in Regional Economic Planning." *Pacific Affairs* 67 (4): 513–31.

Christoffersen, Gaye. 1996a. "Nesting the Sino-Russian Border and the Tumen Project in the Asia-Pacific: Heilongjiang's Regional Relations." *Asian Perspectives* 20 (2): 265–99.

Christoffersen, Gaye. 1996b. "China and the Asia-Pacific: Need for a Grand Strategy." *Asian Survey* 36 (11): 1067–85.

Chu, Shulong. 1997. "Concepts, Structures, and Strategies of Security Cooperation in Asia-Pacific." Manuscript.

Cialdini, Robert. 1984. *Influence: The New Psychology of Modern Persuasion.* New York: Quill Books.

Cialdini, Robert. 1987. "Compliance Principles of Compliance Professionals: Psychologists of Necessity." In *Social Influence: The Ontario Symposium,* vol. 5, ed. Mark P. Zanna, James M. Olson, and C. Peter Herman. Hillsdale, NJ: Lawrence Erlbaum Associates.

Cialdini, R. B., C. A. Kallgren, and R. R. Reno. 1991. "A Focus Theory of Normative Conduct." *Advances in Experimental Social Psychology* 24: 202–31.

CICIR (China Institute of Contemporary International Relations), ed. 1987. *Guoji caijun douzheng yu Zhongguo* (China and the international arms control struggle). Beijing: Shishi Publishing House.

Clark, Ann Marie, Elisabeth Friedman, and Kathryn Hochstetler. 1998. "The Sovereign Limits of Global Civil Society." *World Politics* 51 (1): 1–34.

Claude, Inis. 1966. "Collective Legitimization as a Political Function of the UN." *International Organization* 20:267–79.

Clinton, William Jefferson. 1994a. Press conference, February 6.

Clinton, William Jefferson. 1994b. Press conference, August 3.

Collier, David, and James Mahoney. 1996. "Insights and Pitfalls: Selection Bias in Qualitative Research." *World Politics* 49:56–91.

Congressional Record. 1994. 103rd Cong., 1st sess. Washington, DC.

Congressional Record. 1995. 104th Cong., 1st sess. Washington, DC.

Cortell, Andrew, and James Davis Jr. 1996. "How Do International Institutions Matter? The Domestic Impact of International Rules and Norms." *International Studies Quarterly* 40:451–78.

Cottarelli, Carlo, and Curzio Giannini. 1998. "Inflation, Credibility, and the Role of the International Monetary Fund." Paper on Policy Analysis and Assessment No. 98/12, International Monetary Fund.

Cotton, James. 1996. "China and Tumen River Cooperation: Jilin's Coastal Development Strategy." *Asian Survey* 36 (11): 1086–1101.

Cowhey, Peter. 1993. "Domestic Institutions and the Credibility of International Commitments: Japan and the United States." *International Organization* 47 (2): 299–326.

Crescenzi, Mark J. C. 1999. "Violence and Uncertainty in Transitions." *Journal of Conflict Resolution* 43 (April): 192–212.

Dai, Xinyuan. 1999. *Compliance without Carrots or Sticks.* Ph.D. diss., University of Chicago.

Davis, Phillip A. 1992. "Hill Backs Sending Troops." *Congressional Quarterly Weekly Report,* December 5, 3760.

Desch, Michael. 1996. "War and Strong States, Peace and Weak States?" *International Organization* 50:237–68.

Des Forges, Alison. 1999. *Leave None to Tell the Story.* New York: Human Rights Watch.

Dewitt, David. 1994. "Common, Comprehensive, and Cooperative Security in Asia-Pacific." *CANCAPS Papiers* no. 3 (March).

Dhonte, Pierre. 1997. "Conditionality as an Instrument of Borrower Credibility." Paper on Policy Analysis and Assessment No. 97/2, International Monetary Fund.

Diermeier, Daniel, Joel Ericson, Timothy Frye, and Steven Lewis. 1997. "Credible Commitment and Property Rights: The Role of Strategic Interaction between Political and Economic Actors." In *The Political Economy of Property Rights: Institutional Change and Credibility in the Reform of Central Planned Economies,* ed. D. Weimer. Cambridge: Cambridge University Press.

DiMaggio, Paul J., and Walter W. Powell. 1983. "The Iron Cage Revisited: Institutional Isomorphism and Collective Rationality in Organizational Fields." *American Sociological Review* 48:147–60.

DiMaggio, Paul J., and Walter W. Powell. 1991. "Introduction." In *The New Institutionalism in Organizational Analysis,* ed. Paul J. DiMaggio and Walter W. Powell. Chicago: University of Chicago Press.

Dittmer, Lowell, and Samuel S. Kim. 1993. *China's Quest for National Identity.* Ithaca: Cornell University Press.

Doherty, Carroll J. 1993a. "Foreign Policy: Is Congress Still Keeping Watch?" *Congressional Quarterly Weekly Report,* August 21, 2267.

Doherty, Carroll J. 1993b. "Clinton Calms Rebellion on Hill by Retooling Somalia Mission." *Congressional Quarterly Weekly Report,* October 9, 2750.

Doherty, Carroll J. 1993c. "Foreign Policy: House Sends Mixed Message over Somalia Mission." *Congressional Quarterly Weekly Report,* November 13, 3139.

Doherty, Carroll J. 1994a. "Bosnia: Senate Hands President a Muddled Mandate." *Congressional Quarterly Weekly Report,* May 14, 1233.

Doherty, Carroll J. 1994b. "Senate Defeats GOP Proposal to Limit Clinton on Haiti." *Congressional Quarterly Weekly Report,* July 2, 1814.

Doherty, Carroll J. 1994c. "Senate Declines to Restrict Clinton's Options on Haiti." *Congressional Quarterly Weekly Report,* July 16, 1943.

Doherty, Carroll J. 1994d. "President, Rebuffing Congress, Prepares to Launch Invasion." *Congressional Quarterly Weekly Report,* September 17, 2578.

Doherty, Carroll J. 1994e. "As U.S. Troops Deploy Peacefully, Clinton's Battle Has Just Begun." *Congressional Quarterly Weekly Report,* September 24, 2701.

Doherty, Carroll J. 1994f. "Hill Wary of Putting Strings on Military Mission." *Congressional Quarterly Weekly Report,* October 1, 2816.

Doherty, Carroll J. 1994g. "Congress, after Sharp Debate, Gives Clinton a Free Hand." *Congressional Quarterly Weekly Report,* October 8, 2895.

Doherty, Carroll J. 1994h. "Bosnia: U.S. Policy on Use of Force Puzzles Many Lawmakers." *Congressional Quarterly Weekly Report,* April 16, 906.

Doherty, Carroll J. 1995. "Bosnia: Clinton Vow to Provide Troops Revives War Powers Conflict." *Congressional Quarterly Weekly Report,* October 14, 3158.

Dorian, James P. 1997. "Minerals and Mining in the Russian Far East." In *Politics and Economics in the Russian Far East: Changing Ties with Asia-Pacific,* ed. Tsuneo Akaha. London: Routledge.

Downs, George W., David M. Rocke, and Peter N. Barsoom. 1997. "Designing Multilaterals: The Architecture and Evolution of Environmental Agreements." Paper presented at the annual meeting of the American Political Science Association, Washington, DC, August.

Drazen, Allen. 2000. *Political Economy in Macroeconomics.* Princeton: Princeton University Press.

Drew, Elizabeth. 1994. *On the Edge: The Clinton Presidency.* New York: Simon and Schuster.

Drezner, Daniel W. 1998. "The Cohesion of International Regimes." Paper presented at the annual meeting of the American Political Science Association, Boston.

Drezner, Daniel W. 1999–2000. "The Trouble with Carrots: Transaction Costs, Conflict Expectations, and Economic Inducements." *Security Studies* 9 (autumn/winter): 188–218.

Drezner, Daniel W. 2000. "Bargaining, Enforcement, and Multilateral Sanctions: When Is Cooperation Counterproductive?" *International Organization* 54 (winter): 73–102.

Drezner, Daniel W. 2001. "State Structure, Technological Leadership, and the Maintenance of Hegemony." *Review of International Studies* 27 (January): 3–27.

Drogin, Bob. 1994. "Perry Predicts Yearlong Army Aid for Rwanda." *Chicago Sun-Times,* August 1.

Duchacek, Ivo D. 1970. *Comparative Federalism: The Territorial Dimension of Politics.* New York: Holt, Rinehart, and Winston.

Duchacek, Ivo D. 1986. "International Competence of Subnational Governments: Borderlands and Beyond." In *Across Boundaries: Transborder Interaction in Comparative Perspective,* ed. Oscar J. Martinez. El Paso: Texas Western.

Duchacek, Ivo D. 1990. "Perforated Sovereignties: Towards a Typology of New Actors in International Relations." In *Federalism and International Relations: The Role of Subnational Units,* ed. Hans J. Michelmann and Panayotis Soldatos. Oxford: Clarendon.

Economist. 1996. "Survey: MERCOSUR." *The Economist* (October 12): S1–S33.

Eichengreen, Barry. 1992. *Golden Fetters: The Gold Standard and the Great Depression, 1919–1939.* New York: Oxford University Press.

Eilperin, Juliet, and Helen Dewar. 1999. "GOP Pushes Debate on Kosovo; White House Says Timing Could Undermine Peace Talks." *Washington Post,* March 10, A4.

Eldridge, Robert D. 1997. "The 1996 Okinawa Referendum on U.S. Base Reductions: One Question, Several Answers." *Asian Survey* 37 (10): 879–904.

Evangelista, Matthew. 1995. "Transnational Relations, Domestic Structures, and Security Policy in the USSR and Russia." In *Bringing Transnational Relations Back In: Non-State Actors, Domestic Structures, and International Institutions,* ed. Thomas Risse-Kappen. Cambridge: Cambridge University Press.

Evangelista, Matthew. 1997. "Domestic Structure and International Change." In *New Thinking in International Relations Theory,* ed. Michael W. Doyle and G. John Ikenberry. Boulder: Westview.

Evangelista, Matthew. 1999. *Unarmed Forces: The Transnational Movement to End the Cold War.* Ithaca: Cornell University Press.

Evans, Peter, Harold K. Jacobson, and Robert D. Putnam, eds. 1993. *Double-Edged Diplomacy: International Bargaining and Domestic Politics.* Berkeley: University of California Press.

Evans, Peter, Dierich Rueschemeyer, and Theda Skocpol, eds. 1985. *Bringing the State Back In.* New York: Cambridge University Press.

Eyre, Dana, and Mark Suchman. 1996. "Status, Norms, and the Proliferation of Conventional Weapons: An Institutional Theory Approach." In *The Culture of National Security,* ed. Peter J. Katzenstein. New York: Columbia University Press.

Fairman, David, and Michael Ross. 1996. "Old Fads, New Lessons: Learning from Economic Development Assistance." In *Institutions for Environmental Aid: Pitfalls and Promise,* ed. Robert O. Keohane and Marc A. Levy, 29–51. Cambridge: MIT Press.

Fearon, James. 1994. "Domestic Political Audiences and the Escalation of

Interstate Disputes." *American Political Science Review* 88 (September): 577–92.

Fearon, James. 1998. "Bargaining, Enforcement, and International Cooperation." *International Organization* 52:269–306.

Feld, Werner J., and Robert S. Jordan, with Leon Hurwitz. 1994. *International Organizations: A Comparative Approach.* 3d ed. Westport: Praeger.

Feldman, Elliot J., and Lily Gardner Feldman. 1990. "Canada." In *Federalism and International Relations: The Role of Subnational Units,* ed. Hans J. Michelmann and Panayotis Soldatos. Oxford: Clarendon.

Feldmann, Linda. 1994. "Haiti Invasion 'Option' Splits U.S. Lawmakers." *Christian Science Monitor,* July 15, 3.

Fernandez-Arias, Eduardo, and Mark M. Spiegel. 1998. "North-South Customs Unions and International Capital Mobility." *Journal of International Economics* 46:229–51.

Finer, Samuel E. 1962. *The Man on Horseback.* London: Pall Mall.

Finnemore, Martha. 1993. "International Organizations as Teachers of Norms: The United Nations Educational, Scientific, and Cultural Organization and Science Policy." *International Organization* 47 (4): 565–97.

Finnemore, Martha. 1996a. "Constructing Norms of Humanitarian Intervention." In *The Culture of National Security: Norms and Identity in World Politics,* ed. Peter J. Katzenstein. New York: Columbia University Press.

Finnemore, Martha. 1996b. *National Interests in International Society.* Ithaca: Cornell University Press.

Finnemore, Martha. 1996c. "Norms, Culture, and World Politics: Insights from Sociology's Institutionalism." *International Organization* 50 (spring): 324–49.

Finnemore, Martha, and Kathryn Sikkink. 1998. "International Norm Dynamics and Political Change." *International Organization* 52, no. 4 (autumn): 887–917.

Fisher, Louis. 1995a. *Presidential War Power.* Lawrence: University Press of Kansas.

Fisher, Louis. 1995b. "The Korean War: On What Legal Basis Did Truman Act?" *American Journal of International Law* 89 (January): 21–39.

Fisher, Louis, and David Gray Alder. 1998. "The War Powers Resolution: Time to Say Goodbye." *Political Science Quarterly* 113 (spring): 1–19.

Fortna, V. Page. 1998. "Achieving Durable Peace after Civil War." Paper presented at the annual meeting of the American Political Science Association, Boston.

Franck, Thomas M. 1990. *The Power of Legitimacy among Nations.* New York: Oxford University Press.

Francois, Joseph F. 1999. "Maximizing the Benefits of the Trade Policy Review Mechanism for Developing Countries." Erasmus University, Rotterdam, Netherlands. Typescript.

Frank, Robert. 1985. *Choosing the Right Pond: Human Behavior and the Quest for Status.* New York: Oxford University Press.

Frank, Robert. 1988. *Passions within Reason: The Strategic Role of the Emotions.* New York: Norton.

Frieden, Jeffry. 1994. "Making Commitments: France and Italy in the European Monetary System, 1979–1985." In *The Political Economy of European Monetary Integration,* ed. Barry Eichengreen and Jeffry Frieden, 25–46. Boulder: Westview.

Frieden, Jeffry. 1999. "Actors and Preferences in International Relations." In *Strategic Choice in International Relations,* ed. David A. Lake and Robert Powell. Princeton: Princeton University Press.

Fry, Earl H. 1990. "The United States of America." In *Federalism and International Relations: The Role of Subnational Units,* ed. Hans J. Michelmann and Panayotis Soldatos. Oxford: Clarendon Press.

Frye, Timothy. 1997. "Russian Privatization and the Limits of Credible Commitment." In *The Political Economy of Property Rights: Institutional Change and Credibility in the Reform of Centrally Planned Economies,* ed. D. Weimer. Cambridge: Cambridge University Press.

Fu Chengli. 1994. "Dangdai guoji xingshi zhong de ji ge wenti" (A few questions about the current international situation) *Shijie Xingshi Yanjiu* (Research on the international situation) (Beijing) no. 1 (January 5).

Fudenberg, Drew, and Jean Tirole. 1991. *Game Theory.* Cambridge: MIT Press.

Galvin, Kevin. 1992. "Military Shuts Media, Detains Critics as Constitution Is Suspended." *Associated Press Wire,* April 7.

Garrett, Banning, and Bonnie Glaser. 1994. "Multilateral Security in the Asia-Pacific Region and Its Impact on Chinese Interests: Views from Beijing." *Contemporary Southeast Asia* 16, no. 1 (June): 1–13.

Garrett, Banning, and Bonnie Glaser. 1997. "Does China Want the U.S. out of Asia?" *PacNet Newsletter,* no. 22 (May 30).

Gaubatz, Kurt T. 1996. "Democratic States and Commitment in International Relations." *International Organization* 50 (winter): 109–39.

Geddes, Barbara. 1998. "What Do We Know about Democratization after Twenty Years?" Paper presented at the annual meeting of the American Political Science Association, Boston.

Gerard, H. B., and R. Orive. 1987. "The Dynamics of Opinion Formation." *Advances in Experimental Social Pyschology* 20.

Giavazzi, Francesco, and Marco Pagano. 1994. "The Advantage of Tying One's Hands: EMS Discipline and Central Bank Credibility." In *Monetary and Fiscal Policy.* Vol. 1, *Credibility,* ed. Torsten Persson and Guido Tabellini, 225–46. Cambridge: MIT Press.

Gibson, James L. 1998. "A Sober Second Thought: An Experiment in Persuading Russians to Tolerate." *American Journal of Political Science* 42, no. 3 (July): 819–50.

Gilpin, Robert. 1981. *War and Change in World Politics.* Cambridge: Cambridge University Press.

Goldstein, Avery. 1991. *From Bandwagon to Balance-of-Power Politics:*

Structural Constraints and Politics in China, 1949–1978. Stanford: Stanford University Press.

Goldstein, Judith. 1996. "International Law and Domestic Institutions: Reconciling North American 'Unfair' Trade Laws." *International Organization* 50, no. 4 (autumn): 541–64.

Goldstein, Judith, Miles Kahler, Robert Keohane, and Anne-Marie Slaughter, eds. 2001. "Legalization and World Politics." Special issue of *International Organization* 54 (3).

Gompert, David C. 1996. "The United States and Yugoslavia's Wars." In *The World and Yugoslavia's Wars,* ed. Richard H. Ullman. New York: Council on Foreign Relations.

Goodman, John, and Louis Pauly. 1993. "The Obsolescence of Capital Controls?" *World Politics* 46 (October): 50–82.

Gould, David M. 1992. "Free Trade Agreements and the Credibility of Trade Reforms." *Federal Reserve Bank of Dallas Economic Review* (January):17–27.

Gow, James. *Triumph of the Lack of Will.* New York: Columbia University Press.

Graham, Thomas W. 1994. "Public Opinion and U.S. Foreign Policy Decision Making." In *The New Politics of American Foreign Policy,* ed. David Deese. New York: St. Martin's Press.

Green, Donald P., and Ian Shapiro. 1994. *Pathologies of Rational Choice Theory: A Critique of Applications in Political Science.* New Haven: Yale University Press.

Greenhouse, Steven. 1994. "U.S. Shifts Stress to Haiti Sanctions." *New York Times,* June 9, 3A.

Gregg, Robert W. 1968. "The UN Regional Economic Commissions and Integration in Underdeveloped Regions." In *International Regionalism,* ed. Joseph S. Nye Jr. Boston: Little, Brown.

Grieco, Joseph M. 1988. "Anarchy and the Limits of Cooperation: A Realist Critique of the Newest Liberal Institutionalism." *International Organization* 42 (August): 485–507.

Grieco, Joseph. 1990. *Cooperation among Nations.* Ithaca: Cornell University Press.

Grimmett, Richard F. 1999. "Instances of Use of United States Armed Forces Abroad, 1798–1999." Congressional Research Service Report, May 17.

Grossman, Sanford, and Oliver Hart. 1983. "An Analysis of the Principal-Agent Problem.: *Econometrica* 51:7–45.

Gruber, Lloyd. 2000. *Ruling the World.* Princeton: Princeton University Press.

Guisinger, Alexandra, and Alastair Smith. 2000. "Honest Threats: The Interaction of Reputation and Political Institutions in International Crises." Manuscript, Yale University.

Gunther, Richard, P. Nikiforos Diamandouros, and Hans-Jurgen Puhle. 1995.

"Introduction." In *The Politics of Democratic Consolidation,* ed. Richard Gunther, P. Nikiforos Diamandouros, and Hans-Jurgen Puhle. Baltimore: Johns Hopkins University Press.

Haas, Peter M. 1992a. "Introduction: Epistemic Communities and International Policy Coordination." *International Organization* 46 (1): 1–35.

Haas, Peter M. 1992b. "Banning Chlorofluorocarbons: Epistemic Community Efforts to Protect Stratospheric Ozone." *International Organization* 46 (1): 187–224.

Haas, Peter M. 1998. "Constructing Multilateral Environmental Governance: The Evolution of Multilateral Environmental Governance since 1972." Paper presented at the Center for International Affairs, Harvard University, April 16.

Haggard, Stephan. 2000. *The Political Economy of the Asian Financial Crisis.* Washington, DC: Institute for International Economics.

Haggard, Stephan, and Robert Kaufman. 1995. "The Challenges of Consolidation." In *Economic Reform and Democracy,* ed. Larry Diamond and Marc F. Plattner. Baltimore: John Hopkins University Press.

Hamman, Henry L. 1998. "Remodeling International Relations: New Tools from New Science?" In *International Relations in a Constructed World,* ed. Vendulka Kubalkova, Nicholas Onuf, and Paul Kowert, 173–92. Armonk, NY: M. E. Sharpe.

Harding, Harry. 1987. *China's Second Revolution: Reform after Mao.* Washington, DC: Brookings.

Harding, James. 1994. "Invasion of Haiti Inches a Step Closer," *Financial Times,* August 31.

Harre, Rom. 1979. *Social Being: A Theory for Social Psychology.* Oxford: Blackwell.

Hasenclever, Andreas, Peter Mayer, and Volker Rittberger. 1996. "Interests, Power, Knowledge: The Study of International Regimes." *Mershon International Studies Review* 40, no. 2 (October): 177–228.

Hasenclever, Andreas, Peter Mayer, and Volker Rittberger. 1997. *Theories of International Regimes.* Cambridge: Cambridge University Press.

Hatch, Elvin. 1989. "Theories of Social Honor." *American Anthropologist* 91 (2): 341–54.

Hayes, Monte. 1992. "Peru's President Has Earned His Nickname 'The Emperor'." *Associated Press Wire,* April 9.

Hellman, Joel. 1998. "Winners Take All: The Politics of Partial Reform in Post Communist Transitions." *World Politics* 50 (2): 203–34.

Hendrickson, Ryan C. 1998. "War Powers, Bosnia, and the 104th Congress." *Political Science Quarterly* 113 (2): 214–58.

Hinckley, Barbara. 1994. *Less Than Meets the Eye.* Chicago: University of Chicago Press.

Hoekman, Bernard M., and Petros C. Mavroidis. 1999. "Enforcing Multilateral Commitments: Dispute Settlement and Developing Countries."

Paper prepared for the WTO/World Bank Conference on Developing Countries in a Millennium Round, Geneva, Switzerland, September 20–21.

Holbrooke, Richard. 1998. *To End a War.* New York: Random House.

Horn, Henrik, and Petros C. Mavroidis. 1999. "Remedies in the WTO Dispute Settlement System and Developing Country Interests." World Bank. Typescript.

Huang Tingwei and Song Baoxian. 1987. "Dangqian guoji caijun douzheng de tedian ji zhengce jianyi" (Special characteristics of the current international disarmament struggle and policy proposals). In *Guoji caijun douzheng yu Zhongguo* (China and the international arms control struggle), ed. China Institute of Contemporary International Relations. Beijing: Shishi Publishing House.

Hurd, Ian. 1999. "Legitimacy and Authority in International Relations." *International Organization* 53:379–408.

Hurlburt, Heather. 1997. "Gaining Leverage for International Organizations: Incentives and Baltic-Russian Relations, 1992–1994." In *The Price of Peace,* ed. David Cortright. New York: Rownan and Littlefield.

Hyde-Price, Adrian G. V. 1994. "Democratization in Eastern Europe: The External Dimension." In *Democratization in Eastern Europe: Domestic and International Perspectives,* ed. Geoffrey Pridham and Tatu Vanhanen. London: Routledge.

Hyer, Eric. 1996. "The Sino-Russian Boundary Settlement." *Boundary and Security Bulletin* 4 (2): 90–94.

Ibarra, Luis Alberto. 1995. "Credibility of Trade Policy Reform and Investment: The Mexican Experience." *Journal of Development Economics* 47 (June): 39–60.

Ichilov, Orit. 1990. "Introduction." In *Political Socialization, Citizenship Education, and Democracy,* ed. Orit Ichilov. New York: Teachers College Press.

Ikenberry, G. John. 2000. *After Victory.* Princeton: Princeton University Press.

Ikenberry, G. John, and Charles Kupchan. 1990. "Socialization and Hegemonic Power." *International Organization* 44:283–315.

Institute of Far Eastern Studies (Russian Academy of Sciences). 1995. "Russia's Interests in Northeast Asia and the Prospects for Multilateral Cooperation with NEA Countries in Promoting the Development of Russia's Far East." *Far Eastern Affairs* 3:4–49.

Interview 1996a. Interview with former senior U.S. administration figure involved in Asia policy, Beijing, June.

Interview 1996b. Interview with Canadian embassy officials, Beijing, April.

Interview 1996c. Interview with Singaporean embassy official, Beijing, April.

Interview 1996d. Interview with Chinese intelligence analyst involved in ARF policy process, Beijing, July.

Interview 1996e. Interview with strategic analyst, State Council National Development Research Center, Asia-African Research Institute, Beijing, May.

Interview 1997a. Interview with prominent Canadian academic involved in Track II activities, January.

Interview 1998a. Interview with senior Chinese think tank analysts close to the Asia-Pacific policy process in the Ministry of Foreign Affairs, Beijing, October.

Interview 1998b. Interview with Chinese academic specialist on Asia-Pacific multilateralism, Beijing, October.

Interview 1998c. Interview with senior Chinese think tank analyst specializing in Asia-Pacific regional affairs, Beijing, October.

Interview 1998d. Interview with Canadian embassy official, Beijing, October.

Interview 1999. Interview with Chinese think tank analyst specializing in Asia-Pacific regional affairs, January.

Isen, Alice M. 1987. "Positive Affect, Cognitive Processes, and Social Behavior." *Advances in Experimental Social Psychology* 20:203–53.

Ivanov, Vladimir. 1995. "Russia and Northeast Asia." *Northeast Asia Economic Forum Newsletter* 14:5–12.

Jackman, Robert. 1973. "On the Relations of Economic Development to Democratic Performance." *American Journal of Political Science* 17: 611–21.

Jacobson, Harold K. 1984. *Networks of Interdependence: International Organizations and the Global Political System.* 2d ed. New York: McGraw-Hill.

Jacobson, Harold K., and Michel Oksenberg. 1990. *China's Participation in the IMF, the World Bank, and GATT: Towards a Global Economic Order.* Ann Arbor: University of Michigan Press.

Jacobson, Harold K., William Reisinger, and Todd Matthews. 1986. "National Entanglements in International Organizations." *American Political Science Review* 80 (March): 141–59.

Jaggers, Keith, and Ted Robert Gurr. 1995. "Tracking Democracy's Third Wave with the Polity III Data." *Journal of Peace Research* 32 (November): 469–82.

James, Michael Rabinder. 1998. "Communicative Action and the Logics of Group Conflict." Paper presented at the annual meeting of the American Political Science Association, Boston.

Jehl, Douglas. 1994. "Clinton Seeks UN Approval of Any Plan to Invade Haiti," *New York Times,* July 22.

Jepperson, Ronald L., Alexander Wendt, and Peter J. Katzenstein. 1996. "Norms, Identity, and Culture in National Security." In *The Culture of National Security,* ed. Peter J. Katzenstein. New York: Columbia University Press.

Johnson, James. 1993. "Is Talk Really Cheap? Prompting Conversation between Critical Theory and Rational Choice." *American Political Science Review* 87, no. 1 (March): 74–86.

Johnston, Alastair Iain. 1990. "China and Arms Control in the Asia-Pacific Region." In *Superpower Maritime Strategy in the Pacific,* ed. Frank Langdon and Douglas Ross. London: Routledge Press.

Johnston, Alastair Iain. 1995–96. "China's New Old Thinking: The Concept of Limited Deterrence." *International Security* 20 (winter): 5–43.

Johnston, Alastair Iain. 1998. "China and International Environmental Institutions: A Decision Rule Analysis." In *Energizing China: Reconciling Environmental Protection with Energy Demands of a Growing Economy,* ed. Michael McElroy. Cambridge: Harvard University Press.

Johnston, Alastair Iain. 1999a. "Realism(s) and Chinese Security Policy after the Cold War." In *Unipolar Politics: Realism and State Strategies after the Cold War,* ed. Ethan Kapstein and Michael Mastanduno. New York: Columbia University Press.

Johnston, Alastair Iain. 1999b. "Socialization in International Institutions: The ASEAN Way and IR Theory." Paper prepared for project entitled "The Emerging International Relations of East Asia," sponsored by the University of Pennsylvania and Dartmouth College.

Johnston, Harry, and Ted Dagne. 1997. "Congress and the Somalia Crisis." In *Learning from Somalia: The Lessons of Armed Humanitarian Intervention,* ed. Walter Clarke and Jeffrey Herbst, 191–206. Boulder: Westview.

Jones, Daniel, Stuart Bremer, and J. D. Singer. 1996. "Militarized Interstate Disputes, 1816–1992: Rationale, Coding Rules, and Empirical Patterns." *Conflict Management and Peace Science* 15 (2): 163–213.

Jones, Edward E. 1985. "Major Developments in Social Psychology during the Past Five Decades." In *Handbook of Social Psychology,* ed. Gardner Lindzey and Elliot Aronson. New York: Random House.

Jorgensen, Charlotte, Christian Kock, and Lone Rorbech. 1998. "Rhetoric That Shifts Votes: An Exploratory Study of Persuasion in Issue-Oriented Public Debates." *Political Communication* 15:283–99.

Kahler, Miles. 1993. "Bargaining with the IMF: Two-Level Strategies and Developing Countries." In *Double-Edged Diplomacy: International Bargaining and Domestic Politics,* ed. Peter Evans, Harold Jacobson, and Robert Putnam. Berkeley: University of California Press.

Karns, Margaret P., and Karen A. Mingst. 1987. "International Organizations and Foreign Policy: Influence and Instrumentality." In *New Directions in the Study of Foreign Policy,* ed. Charles F. Hermann, Charles W. Kegley Jr., and James N. Rosenau. Boston: Allen & Unwin.

Katzenstein, Peter J. 1978. *Between Power and Plenty: Foreign Economic Policies of Advanced Industrial States.* Madison: University of Wisconsin Press.

Katzenstein, Peter J. 1978. "Conclusion: Domestic Structures and Strategies of Foreign Economic Policy." In *Between Power and Plenty: Foreign*

Economic Policies of Advanced Industrial States, ed. Peter J. Katzenstein. Madison: University of Wisconsin Press.

Katzenstein, Peter J. 1985. *Small States in World Markets.* Ithaca: Cornell University Press.

Katzenstein, Peter J., Robert O. Keohane, and Stephen D. Krasner. 1998. *"International Organization* and the Study of World Politics." *International Organization* 52, no. 2 (autumn): 645–85.

Keck, Margaret E., and Kathryn Sikkink. 1998. *Activists beyond Borders: Advocacy Networks in International Politics.* Ithaca: Cornell University Press.

Keohane, Robert O. 1983. "The Demand for International Regimes." In *International Regimes,* ed. Stephen D. Krasner, 141–71. Ithaca: Cornell University Press.

Keohane, Robert O. 1984. *After Hegemony: Cooperation and Discord in the World Political Economy.* Princeton: Princeton University Press.

Keohane, Robert O. 1988. "International Institutions: Two Approaches." *International Studies Quarterly* 32:379–96.

Keohane, Robert O. 1989. *International Institutions and State Power.* Boulder: Westview.

Keohane, Robert O. 1990. "Multilateralism: An Agenda for Research." *International Journal* 11 (autumn): 731–64.

Keohane, Robert O. 1997. "The Analysis of International Regimes: Towards a European-American Research Programme." In *Regime Theory and International Relations,* ed. Volker Rittberger. Oxford: Clarendon Press.

Keohane, Robert O., and Lisa Martin. 1995. "The Promise of Institutionalist Theory." *International Security* 20, no. 1 (summer): 39–51.

Keohane, Robert O., and Helen V. Milner. 1996. *Internationalization and Domestic Politics.* Cambridge: Cambridge University Press.

Keohane, Robert O., and Joseph S. Nye Jr. 1974. "Transgovernmental Relations and International Organizations." *World Politics* 27 (1): 39–62.

Keohane, Robert O., and Joseph S. Nye Jr. 1978. *Power and Interdependence.* Boston: Scott, Foresman.

Keohane, Robert O., and Joseph S. Nye Jr. 1989. *Power and Interdependence.* 2d ed. Glenview, IL: Scott, Foresman.

Keohane, Robert O., Peter Haas, and Marc Levy. 1993. "The Effectiveness of International Environmental Institutions." In *Institutions for the Earth,* ed. Peter Haas, Robert O. Keohane, and Marc Levy, 3–24. Cambridge: MIT Press.

Killick, Tony. 1995. *IMF Programs in Developing Countries: Design and Impact.* New York: Routledge.

Kim, Won Bae. 1994. "Sino-Russian Relations and Chinese Workers in the Russian Far East." *Asian Survey* 34 (12): 1064–76.

Kireev, Genrikh. 1997. "Strategic Partnership and a Stable Border." *Far Eastern Affairs* 4:8–22.

Kirkow, Peter. 1998. *Russia's Provinces: Authoritarian Transformation versus Local Autonomy?* New York: St. Martin's.

Kirkow, Peter, and Philip Hanson. 1994. "The Potential for Autonomous Regional Development in Russia: The Case of Primorskiy Kray." *Post-Soviet Geography* 35 (2): 63–88.

Klotz, Audie. 1995. *Norms in International Relations: The Struggle against Apartheid.* Ithaca: Cornell University Press.

Knight, Jack. 1992. *Institutions and Social Conflict.* Cambridge: Cambridge University Press.

Knoke, David. 1994. *Political Networks: The Structural Perspective.* London: Cambridge University Press.

Kohut, Andrew, and Robert C. Toth. 1995. "The People, the Press, and the Use of Force." In *The United States and the Use of Force in the Post-Cold War Era,* a report by the Aspen Strategy Group. Queenstown, MA: Aspen Institute.

Komuro, Norio. 1995. "The WTO Dispute Settlement Mechanism: Coverage and Procedures of the WTO Understanding." *Journal of World Trade* 29 (August): 5–95.

Koremenos, Barbara, Charles Lipson, and Duncan Snidal, eds. 2001. "The Rational Design of International Institutions." Special issue of *International Organization* 55 (4).

Korkunov, Igor. 1994. "On the Project of the Tumenjiang Free Economic Zone in the Territory of Russia, China, and North Korea." *Far Eastern Affairs* 2–3:38–43.

Kouriatchev, Mikhail. 1993. "Economic Cooperation in the Asia-Pacific Region: The Tumen River Area Development Project." *USJP Occasional Paper* 93-06. Harvard: Program on U.S.-Japan Relations.

Kovrigin, Evgenii B. 1997. "Problems of Resource Development in the Russian Far East." In *Politics and Economics in the Russian Far East: Changing Ties with Asia-Pacific,* ed. Tsuneo Akaha. London: Routledge.

Kowert, Paul, and Jeffery Legro. 1996. "Norms, Identity, and Their Limits: A Theoretical Reprise." In *The Culture of National Security,* ed. Peter Katzenstein. New York: Columbia University Press.

Krasner, Stephen D. 1978. "United States Commercial and Monetary Policy: Unraveling the Paradox of External Strength and Internal Weakness." In *Between Power and Plenty: Foreign Economic Policies of Advanced Industrial States,* ed. Peter J. Katzenstein. Madison: University of Wisconsin Press.

Krasner, Stephen D. 1985. *Structural Conflict: The Third World against Global Liberalism.* Berkeley: University of California Press.

Krasner, Stephen D. 1991. "Global Communications and National Power: Life on the Pareto Frontier." *World Politics* 43:336–66.

Krasner, Stephen D. 1995a. "Compromising Westphalia." *International Security* 20:115–51.

Krasner, Stephen D. 1995b. "Power Politics, Institutions, and Transnational Relations." In *Bringing Transnational Relations Back In: Non-State Actors, Domestic Structures, and International Institutions*, ed. Thomas Risse-Kappen. Cambridge: Cambridge University Press.

Krasner, Stephen D. 1999. *Sovereignty: Organized Hypocrisy*. Princeton: Princeton University Press.

Krasner, Stephen D., ed. 1983. *International Regimes*. Ithaca: Cornell University Press.

Krehbiel, Keith. 1991. *Information and Legislative Organization*. Ann Arbor: University of Michigan Press.

Kreps, David M. 1989. "Out-of-Equilibrium Beliefs and Out-of-Equilibrium Behavior." In *The Economics of Missing Markets, Information, and Games*, ed. Frank Hahn, 7–44. New York: Oxford University Press.

Kreps, David M. 1990. "Corporate Culture and Economic Theory." In *Perspectives on Positive Political Economy*, ed. James E. Alt and Kenneth A. Shepsle, 90–143. London: Cambridge University Press.

Krueger, Anne O. 1978. *Foreign Trade Regimes and Economic Development: Liberalization Attempts and Consequences*. Lexington: Ballinger.

Kuklinski, James H., and Norman L. Hurley. 1996. "It's a Matter of Interpretation." In *Political Persuasion and Attitude Change*, ed. Diana C. Mutz, Paul M. Sniderman, and Richard Brody. Ann Arbor: University of Michigan Press.

Kull, Steven. 1996. "What the Public Knows That Washington Doesn't." *Foreign Policy* 101 (winter): 102–15.

Kull, Steven, I. M. Destler, and Clay Ramsay. 1997. *The Foreign Policy Gap: How Policymakers Misread the Public*. College Park, MD: The Center for International and Security Studies at the University of Maryland.

Kydland, Finn E., and Edward C. Prescott. 1977. "Rules Rather Than Discretion: The Inconsistency of Optimal Plans." *Journal of Political Economy* 85:473–91.

Laffey, Mark, and Jutta Weldes. 1997. "Beyond Belief: Ideas and Symbolic Technologies in the Study of International Relations." *European Journal of International Relations* 3 (2) 193–237.

Lake, David A., and Robert Powell. 1997. "International Relations: A Strategic-Choice Approach." In *Strategic Choice and International Relations*, ed. David A. Lake and Robert Powell. Princeton: Princeton University Press.

Lane, Frederic C. 1979. *Profits from Power: Readings in Protection Rent and Violence Controlling Enterprises*. Albany: SUNY Press.

Leeds, Brett Ashley. 1999. "Domestic Political Institutions, Credible Commitments, and International Cooperation." *American Journal of Political Science* 43, no. 4 (October): 979–1002.

Li Yuetang and Zhou Bisong. 1997. *He wuqi yu zhanzheng* (Nuclear weapons and warfare). Beijing: National Defense Industry Press.

Lieber, Robert J. 1997. "Eagle without a Cause: Making Foreign Policy without the Soviet Threat." In *Eagle Adrift,* ed. Robert J. Lieber. New York: Longman.

Lieberthal, Kenneth G. 1992. "Introduction: The 'Fragmented Authoritarianism' Model and Its Limitations." In *Bureaucracy, Politics, and Decision Making in Post-Mao China,* ed. Kenneth G. Lieberthal and David M. Lampton. Berkeley: University of California Press.

Lieberthal, Kenneth G. 1995. *Governing China: From Revolution through Reform.* New York: W. W. Norton.

Lindell, Ulf. 1988. *Modern Multilateral Negotiation: The Consensus Rule and Its Implications in International Conferences.* Lund: Studentlitteratur.

Lindsay, James M. 1994. *Congress and the Politics of U.S. Foreign Policy.* Baltimore: The Johns Hopkins University Press.

Lindsay, James M. 1995. "Congress and the Use of Force in the Post-Cold War Era." In *The United States and the Use of Force in the Post-Cold War Era,* a report by the Aspen Strategy Group. Queenstown, MA: Aspen Institute.

Linz, Juan J. 1978. *Breakdown of Democratic Regimes: Crisis, Breakdown, and Reequilibration.* Baltimore: Johns Hopkins University Press.

Linz, Juan J., and Alfred Stepan. 1996. *Problems of Democratic Transition and Consolidation.* Baltimore: Johns Hopkins University Press.

Lippman, Thomas W. 1994a. "U.S. Troop Withdrawal Ends Frustrating Mission to Save Rwandan Lives." *Washington Post,* October 3.

Lippman, Thomas W. 1994b. "U.S. Costs Mounting in Rwanda, Caribbean." *Washington Post,* August 27.

Lipset, Seymour M. 1959. "Some Social Requisites for Democracy: Economic Development and Political Legitimacy." *American Political Science Review* 53:69–105.

Lipson, Charles. 1991. "Why Are Some International Agreements Informal?" *International Organization* 45 (4): 495–538.

Lipson, Charles. 1999. "Reliable Partners: The 'Promising Advantage' of Democracies as an Explanation of Peace." University of Chicago. Typescript.

Liu Gongliang (IAPCM). 1993. "Comments on the Legislation of the US Congress Nuclear Testing Limits in 1992." (June 3, 1993) JPRS-TND-93-024, July 27.

Liu Xuecheng. 1997. "Confidence Building Diplomacy in the Asia-Pacific Region." *International Review* (China Center for International Studies), no. 1 (January).

Londregan, John B., and Keith T. Poole. 1990. "Poverty, the Coup Trap, and the Seizure of Executive Power." *World Politics* 42 (January): 151–83.

Londregan, John B., and Keith T. Poole. 1996. "Does High Income Promote Democracy?" *World Politics* 49:1–30.

Lovaglia, Michael J. 1995. "Power and Status: Exchange, Attribution, and Expectation States." *Small Group Research* 26, no. 3 (August): 400–427.

Lukin, Alexander. 1998. "The Image of China in Russian Border Regions." *Asian Survey* 38 (9): 821–35.

Lupia, Arthur, and Matthew D. McCubbins. 1998. *The Democratic Dilemma: Can Citizens Learn What They Need to Know?* Cambridge: Cambridge University Press.

Lynch, Marc. 1999. *State Interests and Public Spheres: The International Politics of Jordan's Identity.* New York: Columbia University Press.

Lynne, Nicholas J., and Alexei V. Novikov. 1997. "Refederalizing Russia: Debates on the Ideas of Federalism in Russia." *Publius* 27 (2): 187–203.

MacLaren, Robert. 1980. *Civil Servants and Public Policy: A Comparative Study of International Secretariats.* London: Waterloo.

Makabenta, Leah. 1994. "ASEAN: China Looms Large and Security Meet." *Interpress Service,* July 22.

Malik, J. Mohan. 1995. "China's Policy towards Nuclear Arms Control." *Contemporary Security Policy* 16, no. 2 (August): 1–64.

Malone, David. 1998. *Decision-Making in the UN Security Council: The Case of Haiti.* Oxford: Clarendon Press.

Mansfield, Edward D. 1998. "The Proliferation of Preferential Trading Arrangements." *Journal of Conflict Resolution* 42:523–43.

Mansfield, Edward D., and Jon C. Pevehouse. 1999. "Trade Blocs, Trade Flows, and International Conflict." Ohio State University. Typescript.

Mansfield, Edward D., and Jack Sndyer. 1995. "Democratization and the Danger of War." *International Security* 20 (1): 5–38.

Mansfield, Edward D., Helen V. Milner, and B. Peter Rosendorff. 1998. "Why Democracies Cooperate More: Electoral Control and International Trade Agreements." Paper presented at the annual meeting of the American Political Science Association, Boston.

Marshall, Monty. 1999. *Polity 98 Dataset.* <http://www.bsos.umd.edu/cidcm/polity>.

Martin, Lisa L. 1992. *Coercive Cooperation: Explaining Multilateral Economic Sanctions.* Princeton: Princeton University Press.

Martin, Lisa. 1993a. "Credibility, Costs, and Institutions: Cooperation on Economic Sanctions," *World Politics* 45 (April): 406–32.

Martin, Lisa L. 1993b. "The Rational Choice State of Multilateralism." In *Multilateralism Matters: The Theory and Praxis of an Institutional Form,* ed. John Gerard Ruggie. New York: Columbia University Press.

Martin, Lisa L. 2000. *Democratic Commitments: Legislatures and International Cooperation.* Princeton: Princeton University Press.

Martin, Lisa L., and Beth A. Simmons. 1998. "Theories and Empirical Studies of International Institutions." *International Organization* 52, no. 4 (autumn): 729–57.

Martinez, Oscar J. 1986. "Introduction." In *Across Boundaries: Transborder Interaction in Comparative Perspective,* ed. Oscar J. Martinez. El Paso: Texas Western Press.

Martinez, Oscar J. 1994. "The Dynamics of Border Interaction: New

Approaches to Border Analysis." In *Global Boundaries,* ed. Clive H. Schofield. London: Routledge.

Matthews, Jessica. 1997. "Power Shift." *Foreign Affairs* 73 (March/April): 45–55.

Mattli, Walter. 1999. *The Logic of Regional Integration.* Cambridge: Cambridge University Press.

Mattli, Walter. 2001. "Private Justice in a Global Economy: From Litigation to Arbitration." *International Organization* 55 (4): 921–50.

Maxfield, Sylvia. 1997. *Gatekeepers of Growth: The International Political Economy of Central Banking in Developing Countries.* Princeton: Princeton University Press.

May, Michael, ed. 1999. "A Factual Assessment of the Cox Report. Working paper, Center for International Security and Cooperation," Stanford University.

Mayhew, David R. 1974. *Congress: The Electoral Connection.* New Haven: Yale University Press.

McCubbins, Matthew, and Thomas Schwartz. 1984. "Congressional Oversight Overlooked: Police Patrols versus Fire Alarms." *American Journal of Political Science* 28:165–79.

McCubbins, Matthew, Roger Noll, and Barry Weingast. 1987. "Administrative Procedures as Instruments for Legislative Control." *Journal of Law, Economics, and Organization* 3:243–77.

McNeely, Connie L. 1995. *Constructing the Nation-State: International Organization and Prescriptive Action.* Westport, CT: Greenwood Press.

Mearsheimer, John J. 1994–95. "The False Promise of International Institutions." *International Security* 19 (winter): 5–49.

Menkaus, Ken, and Loius Ortmayer. 1995. "Key Decisions in the Somalia Intervention." *Pew Case Studies in International Affairs,* no. 464. Washington, DC: Institute for the Study of Diplomacy.

Meyer, John W., et al. 1997. "The Structuring of a World Environmental Regime, 1870–1990." *International Organization* 51, no. 4 (autumn): 623–51.

Michalopoulos, Constantine. 1998. "The Participation of the Developing Countries in the WTO." Policy Research Working Paper no. 1906, World Bank. http://www.worldbank.org/html/dec/Publications/Workpapers/WPS1900series/wps1906/wps1906.pdf>.

Michelmann, Hans J. 1990. "Conclusion." In *Federalism and International Relations: The Role of Subnational Units,* ed. Hans J. Michelmann and Panayotis Soldatos. Oxford: Clarendon.

Milgrom, Paul, Douglass North, and Barry Weingast. 1991. "The Role of Institutions in the Revival of Trade: The Law Merchant, Private Judges, and the Champagne Fairs." *Economics and Politics* 2:1–23.

Milner, Helen V. 1988. *Resisting Protectionism: Global Industries and the Politics of International Trade.* Princeton: Princeton University Press.

Milner, Helen V. 1991. "The Assumption of Anarchy in International Relations Theory: A Critique." *Review of International Studies* 17 (January): 67–85.

Milner, Helen V. 1997. *Interests, Institutions, and Information: Domestic Politics and International Relations.* Princeton: Princeton University Press.

Milner, Helen V. 1998. "Rationalizing Politics: The Emerging Synthesis of International, American, and Comparative Politics." *International Organization* 52 (4): 759–86.

Milner, Helen V., and Robert O. Keohane. 1996. "Internationalization and Domestic Politics: An Introduction." In *Internationalization and Domestic Politics,* ed. Helen V. Milner and Robert O Keohane. Cambridge: Cambridge University Press.

Minakir, Pavel A., ed. 1994. *The Russia Far East: An Economic Handbook.* Ed. and trans. Gregory L. Freeze. Armonk: M. E. Sharpe.

Mitchell, Alison. 1999. "In Vote Clinton Sought to Avoid, House Backs a Force for Kosovo." *New York Times,* March 12, A1.

Mitchell, Ronald. 1994. "Regime Design Matters: Intentional Oil Pollution and Treaty Compliance." *International Organization* 48 (3): 425–58.

Miyagi, Etsujiro. 1996. "Redressing the Okinawan Base Problem." *Japan Quarterly* 43 (1): 27–32.

Mochizuki, Mike. 1996. "Toward a New Japan-U.S. Alliance." *Japan Quarterly* 43 (3): 4–16.

Moe, Terry. 1984. "The New Economics of Organization." *American Journal of Political Science* 28:739–77.

Moe, Terry. 1991. "Politics and the Theory of Organization." *Journal of Law, Economics, and Organization* 7:106–29.

Mohr, Lawrence B. 1996. *The Causes of Human Behavior: Implications for Theory and Methods in the Social Sciences.* Ann Arbor: University of Michigan Press.

Moltz, James Clay. 1995. "From Military Adversaries to Economic Partners: Russia and China in the New Asia." *Journal of East Asian Affairs* 9 (1): 157–82.

Moltz, James Clay. 1997. "Russo-Chinese Normalization from an International Perspective: Coping with the Pressures of Change." In *Politics and Economics in the Russian Far East: Changing Ties with Asia-Pacific,* ed. Tsuneo Akaha. London: Routledge.

Moon, Chung-In. 1995. "Economic Interdependence and the Implication for Security in Northeast Asia." *Asian Perspective* 19 (2): 29–52.

Moravcsik, Andrew. 1991. "Negotiating the Single European Act: National Interests and Conventional Statecraft in the European Community." *International Organization* 45:19–56.

Moravcsik, Andrew. 1993. "Introduction: Integrating International and Domestic Theories of International Bargaining." In *Double-Edged Diplomacy: International Bargaining and Domestic Politics,* ed. Peter B.

Evans, Harold Jacobson, and Robert Putnam. Berkeley: University of California Press.

Moravcsik, Andrew. 1997. "Taking Preferences Seriously: A Liberal Theory of International Politics." *International Organization* 51, no. 4 (autumn): 513–53.

Moravcsik, Andrew. 1998. *The Choice for Europe: Social Purpose and State Power from Messina to Maastricht.* Ithaca: Cornell University Press.

Moravcsik, Andrew. 1999. "Supranational Entrepreneurs and International Cooperation." *International Organization* 53:267–306

Morgenthau, Hans. [1948] 1985. *Politics among nations: The Struggle for Power and Peace.* New York: Knopf.

Morrow, James. 1999. "The Strategic Setting of Choices: Signaling, Commitment, and Negotiation in International Politics." In *Strategic Choice and International Relations,* ed. David A. Lake and Robert Powell, 77–114. Princeton: Princeton University Press.

Mower, A. Glenn. 1964. "The Official Pressure Group of the Council of Europe's Consultative Assembly." *International Organization* 18:292–306.

Murphy, Sean D. 1996. *Humanitarian Intervention: The United Nations in an Evolving World Order.* Philadelphia: University of Pennsylvania Press.

Mutz, Diana C., Paul M. Sniderman, and Richard A. Brody. 1996. "Political Persuasion: The Birth of a Field of Study." In *Political Persuasion and Attitude Change,* ed. Diane C. Mutz, Paul M. Sniderman, and Richard A. Brody. Ann Arbor: University of Michigan Press.

Napier, Rodney W., and Matti K. Gershenfeld. 1987. *Groups: Theory and Experience.* 4th edition. Boston: Houghton, Mifflin.

Nass, Klaus Otto. 1989. "The Foreign and European Policy of the German *Länder.*" *Publius* 19:165–84.

Nemeth, Charles J. 1987. "Influence Processes, Problem Solving, and Creativity." In *Social Influence: The Ontario Symposium,* vol. 5, ed. Mark P. Zanna, James M. Olson, and C. Peter Herman. Hillsdale, NJ: Lawrence Erlbaum Associates.

North, Douglass C. 1990. *Institutions, Institutional Change, and Economic Performance.* Cambridge: Cambridge University Press.

North, Douglass C., and Barry Weingast. 1989. "Consitutions and Commitment: The Evolution of Institutions Governing Public Choice in Seventeenth-Century England." *Journal of Economic History* 49:803–32.

Nye, Joseph. 1987. "Nuclear Learning and U.S.-Soviet Security Regimes." *International Organization* 41:371–402.

Olson, Hal F., and Joseph Morgan. 1992. "Chinese Access to the Sea of Japan and Integrated Economic Development in Northeast Asia." *Ocean and Coastal Management* 17 (1): 57–79.

Olson, Mancur. 1965. *The Logic of Collective Action.* Cambridge: Harvard University Press.

Oneal, John R., and Bruce Russett. 1996. "The Classical Liberals Were Right:

Democracy, Interdependence, and Conflict, 1950–1985." *International Studies Quarterly* 41 (2): 267–93.

Pahre, Robert, and Paul Papayoanau, eds. 1997. "Modeling Domestic-International Linkages." Special issue of *Journal of Conflict Resolution* 41 (February).

Palmer, Elizabeth A. 1993. "Somalia: Senate Demands Voice in Policy but Shies from Confrontation." *Congressional Quarterly Weekly Report,* September 11, 2399.

Pan Zhenqiang. 1987. "Dangqian guoji caijun douzheng xingshi yu wo guo de diwei he zuoyong" (The current international disarmament struggle and our country's position and effect). In *Guoji caijun douzheng yu Zhongguo* (China and the international arms control struggle), ed. China Institute of Contemporary International Relations. Beijing: Shishi Publishing House.

Perloff, Richard M. 1993. *The Dynamics of Persuasion.* Hillsdale, NJ: Lawrence Erlbaum Associates.

Petersmann, Ernst-Ulrich. 1997. *The GATT/WTO Dispute Settlement System: International Law, International Organizations, and Dispute Settlement.* London: Kluwer.

Petro, Nicolai N., and Alvin Z. Rubinstein. 1997. *Russia's Foreign Policy: From Empire to Nation-State.* New York: Longman.

Petty, Richard E., Duane T. Wegener, and Leandre R. Fabrigar. 1997. "Attitudes and Attitude Change." *Annual Review of Psychology* 48:609–47.

Pevehouse, Jon C. 2000. *Promotion or Preservation: International Organizations and Democratization.* Ph.D. diss., Ohio State University.

Pomfret, Richard. 1996. *Asian Economies in Transition.* Cheltenham: Edward Elgar.

Pomfret, Richard. 1998. "The Tumen River Area Development Programme." *Boundary and Security Bulletin* 5 (4): 80–88.

Pomper, Miles A. 1998. "House Shies Away from Conflict with Clinton over War Powers." *Congressional Quarterly Weekly Report,* March 21, 0760.

Pomper, Miles A. 1999a. "Congress Wants a Bigger Voice on Sending Troops to Kosovo." *Congressional Quarterly Weekly Report,* February 27, 0499.

Pomper, Miles A. 1999b. "Kosovo Vote, Though Won by Clinton, May Signal New Level of Hill Involvement." *Congressional Quarterly Weekly Report,* March 13, 0621.

Pomper, Miles A. 1999c. "Foreign Aid Compromise is a Success for Clinton Team." *Congressional Quarterly Weekly Report,* 20 November.

Poole, Keith T., and Howard Rosenthal. 1991. "Patterns of Congressional Voting." *American Journal of Political Science* 35 (February): 228–78.

Poole, Keith T., and Howard Rosenthal. 1997. *Congress: A Political-Economic History of Roll Call Voting.* Oxford: Oxford University Press.

Portyakov, Vladimir. 1998. "The Tumenjiang Project and Russia's Interests." *Far Eastern Affairs* 4:49–62.

Portyakov, Vladimir. 1996. "Are the Chinese Coming? Migration Processes in Russia's Far East." *International Affairs* 42 (1): 132–40.

Power, Samantha. 2001. "Bystanders to Genocide." *Atlantic Monthly,* September.

Power, Timothy J., and Mark J. Gasiorowski. 1997. "Institutional Design and Democratic Consolidation in the Third World." *Comparative Political Studies* 30 (April): 123–55.

Pratt, John, and Richard Zeckhauser. 1985. *Principals and Agents.* Boston: Harvard Business School.

Price, Richard. 1998. "Reversing the Gunsights: Transnational Civil Society Targets Landmines." *International Organization* 52, no. 3 (summer): 613–44.

Pridham, Geoffrey. 1994. "The International Dimension of Democratization: Theory, Practice, and Inter-regional Comparisons." In *Building Democracy? The International Dimension of Democratization in Eastern Europe,* ed. G. Pridham, E. Herring, and G. Sanford. New York: St. Martin's Press.

Prunier, Gérard. 1998. *The Rwanda Crisis.* 2d ed. London: Hurst.

Przeworski, Adam. 1991. *Democracy and the Market.* Cambridge: Cambridge University Press.

Przeworski, Adam, Michael Alvarez, Jose Antonio Cheibub, and Fernando Limongi. 1996. "What Makes Democracies Endure?" *Journal of Democracy* 7 (1): 39–55.

Putnam, Robert D. 1988. "Diplomacy and Domestic Politics: The Logic of Two-Level Games." *International Organization* 42 (3): 427–60.

Qu Geping. 1992. "Fazhan wo guo huanjing baohu chanye shi zai bixing" (The development of our country's environmental protection industrial power is necessary). In *Guowuyuan huanjing baohu weiyuanhui wenjian huibian* (Collected documents of the State Council environmental protection committee), vol. 2, ed. State Council Environmental Protection Committee Secretariat. Beijing.

Raustiala, Kal. 1997a. "Domestic Institutions and International Regulatory Cooperation." *World Politics* 49:482–509.

Raustiala, Kal. 1997b. "States, NGOs, and International Environmental Institutions." *International Studies Quarterly* 41:719–40.

Reinhardt, Eric. 1996. *Posturing Parliaments: Ratification, Uncertainty, and International Bargaining.* Ph.D. diss., Columbia University.

Reinhardt, Eric. 1998. "Adjudication without Enforcement Can Be Influential." Emory University. Typescript.

Reinhardt, Eric. 1999. "Aggressive Multilateralism: The Determinants of GATT/WTO Dispute Initiation, 1948–1998." Paper presented at the annual meeting of the International Studies Association, Washington, DC, February 17–20.

Remington, Thomas F. 1999. *Politics in Russia.* New York: Longman.

Ripsman, Norrin M. 2002. *Peacemaking by Democracies: The Effect of State*

Autonomy on the Post-World-War Settlements. University Park: Penn State University Press.

Ripsman, Norrin M., and Jean-Marc F. Blanchard. 2000. "Contextual Information and the Study of Trade and Conflict: The Utility of an Interdisciplinary Approach." In *Beyond Boundaries? Disciplines, Paradigms, and Theoretical Integration in International Studies,* ed. Rudra Sil and Eileen M. Doherty. Albany: SUNY Press.

Risse, Thomas. 1997. "Let's Talk." Paper presented at the annual meeting of the American Political Science Association, Washington, DC, August.

Risse, Thomas. 2000. "'Let's Argue!': Communicative Action in World Politics." *International Organization* 54 (1): 1–40.

Risse-Kappen, Thomas. 1995a. *Cooperation among Democracies: The European Influence on U.S. Foreign Policy.* Princeton: Princeton University Press.

Risse-Kappen, Thomas. 1995b. "Bringing Transnational Relations Back In: Introduction." In *Bringing Transnational Relations Back In: Non-State Actors, Domestic Structures, and International Institutions,* ed. Thomas Risse-Kappen. Cambridge: Cambridge University Press.

Risse-Kappen, Thomas, ed. 1995. *Bringing Transnational Relations Back In: Non-State Actors, Domestic Structures, and International Institutions.* Cambridge: Cambridge University Press.

Rodrik, Dani. 1989a. "Promises, Promises: Credible Policy Reform via Signaling." *Economic Journal* 99 (September): 756–72.

Rodrik, Dani. 1989b. "Credibility of Trade Reform—A Policy Maker's Guide." *World Economy* (March): 1–16.

Rodrik, Dani. 1995. "Why Is There Multilateral Lending?" Working paper 5160, National Bureau of Economic Research, Cambridge, MA.

Rodrik, Dani. 1996. "Understanding Economic Policy Reform." *Journal of Economic Literature* 34 (March): 9–41.

Rodrik, Dani. 1997. *Has Globalization Gone Too Far?* Washington, DC: Institute for International Economics.

Rogowski, Ronald. 1989. *Commerce and Coalitions.* Princeton: Princeton University Press.

Rogowski, Ronald. 1999. "Institutions as Constraints on Strategic Choice." In *Strategic Choice and International Relations,* ed. David A. Lake and Robert Powell, 155–36. Princeton: Princeton University Press.

Root, Hilton. 1994. *The Fountain of Privilege: Political Foundations of Markets in Old Regime France and England.* Berkeley: University of California Press.

Rosner, Jeremy D. 1995–96. "The Know-Nothings Know Something." *Foreign Policy* 101 (winter): 116–29.

Rotte, Ralph. 1998. "International Commitment and Domestic Politics: A Note on the Maastricht Case." *European Journal of International Relations* 4:131–42.

Rozman, Gilbert. 1997a. "Cross-National Integration in Northeast Asia: Geopolitical and Economic Goals in Conflict." *East Asian Studies* (spring/ summer): 6–43.

Rozman, Gilbert. 1997b. "Troubled Choices for the Russian Far East: Decentralization, Open Regionalism, and Internationalism." *Journal of Asian Affairs* 11 (2): 537–69.

Rozman, Gilbert. 1998. "Sino-Russian Relations in the 1990s: A Balance Sheet." *Post-Soviet Affairs* 14 (2): 93–113.

Ruggie, John G. 1993. *Multilateralism Matters: The Theory and Praxis of an Institutional Form.* New York: Columbia University Press.

Ruggie, John G. 1998. *Constructing the World Polity: Essays on International Institutionalization.* London: Routledge.

Ruggiero, Renato. 1998. "Statement by the Director-General, General Council, 24 April 1998." World Trade Organization. <http://www.wto .org/wto/speeches/state17.htm>.

Rule, Brendon Gail, and Gay L. Bisanz. 1987. "Goals and Strategies of Persuasion: A Cognitive Schema for Understanding Social Events." In *Social Influence: The Ontario Symposium,* vol. 5, ed. Mark P. Zanna, James M. Olson, and C. Peter Herman. Hillsdale, NJ: Lawrence Erlbaum Associates.

Russett, Bruce, John Oneal, and David R. Davis. 1998. "The Third Leg of the Kantian Tripod: International Organizations and Militarized Disputes, 1950–1985." *International Organization* 52 (summer): 441–67.

Sandholtz, Wayne. 1993. "Choosing Union: Monetary Politics and Maastricht." *International Organization* 47 (winter): 1–39.

Sartori, Anne. 2002. "The Might of the Pen: A Reputational Theory of Communication in International Disputes." *International Organization* (winter): 121–49.

Schelling, Thomas. 1960. *The Strategy of Conflict.* Cambridge: Harvard University Press.

Schiff, Maurice, and L. Alan Winters. 1997. "Regional Integration as Diplomacy." Working paper, World Bank, April.

Schmitter, Phillipe. 1996. "The Influence of the International Context upon the Choice of National Institutions and Policies in Neo-Democracies." In *The International Aspects of Democratization: Europe and the Americas,* ed. Laurence Whitehead. Oxford: Oxford University Press.

Schoppa, Leonard. 1993. "Two-Level Games and Bargaining Outcomes: Why *Gaiatsu* Succeeds in Japan in Some Cases but Not in Others." *International Organization* 47 (3): 353–86.

Schoppa, Leonard. 1997. *Bargaining with Japan: What American Pressure Can and Cannot Do.* New York: Columbia University Press.

Schultz, Kenneth A. 1998. "Domestic Opposition and Signaling in International Crises." *American Political Science Review* 92 (December): 829–44.

Scott, James Wesley. 1989. "Transborder Cooperation, Regional Initiatives, and Sovereignty Conflicts in Western Europe: The Case of the Upper Rhine Valley." *Publius* 19:139–56.

Sell, Susan. 1998. *Power and Ideas: North-South Politics of Intellectual Property and Antitrust*. Albany: SUNY Press.

Sevilla, Christina R. 1998. "Explaining Patterns of GATT/WTO Trade Complaints." Working paper no. 98-1, Weatherhead Center for International Affairs, Harvard University.

Shanks, Cheryl, Harold K. Jacobson, and Jeffrey H. Kaplan. 1996. "Inertia and Change in the Constellation of International Governmental Organizations." *International Organization* 50 (autumn): 593–627.

Shi Chunlai, and Xu Jian. 1997. "Preventive Diplomacy Pertinent to the Asia-Pacific." *International Review* (China Center for International Studies), no. 4 (July).

Shirk, Susan. 1993. *The Political Logic of Economic Reform in China*. Berkeley: University of California.

Simmons, Beth. 1995. *Who Adjusts? Domestic Sources of Foreign Economic Policy during the Interwar Years*. Princeton: Princeton University Press.

Singer, J. David, and Melvin Small. 1994. *Correlates of War Project: International and Civil War Data, 1816–1992*. Study no. 9905. Ann Arbor, MI: Inter-University Consortium for Political and Social Research.

Siverson, Randolph M., and Juliann Emmons. 1991. "Birds of a Feather: Democratic Political Systems and Alliance Choices in the Twentieth Century." *Journal of Conflict Resolution* 35:285–306.

Slaughter, Anne-Marie. 1997. "The *Real* New World Order." *Foreign Affairs* 76 (September/October): 183–97.

Smith, R. Jeffrey. 1994. "U.S. Mission to Rwanda Criticized." *Washington Post*, September 5.

Smith, Gary. 1996. "Multilateralism and Regional Security in Asia: The ASEAN Regional Forum and APEC's Geopolitical Value." Center for International Affairs, Harvard University, June. Manuscript.

Smith, Michael E. 1998. "Congress, the President, and the Use of Military Force: Cooperation or Conflict in the Post-Cold War Era?" *Presidential Studies Quarterly* 28 (winter): 36–50.

Smith, Mitchell P. 1997. "The Commission Made Me Do It: The European Commission as a Strategic Asset in Domestic Politics." In *At the Heart of the Union: Studies of the European Commission,* ed. Neill Nugent, 167–86. New York: St. Martin's Press.

Sniderman, Paul M., Richard A. Brody, and Philip E. Tetlock. 1991. *Reasoning and Choice: Explorations in Political Psychology*. New York: Cambridge University Press.

Snyder, Jack. 1991. *Myths of Empire: Domestic Politics and International Ambition*. Ithaca: Cornell University Press.

Sobel, Richard. 1996. "U.S. and European Attitudes toward Intervention in the Former Yugoslavia: *Mourir pour la Bosnie?*" In *The World and Yu-*

goslavia's Wars, ed. Richard H. Ullman. New York: Council on Foreign Relations.

Soldatos, Panayotis. 1990. "An Explanatory Framework for the Study of Federated States as Foreign-Policy Actors." In *Federalism and International Relations: The Role of Subnational Units,* ed. Hans J. Michelmann and Panayotis Soldatos. Oxford: Clarendon.

Solingen, Etel. 1994. "The Political Economy of Nuclear Restraint." *International Security* 19, no. 2 (fall): 126–69.

South Centre. 1999. "Issues Regarding the Review of the WTO Dispute Settlement Mechanism." Trade-Related Agenda, Development, and Equity Working Paper no. 1, South Centre. <http://www.southcentre.org/publications/trade/dispute.pdf>.

Steiner, Jurg. 1974. *Amicable Agreement versus Majority Rule: Conflict Resolution in Switzerland.* Raleigh: University of North Carolina Press.

Stephan, John J. 1994. *The Russian Far East: A History.* Stanford: Stanford Univeristy Press.

Stone, Randall. 1996. *Satellites and Commissars.* Princeton: Princeton University Press.

Stone, Randall. 1997. "Russian and the IMF: Reputation and Unrestricted Bargaining." Paper presented at the annual meeting of the International Studies Association, Toronto, Canada.

Stone, Randall. 2002. *Lending Credibility: The International Monetary Fund and the Post-Communist Transition.* Princeton: Princeton University Press.

Strang, David, and Patricia Mei Yin Chang. 1993. "The International Labor Organization and the Welfare State: Institutional Effects on National Welfare Spending, 1960–80." *International Organization* 47:235–62.

Strange, Susan. 1996. *The Retreat of the State: The Diffusion of Power in the World Economy.* Cambridge: Cambridge University Press.

Stryker, Sheldon, and Anne Statham. 1985. "Symbolic Interaction and Role Theory." In *Handbook of Social Psychology,* vol. 1, ed. Gardner Lindzey and Elliot Aronson. New York: Random House.

Summers, Robert, Alan Heston, Daniel A. Nuxoll, and Bettina Aten. 1995. *The Penn World Table (Mark 5.6a).* Cambridge, MA: National Bureau of Economic Research.

Thompson, Alexander. 2000. "Framing Foreign Policy: Statecraft and International Organizations." Paper presented at the annual meeting of the American Political Science Association, Washington, DC, August 31–September 3.

Thompson, Alexander. 2001. "Channeling Power: International Organizations and the Politics of Coercion." Ph.D. diss., University of Chicago.

Thompson, Alexander, and Duncan Snidal. 2000. "International Organization." In *Encyclopedia of Law and Economics,* vol. 5, ed. Boudewijn Bouckaert and Gerrit De Geest, 692–722. Northhampton, MA: Edward Elgar.

Tirole, Jean. 1986. "Hierarchies and Bureaucracies: On the Role of Collusion in Organization." *Journal of Law, Economics, and Organization* 2: 181–214.

Toloraya, Georgi D. 1996. "Russian Perception of Northeast Asia Cooperation: Pros and Cons." *Northeast Asia Economic Forum Newsletter* 17: 2–9.

Tomikhin, Evgeni. 1997. "The Tumangan Project with the Agreements Signed." *Far East Affairs* 3:91–95.

Tonelson, Alan. 2000. *The Race to the Bottom.* Boulder: Westview.

Towell, Pat. 1993a. "Behind Solid Vote on Somalia: A Hollow Victory for Clinton." *Congressional Quarterly Weekly Report,* October 16, 2823.

Towell, Pat. 1993b. "Cover Story: Clinton's Policy Is Battered, but His Powers Are Intact." *Congressional Quarterly Weekly Report,* October 23, 2896.

Towell, Pat. 1994. "On Issue of Using Military Abroad House Marches to a Different Drum." *Congressional Quarterly Weekly Report,* May 28, 1402.

Towell, Pat. 1995a. "Bosnia: House Opposes Peacekeeping Role, Delays Vote on Cutoff of Funds." *Congressional Quarterly Weekly Report,* November 4, 3390.

Towell, Pat. 1995b. "Hill Set for Full-Scale Debate on U.S. Peacekeeping Role." *Congressional Quarterly Weekly Report,* November 25, 3602.

Towell, Pat. 1995c. "Congress Reluctantly Acquiesces in Peacekeeping Mission." *Congressional Quarterly Weekly Report,* December 2, 3668.

Towell, Pat. 1995d. "Congress Torn over Response as Deployment Begins." *Congressional Quarterly Weekly Report,* December 9, 3750.

Towell, Pat. 1997. "Congress Gives Clinton Leeway to Extend Bosnia Mission." *Congressional Quarterly Weekly Report,* September 27, 2321.

Towell, Pat. 1998a. "Democrats Parry GOP Thrusts on China Policy, Bosnia Mission." *Congressional Quarterly Weekly Report,* June 27, 1781.

Towell, Pat. 1998b. "Senate Passes Defense Spending Bill, Backing U.S. Troop Levels in Balkans." *Congressional Quarterly Weekly Report,* August 1, 2123.

Towell, Pat and Donna Cassata. 1995a. "House Votes to Block Clinton from Sending Peacekeepers." *Congressional Quarterly Weekly Report,* November 18, 3549.

Towell, Pat and Donna Cassata. 1995b. "Congress Takes Symbolic Stand On Troop Deployment." *Congressional Quarterly Weekly Report,* December 16, 3817.

Trade and Development Centre. 1999. "An Advisory Centre on WTO Law." Typescript. <http://www.itd.org/links/acwlintro.htm>.

Tumen Secretariat. 1997. "Overview of Recent Foreign Investment Trends and Major Achievements in the Tumen River Economics Development Area, 1996–1997."

Turner, John C. 1987. *Rediscovering the Social Group.* Oxford: Basil Blackwell.

Turner, Jonathan. 1988. *A Theory of Social Interaction.* Stanford: Stanford University Press.

Underdal, Arild. 1998. "Explaining Compliance and Defection: Three Models." *European Journal of International Relations* 4 (March): 5–30.

United Nations. Security Council. 1994. *Resolution 929.* Adopted June 22.

U.S. Congress. 1989. "Instances of Use of United States Armed Forces Abroad, 1798–1989." Congressional Research Service Report, December 4.

Valliant, Robert. 1997. "The Political Dimension." In *Politics and Economics in the Russian Far East: Changing Ties with Asia-Pacific,* ed. Tsuneo Akaha. London: Routledge.

Velasco, Andrés. 1997. "When Are Fixed Exchange Rates Really Fixed?" *Journal of Development Economics* 54 (October): 5–25.

Vogel, David. 1995. *Trading Up: Consumer and Environmental Regulation in a Global Economy.* Cambridge: Harvard University Press.

Wallace, William. 1994. *Regional Integration: The Western European Experience.* Washington, DC: Brookings Institution.

Wallach, Lori, and Michelle Sforza. 1999. *Whose Trade Organization? Corporate Globalization and the Erosion of Democracy.* Washington, DC: Public Citizen.

Wallander, Celeste. 1999. *Mortal Friends, Best Enemies: German-Russian Cooperation after the Cold War.* Ithaca: Cornell University Press.

Walt, Stephen M. 1987. *The Origins of Alliances.* Ithaca: Cornell University Press.

Waltz, Kenneth. 1959. *Man, the State, and War: A Theoretical Analysis.* New York: Columbia University Press.

Warburg, Gerald Felix. 1989. *Conflict and Consensus.* New York: Harper and Row. Publishers.

Weaver, R. Kent. 1986. "The Politics of Blame Avoidance." *Journal of Public Policy* 6(4): 371–98.

Weber, Axel. 1991. "EMS Credibility." *Economic Policy* 12 (April): 57–102.

Weingast, Barry. 1995. "The Economic Role of Political Institutions: Market-Preserving Federalism and Economic Development." *Journal of Law, Economics, and Organization* 11 (1): 1–30.

Wendt, Alexander. 1987. "The Agent-Structure Problem in International Relations Theory." *International Organization* (summer): 335–70.

Wendt, Alexander. 1994. "Collective Identity Formation and the International State." *American Political Science Review* 88 (June): 384–96.

Wendt, Alexander. 1999. *Social Theory of International Politics.* Cambridge: Cambridge University Press.

Wetherell, Margaret. 1987. "Social Identity and Group Polarization." In *Rediscovering the Social Group,* ed. John C. Turner. Oxford: Basil Blackwell.

Whalley, John. 1996. "Why Do Countries Seek Regional Trade Agreements?" Working paper 5552, National Bureau of Economic Research, Cambridge, MA.

Whitehead, Laurence. 1989. "The Consolidation of Fragile Democracies: A

Discussion with Illustrations." In *Democracy in the Americas,* ed. Robert Pastor. New York: Holmes and Meier.

Whitehead, Laurence. 1993. "Requisites for Admission." In *The Challenge of Integration: Europe and the Americas,* ed. P. H. Smith. New Brunswick, NJ: Transaction.

Whitehead, Laurence. 1996. *The International Aspects of Democratization: Europe and the Americas.* Oxford: Oxford University Press.

Williams, Michael C. 1997. "The Institutions of Security." *Conflict and Cooperation* 32 (3): 287–308.

Wilson, James Q. 1973. *Political Organizations.* New York: Basic Books.

Woods, James L. 1997. "U.S. Government Decisionmaking Processes during Humanitarian Operations in Somalia." In *Learning from Somalia: The Lessons of Armed Humanitarian Intervention,* ed. Walter Clarke and Jeffrey Herbst, 151–72. Boulder: Westview.

World Bank. 1998. *The World Development Indicators.* CD-ROM.

World Trade Organization. 1999. "Preparations for the 1999 Ministerial Conference, Technical Assistance, Communication from Kenya on Behalf of the African Group." WT/GC/W/299, August 6.

Wormuth, Francis D., and Edwin B. Firmage. 1989. *To Chain the Dog of War.* 2d ed. Urbana: University of Illinois Press.

Wu Chenhuan and David R. Shaffer. 1987. "Susceptibility to Persuasive Appeals as a Function of Source Credibility and Prior Experience with Attitudinal Object." *Journal of Personality and Social Psychology* 52 (4).

Wu Yun. 1996. "China's Policies towards Arms Control and Disarmament: From Passive Responding to Active Leading." *Pacific Review* 9 (4): 577–606.

Wu Zhan. 1994. "Some Thoughts on Nuclear Arms Control." Conference on South Asia Arms Control, Shanghai, March.

Wu Zheng. 1996. "Quanmian jinzhi he shiyan tiaoyue tanpan jinzhan qingkuang" (The state of development of the negotiations on the comprehensive nuclear test ban treaty). *Guowai he wuqi dongtai* (Trends in foreign nuclear weapons) 3 (May 8): 9–10.

Young, Oran. 1980. "International Regimes: Problems of Concept Formation." *World Politics* 32:331–56.

Young, Oran. 1992. "The Effectiveness of International Institutions: Hard Cases and Critical Variables." In *Governance without Government: Order and Change in World Politics,* ed. James Rosenau and Ernst-Otto Czempiel. Cambridge: Cambridge University Press.

Yu Lixing. 1993. "Dangqian Wo Guo Bianjing Maoyi de Wenti Ji Tiaokong Duice" [About current frontier trade problems and their regulation measures in China]. *Jingji Yanjiu* [Economic research monthly] 10: 67–70.

Yuan, Jing-dong. 1996. "Conditional Multilateralism: Chinese Views on Order and Regional Security." *CANCAPS Papiers,* no. 9 (March).

Zabrovskaya, Ludmila. 1995. "The Tumanggang Project: A View from Primorie." *Far Eastern Affairs* 1:34–38.

Zhang, Ming. 1995. *Major Powers at a Crossroads: Economic Interdependence and an Asia Pacific Security Community.* Boulder: Lynne Rienner.

Zhang, Yunling. 1998. "Zonghe anquanguan ji dui wo guo YaTai anquan de lilunxing kaolu" (The concept of comprehensive security and some theoretical thoughts about China and Asia-Pacific security). Beijing: Chinese Academy of Social Sciences, Asia-Pacific Research Institute, December.

Zhao, Quansheng. 1991. "Domestic Factors of Chinese Foreign Policy: From Vertical to Horizontal Authoritariansim." In *China's Foreign Relations,* ed. Allen S. Whiting. Newbury Park, CA: Sage.

Zimbardo, Philip G., and Michael R. Leippe. 1991. *The Psychology of Attitude Change and Social Influence.* New York: McGraw-Hill.

Zinberg, Yakov. 1996. "The Vladivostok Curve: Subnational Intervention into Russo-Chinese Border Agreements." *Boundary and Security Bulletin* 4 (3): 76–86.

Zou Yunhua. 1998. "China and the CTBT Negotiations." Manuscript, Stanford Center for International Security and Cooperation, October.

Contributors

Daniel W. Drezner is an assistant professor of political science at the University of Chicago. He is the author of *The Sanctions Paradox* (1999).

Jean-Marc F. Blanchard is a lecturer with the International Relations Program at the University of Pennsylvania. He is the coeditor of *Power and the Purse* (2000).

Alastair Iain Johnston is a professor in the Government Department at Harvard University. He is the author of *Cultural Realism: Strategic Culture and Grand Strategy in Chinese History* (1995).

Jon C. Pevehouse is an assistant professor of political science at the University of Wisconsin.

Eric Reinhardt is an assistant professor of political science at Emory University.

Kenneth A. Schultz is an associate professor of political science at the University of California, Los Angeles. He is the author of *Democracy and Coercive Diplomacy* (2001).

Duncan Snidal is associate professor of political science at the University of Chicago.

Alexander Thompson is an assistant professor of political science at Ohio State University.

Index

Abbott, Kenneth W., 118, 188, 216, 221
Abramson, Hillel, 189n. 10
Acharya, Amitav, 161, 192n. 30
actors, subnational. *See* subnational actors
Adler, Emanuel, 52, 73n. 11, 141n. 3
Afghanistan, 108
Agénor, Pierre-Richard, 77
Aguero, Felipe, 34
Alexseev, Mikhail A., 69, 70
Anderson, Jennifer, 57, 68, 69, 73n. 15
Archer, Clive, 27
Arnold, R. Douglas, 110
ASEAN (Association of Southeast Asian Nations) Regional Forum (ARF). *See* Association of Southeast Asian Nations (ASEAN) Regional Forum (ARF)
Asiwaju, Anthony I., 73n. 12
Association of Southeast Asian Nations (ASEAN) Regional Forum (ARF), 17, 70, 191n. 26, 222, 223, 224. *See also* China, participation in the ASEAN Regional Forum (ARF)
Auerswald, David P., 111, 141n. 3
Australia, 71
Axelrod, Robert, 7, 17, 79, 98, 149, 193n. 40
Axsom, Danny, 155

Ball, R., 77
Banks, Arthur S., 39
Banks, Jeffrey, 10

bargaining, political, 4–5. *See also* cooperation, international
Barnum, Christopher, 193n. 40
Barshefsky, Charlene, 104n. 15
Barsoom, Peter N., 186
Bar-Tal, Daniel, 153
Basle Committee on Banking Supervision, 5
Beck, Nathaniel, 42
Berger, Charles R., 152, 190n. 18
Berger, Peter L., 150
Betz, Andrew L., 165
Bilveer, S., 73n. 15
Bird, Graham, 77
Bisanz, Gay L., 152
Blanchard, Jean-Marc F., 72nn. 2, 10, 73n. 16, 74nn. 20, 33
Bleaney, Michael, 77
bloc, Eastern. *See* Eastern bloc
Bollen, Kenneth, 40
Booster, Franklin J., 165
Bosnia, 105. *See also* intervention, humanitarian, in Bosnia
Braithwaite, John, 2, 9
Brody, Richard A., 152, 154
Broz, J. Lawrence, 212
Bulgaria, 206
Bundesbank, German, 52
Burns, Katherine G., 50, 70
Burton, Michael, 31
Busch, Marc L., 27
Bush, George H. W., 129
Byrd, Robert, 127, 136

Calvo, Guillermo A., 30, 32, 37
Cameron, David R., 52
Canada, 51